Praise for *American Vegan Kitchen*

American Vegan Kitchen is thoroughly enjoyable, full of pleasant nostalgia, well-seasoned vegan recipes, and scrumptious photos. Just about any North American can find a delicious vegan version of a childhood (or lifelong!) comfort food. The author provides clear instructions, good information, and recipes designed for maximum flavor. This book will be well-used in any vegan kitchen.

– Bryanna Clark Grogan, author of *Nonna's Italian Kitchen* and *The Fiber for Life Cookbook*

With so many great dinner destinations, *American* vegan will want to take.

– Terry Hope Romero, co-author of *Vegan Cook*

Imagine taking classic American favorites for breakfast, lunch, dinner, side dishes, and dessert, and veganizing them in the most exciting ways imaginable. That's just what Tamasin Noyes has done here. *American Vegan Kitchen* offers a staggering assortment of the best American-style comfort food that I've ever seen.

– Erik Marcus, author of *The Ultimate Vegan Guide* and publisher of Vegan.com

Tami Noyes has a special gift for creating luscious co_
dedicated herbivore or an omnivore dipping your to
Kitchen offers a plethora of down-home recipes to pl
making Tami's easy, satisfying dishes over and over aga

– Dynise Balcavage, author of *The Urban Vegan* co

After years of whetting our "vegan appetites" online, T
filled with the kind of irresistible recipes she's known f
her marvelous dishes. *American Vegan Kitchen* is sure t
bookshelves everywhere.

– Celine Steen, author of *500 Vegan Recipes*

2-10

American Vegan Kitchen

Delicious Comfort Food
from Blue Plate Specials
to Homestyle Favorites

Tamasin Noyes

VEGAN HERITAGE PRESS

Woodstock • Virginia

American Vegan Kitchen: Delicious Comfort Food from Blue Plate Specials to Homestyle Favorites, copyright © 2010 **by Tamasin Noyes**

First printing, February 2010

10 9 8 7 6 5 4 3 2 1 paperback

ISBN-13: 978-0-9800131-1-5
ISBN-10: 0-9800131-1-9

COVER PHOTOS: Front Cover (clockwise from bottom): Blueberry-Oat Short Stack (page 38); All-American Incrediburger with Midway French Fries (page 122 and 166); New York-Style Cheesecake (page 192); Mom's Noodle Soup (page 76). **PHOTO INSERT:** Food styling and photographs by Tamasin Noyes © 2010.

Vegan Heritage Press books are available at quantity discounts. For information about this and upcoming titles, please visit our website at www.veganheritagepress.com or write the publisher at Vegan Heritage Press, P.O. Box 628, Woodstock, VA 22664-0628.

Printed in Canada

Dedication

For Jim, my best friend. Thank you for filling my life with laughter and love.

For my Mom, Jackie Schwind. Thank you for teaching me that food is one of many ways to show love, and for always keeping the cookie crock full.

And for Kevin, always.

My mom's traditional recipe is now Apricot Cream Cheese Cookies (page 194). See a photo of them on page 6 of the photo insert.

Contents

Acknowledgments

Thanks to the testers who helped with *American Vegan Kitchen*. You are a wonderfully creative and thoughtful group who diligently and enthusiastically helped me hone these recipes. Thank you for the hours spent in the kitchen (and on the computer!) in making this cookbook what it is. When looking at this cookbook, it's your generous input that stands out to me. It's been an honor and pleasure to have you share in this experience. Thank you for being the best group of testers ever: Liz Wyman, Celia Ozereko, Kirsten Lakso, Aimee Kluiber, Amy Madden, Amy Mekemson, Kimberly Eads, Clea Mahoney, Courtney Blair, Kim Lahn, Tara Smith, Elaine Trautwein, Stephanie Roy, Sünne Kayser, and Jenn Lynskey.

Many thanks to the incredible cookbook authors who have supported and encouraged me along the way: Isa Chandra Moskowitz, Robin Robertson, Terry Hope Romero, Dynise Balcavage, and Celine Steen, as well as all the wonderful vegan bloggers, for their inspiration, amazing food, and for creating such a fun and exciting community.

A special and heartfelt thanks to Jon Robertson and the staff at Vegan Heritage Press. I sincerely appreciate this incredible opportunity. Thank you for your guidance and support in making this book happen and for everything you do.

Welcome to *American Vegan Kitchen*

Most of us remember a favorite neighborhood "hang-out"– a familiar coffee shop, cafe, or diner that felt like a home away from home. It was a place where all pretense stopped, where you could dress however you liked, and you were sure to get a great meal. Such places had a cozy feeling that was a lot like eating at home, as though the proprietors were trying to provide an extension of your own kitchen – and they actually were.

Diners and mom-and-pop eateries intentionally try to emulate familiar home cooking. They serve meatloaf, mashed potatoes, and green beans, and other "blue plate specials," along with mac and cheese, a soup of the day, and, of course, fresh cakes and pies. With a menu of homestyle dishes, they attract locals, from busy workers who don't have time to cook, to couples wanting a night out, or families giving Mom a night off from cooking. These restaurants also appeal to travelers who come inside for a meal that reminds them of home.

The problem for vegans, of course, is that many of these dishes simply aren't vegan. Most of us didn't grow up in a vegan household, either. Unless we happen to live near a vegan restaurant, the only way to enjoy these familiar favorites is to make them ourselves in our own kitchens. That's what *American Vegan Kitchen* is all about.

Over the years, I've cooked for many people, vegans and omnivores alike. This has allowed me to discover dishes that appeal to both camps and to develop a collection of recipes that all my guests enjoy. Cooking for others is a fun and friendly sharing experience that continues to be a big part of my life. The reason is simple: Rather than try to "convert" people, I choose to eat (and cook) by example.

With *American Vegan Kitchen,* you can enjoy starters and snacks such as Movie Night Potato Skins (page 48), Cafe Spinach Dip (page 64), and Spicy Balsamic Maple Wingz (page 49). Add a bowl of soup, and you've got the makings of a delicious meal without a lot of trouble. A favorite in my house is the Smoky Cauliflower and Bean Soup (page 75). You want tradition? Make Mom's Noodle Soup (page 76) and be sure to add her secret ingredient: Love.

Several salads in this book can be meals in themselves, or they can be enjoyed as a perfect addition to a sandwich platter. The Deli Potato Salad (page 96), made with fresh herbs, is ideal alongside a burger or sandwich, while the Midtown Greek Salad with Faux Feta (page 86) can stand on its own.

Don't forget those Blue Plate Specials, either. My husband Jim and I love the creamy Tuna-Free Noodle Casserole (page 133), the Brewpub Tater-Tot Pie (page 152), and the Seitan and Herb Dumplings (page 134).

Perennial favorites from the earliest diner traditions are the sandwiches, and the Sandwich Board chapter is filled with tempting choices. Try the All-American Incrediburger (page 122) with Midway French Fries (page 166) and Midwest Vinegar Slaw (page 98) on the side. Do you feel like traveling? You can cook your way across the country with a Chicago-Style Deep-Dish Pizza (page 158), a Cajun Pot Pie (page 149), and Almost-Philly Cheese Steak Sandwiches (page 121).

Where American comfort food is concerned, change has been good. Like our country and our taste, our cuisine has evolved over the years. American comfort food isn't just meat and potatoes anymore. It reflects the richness of various world cultures. To honor our cultural diversity, *American Vegan Kitchen* includes offerings from Chinatown, Little Italy, the Latino community, and a little soul food.

So, go ahead and linger in Little Italy with my homemade pizzas and dishes, such as Pesto Lasagna with Slow-Roasted Tomatoes and Mushrooms (page 155) or Italian-Style Seitan with Linguine (page 138) — sumptuous main dishes for any night. If you're in the mood for something south of the border, enjoy classic dishes like Wet Bean Burritos (page 146) and the Tex-Mex Taco Salad (page 101). For soul food, try Southern-Style Rice and Red Beans (page 172) and Sweet Garlicky Ribz (page 150).

Also, be sure to save room for dessert. Try a seasonal delight, such as the Peachy Keen Cobbler (page 184), or the truly decadent New York-Style Cheesecake (page 192). Oh yes — and did I mention Mom's Apple Pie (page 178)?

With the more than 200 recipes in this book, you'll be able to recreate your favorite nostalgic dishes in the comfort of your own American vegan kitchen.

BASICS

Years ago, when my husband Jim and I were traveling through Vermont, we found ourselves looking for a place to eat. Without high expectations, we wandered into a diner to see how we'd fare. Once inside, we were surprised to see several vegan items on a chalkboard behind the counter. After enjoying a thick veggie burger and fries, we continued on our annual trip. When we returned the following year, we couldn't believe it when our server remembered us. We felt welcomed and right at home. It was this little diner that brought back memories of the comfort foods I enjoyed before I became vegan, and it inspired the idea of writing an American vegan comfort food cookbook.

The American Vegan Kitchen

When you think about it, American cooking is synonymous with nostalgic comfort food. Most everyone can remember their favorite dishes: a stack of pancakes on a sunny morning in a corner cafe; a big delicious burger made just right with a side of fries and a garlicky deli pickle; or maybe French toast, an omelet, or a well-stuffed sandwich that you devoured while sitting at a diner counter, eyeing the dessert case near the cash register.

In *American Vegan Kitchen,* I have assembled my favorite vegan versions of the comfort foods I enjoyed at friendly neighborhood eateries, as well as in my mom's kitchen. The book provides recipes for the foods we grew up with, but made one-hundred percent vegan. This means they contain no animal products of any kind. *American Vegan Kitchen* gives you casual, satisfying comfort food at its very best. The book shows you how to create restaurant and homestyle dishes for breakfast, lunch, dinner, and desserts, whenever the mood strikes, without leaving the comfort of your home.

If you're like me, these vegan improvements on old standards will become your new go-to dishes when you just want to eat something delicious at home. You'll also find that by using familiar cooking styles and great healthful ingredients, it doesn't take long to get a wonderful meal on the table.

My kitchen is the heart of my home, and I've learned over the years that a little preparation goes a long way toward successful cooking. In this chapter, I explain some basics about the ingredients that make vegan cooking so versatile, and a little about the equipment that I use. Let's look at the ingredients first.

Tofu

Tofu is made from cooked soybeans that are processed into soy milk, then mixed with a coagulant and pressed into blocks, not unlike the process of making cheese. Tofu is high in protein and B vitamins, and it is low in saturated fat with zero cholesterol. Some brands of tofu are calcium enriched. Though bland in flavor, the key to making tofu taste great is knowing how to prepare it.

Regular Tofu: Various kinds of tofu are available in supermarkets, natural food stores, and Asian groceries, the most common type being the "regular" (or Chinese-style) tofu. It is sold in dense cakes packed in water and must be kept refrigerated. Regular tofu is available in soft, firm, and extra-firm textures, although extra-firm regular tofu is the type used most frequently in *American Vegan Kitchen.* Regular tofu is commonly found unseasoned, which allows it to absorb the flavors of marinades and seasonings as it cooks. Before using tofu, it must be drained (and sometimes pressed) to eliminate extra moisture and help it absorb flavors. Regular tofu may be frozen and thawed to create a chewier texture. If you're not using the whole block of tofu, keep the unused portion in the container, though the water should be changed daily to maintain freshness. Always check the "sell by" date when buying tofu. Regular tofu is also available smoked, seasoned, and marinated in a variety of flavors.

Pressing Regular Tofu: To press regular tofu, drain the packing water and cut the block into quarters. Depending on how the tofu will be cut for a recipe, it can be pressed even more quickly by cutting it into eight slabs rather than four. Place the tofu between two cutting boards and a clean dish towel (or paper towels). Leave the tofu pressed this way for an hour, changing the towels once or twice as they get soaked. Different brands of tofu contain different amounts of water so the need to change the towels will vary. After pressing, the tofu is ready to marinate or be used in your favorite recipes.

Silken Tofu: Sometimes called Japanese-style, silken tofu is usually sold in aseptic packages that require no refrigeration until opened. Silken tofu is also available in soft, firm, and extra-firm textures. Extra-firm silken tofu is used in some dessert recipes in this book. It requires no draining or pressing before using.

Tempeh

Tempeh is believed to have originated in Indonesia, where it's still a primary source of protein. Like tofu, tempeh is made from soybeans. Instead of using soy milk, whole soybeans are softened, dehulled, and partially cooked. In a process similar to the making of yogurt, the beans are pressed into cakes and allowed to ferment. A four-ounce serving of tempeh provides forty-one percent of the daily suggested protein requirement. It's also rich in riboflavin, magnesium, manganese, and copper.

Tempeh should always be stored in the refrigerator, though it freezes well without affecting the texture. Like tofu, be sure to check the "sell by" date when purchasing. Some people detect a slight bitterness in tempeh. To counteract that taste, simmer tempeh in a large skillet with enough water to cover for 15 minutes before using. Simmering also helps the tempeh absorb marinades and other seasonings. Other than this optional step, little prep work is required for tempeh.

Seitan

Of the "big three" vegan protein foods, seitan is my favorite. Sometimes called "wheat meat" or gluten, meaty seitan was first made in Japan and China by Buddhists who observed a vegetarian diet. Traditional seitan is made by combining whole wheat flour and water to create a dough that undergoes multiple rinsings to remove the bran and starch. This creates a densely textured mass of gluten, which is known as seitan after it is cooked.

In the United States, seitan gained in popularity due to interest in the macrobiotic diet in the 1980s. Today, seitan is an ingredient in many "faux meats" available in supermarkets. Seitan is protein rich, packing twice as many grams per serving as tofu. It's also rich in amino acids and, like all vegan foods, cholesterol free.

Making Seitan the Easy Way: In this book, I provide a convenient method to make seitan using vital wheat gluten, wheat flour with the bran and starch already removed. Also called "wheat gluten flour," vital wheat gluten can be found at natural food stores and well-stocked supermarkets. It is also available online from companies such as Bob's Red Mill.

Save the Broth

When making seitan, save the cooking broth to use next time you make a batch. This enriched broth makes the new recipe even richer. Each time you finish, just strain the broth into a container and freeze. After using the enriched broth a few times, you'll see how your seitan flavor improves each time you make it. As an added bonus, the seitan broth can be reused in soups, sauces, risottos, or other dishes.

The texture of seitan varies, depending on whether you simmer it on top of the stove, cook it in a slow cooker, or bake it in the oven. For a more sausage-like or cold cut style, the seitan can be wrapped in foil and steamed. After the seitan is cooked in any one of these ways, it is ready for use in other recipes.

Making homemade seitan is much less expensive than buying it ready-made, plus you can adjust the seasonings to create various flavors. You can make a rich "beefy" flavor with Savory Seitan (page 5) or a more mellow flavor with Seitan Lite (page 6). You can even create a spicy "sausage-like" flavor with Vegan Sausage Links (page 41).

Freezing Seitan: Most of the seitan recipes in *American Vegan Kitchen* yield about two pounds of seitan, making it easy to keep some in the freezer for another meal. Seitan can be frozen, with or without broth, in plastic containers or freezer bags. For easiest use, divide your seitan into serving sizes and package them individually. You can then pull out a package to thaw and have dinner on the table in no time. If you plan to use the seitan within a few days, it can also be refrigerated. In fact, the texture of seitan firms up after cooling, which makes it easy to slice.

Alternatively, you can buy prepared seitan at a natural food store or well-stocked supermarket and use it in any of the recipes in this book calling for seitan. If you want to make your own seitan, here are the two basic recipes for the Savory Seitan and Seitan "Lite" called for in several of the recipes in *American Vegan Kitchen*.

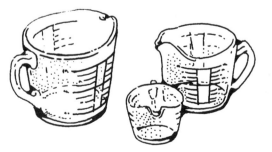

Savory Seitan

This recipe makes cutlets that can be used in a variety of recipes. Instead of soy sauce, you can substitute tamari or liquid aminos, such as Braggs. Makes about 2 pounds or 10 (3-ounce) cutlets. Instructions follow for using this recipe to make seitan roasts in a slow cooker.

2 1/2 cups vital wheat gluten
1/4 cup nutritional yeast
1/4 cup soy flour
1/4 cup soy sauce
2 tablespoons ketchup
1 tablespoon olive oil
1 teaspoon browning sauce, optional
1/4 cup dry red wine, or additional broth
1 1/2 cups plus 4 cups chilled vegetable broth, divided
3 cloves garlic, minced
1 tablespoon canola oil

TIP

If you make seitan at home and aren't happy with its texture, just grind it up in a food processor and season it for use in dishes such as tacos, chili, loaves, or casseroles.

1. In a medium bowl, combine the vital wheat gluten, yeast, and flour. Set aside.

2. In a small bowl, combine the soy sauce, ketchup, olive oil, browning sauce (if using), wine, 1 1/4 cups of the vegetable broth, and the garlic. Mix well, then add to the dry ingredients. Stir together with a wooden spoon, adding the remaining 1/4 cup broth, if needed, to make a firm but workable dough. Knead for about 2 minutes, or until a cohesive dough is formed.

3. Let the dough rest for 15 minutes, then divide it into 10 dough balls. Place a dough ball between two sheets of parchment paper and use a rolling pin to roll it out to 1/4-inch thickness. The cutlet will shrink some during cooking, so make it about 1-inch larger than you want it to be when cooked. Continue with the remaining dough balls, keeping the cutlets separated so they don't stick together.

4. Preheat the oven to 300°F. Heat the canola oil in a large skillet over medium heat. Working in batches, add the cutlets and cook until browned, about 4 minutes. Turn and cook on the other side until browned, about 3 minutes. Place the cutlets in a large roasting pan and cover with the 4 cups of broth. Cover the pan tightly with foil and place in the oven. Bake 1 hour, turning once. Let the cutlets cool in the broth. The seitan is now ready to use or store until needed.

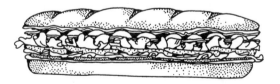

Slow Cooker Version (for roasts): Seitan "roasts" are versatile because they can be sliced, diced, and chopped to use as desired in recipes. Follow the recipe above, but instead of making the cutlets in step two, divide the dough into 4 equal pieces and shape into balls. Place them in a slow cooker and add enough broth to cover (about 6 cups). Cook on low for 8 hours. Let cool in the slow cooker. The seitan is now ready to use or store until needed. Makes 2 pounds or 4 (8-ounce) roasts.

Seitan Lite

These flavorful cutlets are slow-simmered in the oven and can be used anytime you want a tender, lighter tasting, seitan. In addition to using in the seitan recipes in this book, these cutlets may be substituted in many of the recipes calling for tempeh or extra-firm tofu. Makes 10 (3-ounce) cutlets.

CUTLETS:
1/2 cup cooked chickpeas
3/4 to 1 cup vegetable broth
2 cloves garlic, minced
2 tablespoons dry white wine
1 tablespoon olive oil
1 teaspoon onion powder
1/2 teaspoon garlic powder
1 tablespoon "chicken-flavored" vegan
  bouillon paste, optional
1 1/2 cups vital wheat gluten
1/4 cup nutritional yeast
1/4 cup soy flour

COOKING BROTH:
4 cups chilled vegetable broth
3 tablespoons nutritional yeast
2 cloves garlic, minced
1 teaspoon dried thyme
1 teaspoon dried rosemary
1 teaspoon dried parsley
1/2 teaspoon onion powder
1/2 teaspoon garlic powder
1/4 teaspoon white pepper
1 tablespoon prepared yellow mustard
Salt

1. *Cutlets:* Combine the chickpeas and broth in a blender and blend until smooth. Add the garlic, wine, oil, onion powder, garlic powder, and bouillon, if using. Blend again to combine. Set aside.

2. In a large bowl, combine the vital wheat gluten, yeast, and soy flour. Whisk together. Then add the blended mixture, stirring to combine. If the mixture is not holding together well, add another 1 to 2 tablespoons of either the broth or vital wheat gluten to make a workable dough. Place the dough on a work surface and knead a few minutes, until the mixture is cohesive. Divide into ten equal pieces and shape into balls. Set aside for 10 minutes.

3. *Broth:* Preheat the oven to 300°F. While the dough balls are resting, prepare the cooking broth. In a large roasting pan, combine the broth, yeast, garlic, thyme, rosemary, parsley, onion powder, garlic powder, white pepper, mustard, and salt to taste. Mix well.

4. Using a rolling pin, roll out the dough balls, one at a time, between 2 pieces of parchment paper. They should be about 1/4-inch thick or less. Transfer to the pan with the broth. Continue until all the cutlets are rolled out. It's fine if they touch or overlap. Cover the pan tightly with foil. Bake for 1 hour. Turn the oven off and leave the cutlets in the oven for one hour. Let cool completely. The cutlets are now ready to use or store until needed.

Other Essential Ingredients

Beans

Beans are another wonderful source of protein. They are available dried or pre-cooked in cans. Dried beans can be cooked on the stove top or in a pressure cooker. Canned beans should be rinsed and drained prior to use. Whether you cook your beans at home or buy canned, it's best to use organic beans whenever possible.

Cooking Beans: For dried beans, pick through them to remove any nonbean material and rinse well with water. Place the beans in a large bowl, adding enough water to cover the beans by 3 to 4 inches. Refrigerate overnight. (NOTE: Lentils and split peas don't require soaking, but should still be picked through.) The next day, drain the soaked beans and transfer them to a large saucepan or soup pot. Add about 3 cups of water for each cup of beans. Bring to a boil, then reduce the heat to simmer. Depending on the type and age of the beans, cooking time will take from 30 minutes to 1 1/2 hours. Dried herbs, spices, or garlic may be added to the beans for flavor, but not until the last half hour of simmering. At that time, salt may also be added. Adding salt too early in the cooking process causes the beans to soften more slowly. Test for desired doneness, then drain.

If you prepare your own beans from scratch, the cooked beans can be portioned into desired serving sizes and frozen for convenience. I generally freeze cooked beans in 1 1/2 cup amounts to be roughly equal to that in a 15-ounce can. When you're cooking beans for a specific recipe, it's a great idea to cook extra so you can have them on hand for other meals.

Texturized Vegetable Protein

Sometimes called texturized soy protein or TVP, texturized vegetable protein is made from defatted soy flour. It is mixed into a dough, then processed through an extruder. TVP is available in two sizes: granular and chunk. The popularity of texturized vegetable protein ebbs and flows. As some people endeavor to eat ever lower on the food chain, they strive for purity, steering clear of any processed foods. For others, texturized vegetable protein provides an economical source of protein. TVP absorbs flavors well and brings a "meaty" texture to dishes. Bob's Red Mill is a high quality brand available in supermarkets and natural food stores; it can also be purchased online. Texturized vegetable protein makes a great substitute for ground beef in recipes such as tacos, chilis, or spaghetti sauce. While some flavored varieties exist, the recipes in this book only call for unflavored.

Since it's a dried product, texturized vegetable protein is usually reconstituted before being used in a recipe. To do this, use 1 cup hot water or broth for each 7/8 cup dry granules. Be sure to use a bowl that will allow for some expansion. If desired, the reconstituting water may be seasoned. Specific directions and ratios for reconstituting are included in the recipes. If using texturized vegetable protein in a soup or stew that will cook for 30 minutes or longer, rehydration may not be necessary.

Nutritionally, texturized vegetable protein is a good source of protein and iron, and it is also low in fat. Store it airtight at room temperature. If texturized vegetable protein isn't available, minced seitan may be substituted, using eight ounces of seitan to one cup of dry texturized vegetable protein. Other alternatives include frozen or refrigerated vegan burger crumbles, available in supermarkets and natural food stores.

Grains

To make the recipes in this cookbook, you probably already have on hand all the grains that you'll need. Rice dishes can be made with your favorite long grain rice. Couscous (both regular and the larger grained Israeli variety), barley, oats, and quinoa may be used as well. You should also keep a few types of pasta on hand, such as cappelini, spaghetti, and elbows. Grains and pastas should be stored in airtight containers. Specific directions for cooking grains are included in each recipe where they are used.

Vegetables and Fruits

My standard vegetable and fruit shopping list really doesn't vary a lot from week to week. However, I do try to buy most of my produce fresh and organic from local sources. Peas, corn, and out-of-season berries are the exceptions to my fresh purchases. While I prefer them fresh, frozen will get the job done in most dishes. Remember, be sure to wash any produce before using it in a recipe.

Flours

Flours are used in a variety of ways in *American Vegan Kitchen.* It's a good idea to keep a variety on hand, including all-purpose flour, whole wheat flour, bread flour, and whole wheat pastry flour. My preference happens to be white whole wheat. In most non-yeasted recipes, whole wheat pastry flour may be substituted for half of the all-purpose flour with little effect on the results. Vital wheat gluten is used in all the seitan recipes, sometimes along with soy flour, chickpea flour, or tapioca flour. I use the "scoop and scrape" method in measuring. This is done by dipping the cup into the flour and then leveling it, rather than spooning flour into the cup. Keep flours in airtight containers for longer life.

Broth

It's time for a little confession. I rarely make my own vegetable broth. With my freezer space already crowded with breads, several kinds of seitan, tempeh, and frozen beans, I usually rely on quick and easy vegan vegetable broth that is sold in aseptic containers. Other good alternatives are bouillon paste or cubes reconstituted in water. To boost the flavor of any broth, you can add flavorings that complement the dish you're making, such as a little soy sauce or tamari, miso, a bouillon cube, or vegan bouillon paste, a tablespoon of tomato paste, wine, some extra herbs, or maybe a little chili paste. It's important to be aware of the sodium content in the broth you purchase; some are higher than others or contain other preservatives. For the recipes in this book, you may need to adjust the salt level accordingly if your broth tends toward the salty side.

If you prefer to make your own broth, it's an easy process and can be very satisfying. Vegetable broth can be made using a wide variety of ingredients. It can be tailored to emphasize the flavors of a particular dish, or simply made to suit your own taste. Making broth leaves lots of room for creativity and flexibility, but keep in mind that the flavor of a broth generally intensifies as it is cooked again in a soup or other recipe, so it's best to season it lightly to start. The flavors may be boosted or salt added when it's used in cooking, if desired. Cruciferous vegetables, such as cauliflower, broccoli, and cabbage, should be avoided in stocks as their flavors tend to dominate. Here is an easy recipe that can be adapted to your own preferences.

Basic Vegetable Broth

Makes 2 quarts

1 tablespoon olive oil
1 medium onion, cut into 1-inch dice
5 cloves garlic, halved
3 large carrots, cut into 1-inch pieces
1 shallot, quartered
1 scallion, chopped
2 russet potatoes, scrubbed and chopped
   into 2-inch chunks
10 cremini mushrooms, halved
1/4 cup dry red wine, optional
1 tablespoon soy sauce
10 cups water
1/2 cup chopped fresh parsley
1 teaspoon All-American Spice Blend
   (page 13) or other spice blend
1 teaspoon dried thyme
1/2 teaspoon dried rosemary
1/4 teaspoon white peppercorns
1/2 teaspoon salt
1/8 teaspoon black pepper

1. In a large soup pot, heat the oil over medium heat. Add the vegetables and cook 5 to 10 minutes, stirring occasionally, until fragrant.

2. Add the remaining ingredients and simmer, partially covered, for 1 1/2 to 2 hours. The broth is done when it is a rich golden brown color.

3. Strain and use as desired. The broth can be divided into tightly sealed containers and refrigerated for up to 1 week or frozen for 2 months.

Dairy Alternatives

In this book, the primary milk used is unsweetened soy milk. It is widely available, and it works well in recipes. You may substitute other non-dairy milks for those specified in my recipes, but the results may vary. If substitutions are a problem, it will be noted in the recipe. Soy creamer is also used in some recipes. It's a thicker, richer version of soy milk. Vegan margarines are increasingly available. I always keep some in the refrigerator as well as the freezer. Vegan cream cheese and sour cream are also available, with new brands and flavors being developed all the time. In this book, the plain versions are used in recipes. Be sure to buy the non-hydrogenated products when possible. All dairy substitutes should be stored in the refrigerator. As always, watch the "sell by" dates. For those living in less populated areas, many vegan products can be ordered from a variety of online companies (see Resources, page 199).

Instead of Eggs

Years ago, when I started cooking vegan, I was amazed at how often eggs could just be left out of a recipe. In certain baked goods, a substitute helps. In this book, the one most often used is ground flaxseed, which can be made into a gel-like substance. Grind the seeds in a coffee or spice grinder when you need it. A time-saving tip is to grind more than you need, then store it in the freezer, as it can turn rancid. Flaxseed is also a good source of omega-3 fatty acids. Soy yogurt and applesauce, both of which can be used to replace eggs in conventional recipes, are also used in this book.

Egg Substitutes

In traditional cooking, eggs are used for their leavening properties to create a better texture or to bind the ingredients in a recipe. Here are some of the most common egg substitutes and how they are best used:

Ground flaxseed: Combine 1 tablespoon with 3 tablespoons hot water. Stir together vigorously to thicken. This flaxseed mixture works well in any baked goods. It is the substitute I use the most because it is a good leavener, and it retains the texture most often expected in baked goods.

Silken or soft tofu: Blend 1/4 cup in a blender until smooth for each egg in a recipe. This adds some moisture to baked goods and works well in recipes such as pancakes, waffles, quick breads and other recipes that don't require as much rising. This is best used to bind rather than leaven.

Applesauce: Substitute 1/4 cup for each egg in a recipe. The other properties are the same as those listed for silken tofu.

Vegan soy yogurt and **vegan mayonnaise** may also be used in a ratio of 1/4 cup per egg, as used in Maple Cupcakes with Cinnamon Cream Cheese Frosting (page 191). These provide some leavening when combined with other ingredients, such as baking powder. **Curdled soy milk** works in the same manner. Specific directions are provided in each recipe.

Sweeteners

In this book, the most commonly used sweeteners are sugar, brown sugar, maple syrup, molasses, and agave nectar. Since white table sugar is usually refined with bone char, you can substitute a vegan sugar, such as Florida Crystals, turbinado sugar, or beet sugar. These are available in well-stocked supermarkets and natural food stores. Although more expensive than the non-vegan versions, vegan brown sugar and confectioners' sugar are also available. Dry sweeteners may be used interchangeably, but keep in mind that brown sugar imparts a slight molasses flavor. My preference is turbinado sugar, sometimes called raw sugar, in its finest granulated form, because it integrates more easily into a mixture.

Of the liquid sweeteners, agave imparts the least flavor and is the most adaptable. Maple syrup, while expensive, imparts a great flavor in some dishes, but may be overpowering in others. My preference is Grade B maple syrup. It's less expensive and has a wonderful depth of flavor. Molasses is strongly flavored, and it is generally used sparingly.

As a general rule, in converting your own recipes, it's best to replace a dry sweetener with another dry sweetener, or a liquid sweetener with another liquid sweetener. It's also important to keep in mind that when substituting a liquid sweetener, such as agave nectar for sugar, it will increase the moisture in the finished product unless the other liquid ingredients are slightly reduced.

Oils

In *American Vegan Kitchen,* I try to use as little oil as possible. For most dishes, I find myself reaching for canola or olive oil. However, I also keep some peanut oil (for Asian cooking), toasted sesame oil (for Asian and dishes that need some depth), and chili oil, just because it's spicy. All oils should be stored in a cool place; sesame and chili oils should be refrigerated.

Herbs and Spices

Herbs and spices can turn good food into great food. All it takes is a few magic ingredients to make a recipe's basic flavors pop. This book uses a lot of herbs and spices. If you're in the mood for a dish and are missing one of them, don't let that stop you from tackling the recipe. Make adjustments using the ingredients you have on hand and cook to taste, adjusting herbs and spices to please your palate.

Dried herbs and spices used in this book include basil, cayenne, chili powder, cinnamon, coriander, cumin, five-spice powder, garlic powder, onion powder, oregano, parsley, red pepper flakes, rosemary, tarragon, thyme, turmeric, and others. I also make my own All-American Spice Blend (page 13), an all-purpose kitchen seasoning used to enhance the flavor of certain recipes in this book. Feel free to change the blend to suit your taste or use a commercial blend, if you prefer.

The potency of dried herbs decreases over time, so be aware of that when cooking. It's especially nice to pair fresh herbs with their dried counterparts to create layers in a dish. Dried herbs should be stored airtight, while fresh should be stored in the refrigerator.

Nutritional Yeast

Nutritional yeast adds a "cheesy" flavor to recipes. It's high in protein and vitamin B complex, including B-12, and is most commonly sold in flake form, though it is sometimes available as a powder. It is quite different from other types of yeast. Active dry yeast, for example, is used as a leavener in baking, while brewer's yeast is employed in the production of beer and is not used in cooking.

Nutritional yeast is available in well-stocked supermarkets and natural food stores. The most widely available brands are Red Star and Bob's Red Mill. Nutritional yeast does not require refrigeration but should be stored in an airtight container.

NOTE: For a quick and easy snack, try sprinkling a little nutritional yeast on popcorn that you've dressed with a little melted vegan margarine.

Marinade Magic

Would you like to make a good meal even better? Make a marinade and let your tofu, tempeh, or seitan marinate for an hour or longer before cooking. Marinades take only minutes to prepare. When making a marinade, taste it before adding the ingredients you want to marinate, adjusting the seasonings as needed. Here are the elements that will make your marinade successful:

- Oil: Helps the protein retain its texture and moisture. For increased flavor, use chile oil or toasted sesame oil.

- Acid: Acids work into the protein to boost the flavor. To create various effects, try different vinegars, fresh citrus juices, and wine.

- Paste: Using a thicker ingredient, such as tomato paste, ketchup, or maple syrup, helps the marinade cling to the food.

- Sweeteners: These include white sugar, brown sugar, agave nectar, maple syrup, molasses, and brown rice syrup. The liquid sweeteners also help the marinade cling to the food.

- Spices and herbs: The sky is the limit here. Fresh or fried herbs (always use less of dried), garlic, onion, prepared mustard, lemon pepper, white pepper, or any spices you like.

- Broth: When creating a flavor-packed marinade, don't forget broth. It will help extend your marinade so you'll have plenty to coat the tofu, tempeh, or seitan, without losing flavor.

- Seasonings: Marinades need salt and pepper to really bring out the flavors. Besides regular salt and pepper, consider tamari, soy sauce, and vegan Worcestershire sauce. If you will be adding broth, it's best to add the salt last.

Since some vinegars react with metal, it's best to use a shallow glass pan, plastic container, or even a ziplock bag to marinate.

All-American Spice Blend

Makes about 1/2 cup

A little of this and a little of that combine to create a zesty spice blend that reflects the American melting pot. Flavorful and versatile, add a teaspoon to your favorite soup or use it to season flour for breading seitan. This spice blend is used in several recipes throughout the book. If you're missing one of the spices in this blend, you can modify the recipe by substituting different spices or adding more of another spice in the recipe.

1 tablespoon ground cumin
1 tablespoon cayenne
1 tablespoon onion powder
1 tablespoon smoked paprika
2 teaspoons garlic powder
1 teaspoon ground coriander
1 teaspoon salt
1 teaspoon dried parsley
1/2 teaspoon black pepper
1/2 teaspoon dried mustard
1/2 teaspoon red pepper flakes
1/4 teaspoon ground allspice
1/8 teaspoon ground cloves

1. Combine all ingredients in a small skillet over medium heat. Stirring constantly, toast for 2 minutes, or until fragrant.

2. Remove from the heat and allow to cook completely. Store in an airtight container.

Cookware

Along with quality ingredients, it's important to have tools that will help make cooking easier. Cookware is one of the bigger investments most of us make, but it will hold a permanent place in your kitchen. My favorite cookware is cast iron. I like it for its even heat distribution, the fact that it can go from stovetop to oven, and, when properly seasoned, it is virtually nonstick. If your budget and cupboard space will allow, a 10 to 12-inch nonstick skillet also comes in handy for omelets or French toast. Saucepans in a variety of sizes are needed, as are colanders and cutting boards. A large roasting pan is helpful for cooking seitan, but not necessary.

Knives don't have to be expensive ones, but they do need to be sharp and comfortable in your hand. The three I use the most are a paring knife for peeling and slicing; a santoku knife (an all-purpose knife that resembles a short cleaver) for chopping; and a serrated knife for slicing seitan, tempeh, breads, and fragile ingredients.

You don't need a lot of specialty appliances to make the recipes in this cookbook, but a steamer of some sort comes in handy, as does a blender or a food processor. In addition, an electric mixer is needed for some recipes. While a deep fryer is the easiest way to fry, a large heavy bottomed skillet may be used instead (see Before You Deep Fry on page 67). Occasionally, a recipe calls for a slow cooker, but in most cases alternate directions are provided if you don't have one.

Now, it's time to get cooking in your own American vegan kitchen.

Celebrate All Year 'Round with *American Vegan Kitchen*

Celebrations always feature food, so why not make food the cause for celebration? Here's a list of food-specific holidays that will give you even more reasons to cook from this book. These holidays are the perfect times to try new recipes:

January 4 – **National Spaghetti Day:** Spaghetti Pie with Arrabbiata Sauce
January 6 – **Bean Day:** Corn and Bean Chowder
January 27 – **Chocolate Cake Day:** Spiced Chocolate Pudding Cake
February – **National Cherry Month:** Cherry Turnovers, Cherry Chocolate Bread Pudding
February – **Potato Lover's Month:** Movie Night Potato Skins, Loaded Baked Potato Soup
February (second week) – **Great American Pizza Bake:** Chicago-Style Deep Dish Pizza
February (second week) – **Kraut and Frankfurter Week:** Diner Brats with Kraut
February 4 – **Homemade Soup Day:** 'Big Soup' Minestrone
February 7 – **National Fettuccine Alfredo Day:** Fettuccine Alfredo
February 26 – **National Chili Day:** Chase-the-Chill Chili
March 1 – **National Peanut Butter Lover's Day:** Crispy Bottom Peanut Butter Pie
March 14 – **National Potato Chip Day:** Handcut Potato Chips
March 18 – **Oatmeal Cookie Day:** Oatmeal Raisin Cookies
March 20 – **National Ravioli Day:** St. Louis T-Ravs
March 23 – **National Chip and Dip Day:** Everybody's Favorite Taco Dip
March 26 – **Spinach Day:** Cafe Spinach Dip, Portobello Popeye Club Sandwiches
April (entire month) – **National Soy Foods Month:** Red-Eye Tofu and Vegetable Skewers
April 7 – **National Coffee Cake Day:** Around-the-Clock Coffee Cake
April 13 – **National Peach Cobbler Day:** Peachy Keen Cobbler
April 16 – **Day of the Mushroom:** Smokin' BBQ Portobello Sandwiches
April 19 – **Garlic Day:** Sweet Garlicky Ribz
April 26 – **National Pretzel Day:** Roasted Garlic Pretzels
May 5 – **Cinco de Mayo:** Wet Bean Burritos, Mexicali Seitan, Tex–Mex Taco Salad
May 15 – **National Chocolate Chip Day:** Chocolate Chip Quick Cake
May 26 – **National Cherry Dessert Day:** Cherry Chocolate Bread Pudding with Vanilla Sauce
Memorial Day Monday – **National Hamburger Day:** All-American Incrediburgers

June (first Friday) – **National Doughnut Day:** Darngood Donut Bites

June 7 – **National Chocolate Ice Cream Day:** Double-Dark Mississippi Mud Pie

June 22 – **National Onion Rings Day:** Beer-Battered Onion Rings, Baked Onion Rings

July 3 – **Eat Beans Day:** Baked Beans, Three-Bean Salad

July 13 – **National French Fries Day:** Midway French Fries

July 14 – **Macaroni Day:** Homestyle Macaroni Salad, Mustard Mac Slaw

July 15 – **National Tapioca Pudding Day:** Mom's Tapioca Pudding

July 26 – **National Coffee Milkshake Day:** Vanilla Espresso Shake

July 30 – **National Cheesecake Day:** New York-Style Cheesecake

August 4 – **National Lasagna Day:** Pesto Lasagna with Slow-Roasted Tomatoes

August 5 – **National Waffle Day/National Peach Month:** Spiced Sour Cream Waffles with Peaches

August 10 – **National Banana Split Day:** Banana Split Cake

August 19 – **National Potato Day:** Cheezy Tofu Potato Skillet

August 28 – **National Cherry Turnover Day:** Cherry Turnovers

September 10 – **National TV Dinner Day:** Make your own Combo and watch a rerun

September 15 – **National Linguine Day:** Italian-Style Seitan with Linguine

September 26 – **National Pancake Day:** Cinnamon Flapjacks, Blueberry Oat Short Stack

September 28 – **Drink Beer Day:** Seitan Brew Stew

October (third week) – **National Kraut Sandwich Week:** Fork-and-Knife Reubens

October 4 – **Taco Day:** 21st Century Tacos

October 6 – **National Noodle Day:** Tuna–free Noodle Casserole

October 9 – **Sub/Hoagie/Hero/Grinder Day:** Seitan Po' Boys, Almost-Philly Cheese Steak Sandwiches

October 17 – **National Pasta Day:** Italian Big Bowl

October 29 – **National Oatmeal Day:** Oatmeal Raisin Cookies

November (the entire month) – **It's Vegan Month:** Celebrate with any of your favorite dishes

November (the entire month) – **Raisin Bread Month:** Very Vanilla Raisin Bread

November 3 – **National Sandwich Day:** Ultimate Tempeh Salad Sandwich, Greek Town Gyro

November 5 – **Doughnut Appreciation Day:** Darngood Donut Bites

November 9 – **Cook Something Bold and Pungent Day:** Seitan Goulash with Kraut

November 17 – **Homemade Bread Day:** Sandwich Bread, Yankee Cornbread

November 23 – **National Espresso Day:** Vanilla Espresso Shake

December 2 – **Apple Pie Day:** Apple Butterscotch Pie, Mom's Apple Pie

December 4 – **National Cookie Day:** Apricot Cream Cheese Cookies

About the Icons

 Make Ahead: Indicates recipes that taste best if prepared in advance or that can be assembled ahead of time for convenience.

 Quick: Indicates recipes that can be made in 30 minutes or less.

 Kid-Friendly: Indicates recipes that are especially appealing to children.

RISE AND SHINE

This chapter is filled with plenty of delectable ways to start the day, all animal-free and full of flavor. With these recipes, you can enjoy palate-pleasing vegan versions of your favorite breakfast foods around the clock. You'll find old standards as well as breakfasts inspired by regional specialties. From the Southwest, you can enjoy the zesty Tofu Rancheros, Mexican-Style "Beans-on-Bread" or savor the Yankee Cornbread with Blueberry Sauce from New England. How about some Cinnamon Flapjacks or Spiced Sour Cream Waffles with Peaches? Whether you prefer to start your day with an omelet, some pancakes, or just a muffin, the recipes in this chapter can help you rise and shine.

Very Vanilla Raisin Bread

Makes 1 loaf

Nothing turns a house into a home better than the aroma of freshly baked bread. If you've never baked bread before, this luscious loaf is reason enough to take the plunge and make your own (be sure to read Bread Basics, page 126). If you have leftovers, the slices make incredible toast or French toast.

1/2 cup raisins
2 tablespoons pure vanilla extract
1/4 cup warm water
1 1/2 tablespoons sugar, divided
2 teaspoons active dry yeast
3/4 cup soy milk
1 tablespoon apple cider vinegar
2 tablespoons canola oil
2 1/2 to 2 3/4 cups all-purpose flour
1 teaspoon salt
Raisin Bread Glaze (recipe follows),
   optional

1. In a small bowl, combine the raisins and the vanilla and set aside for one hour, or microwave on high for one minute.

2. In another small bowl, combine the warm water with 1/2 tablespoon sugar. Add the yeast and set aside until bubbly, about 3 minutes. In a separate bowl, combine the soy milk and vinegar and set aside for 3 minutes to curdle. Add the canola oil and set aside.

3. In a large bowl, combine 2 1/2 cups of the flour, the remaining 1 tablespoon sugar, and salt. Add the yeast mixture and the soy milk mixture. Stir together to form a cohesive soft dough, adding more flour if needed to make it manageable.

4. Transfer the dough to a lightly floured work surface. Knead 10 minutes, until smooth and elastic. During the last 2 minutes, knead the raisin mixture into the dough and shape the dough into a ball.

5. Lightly oil a large bowl. Place the dough into the bowl and cover with a clean towel. Let rise in a warm, draft free place for 60 to 90 minutes, or until you can poke your finger in the dough and the indentation doesn't fill in immediately. Lightly oil an 8-inch bread pan. Set aside.

6. Return the dough to a lightly floured work surface. Gently flatten the dough, then shape into a loaf, by folding both ends in and rolling the sides together. Transfer the loaf to the prepared pan and cover with a clean towel. Let rise another 45 minutes, checking again with the finger test. Preheat the oven to 375°F.

7. Bake for 20 minutes, then check to see if the top is getting too brown. If so, cover with foil. Continue to bake another 20 to 25 minutes, or until the bottom of the loaf sounds hollow when tapped with your knuckles. Remove from the pan and cool on a wire rack. Cool completely before slicing. Serve as is or drizzle the cooled loaf with the glaze.

Raisin Bread Glaze

For easy clean-up, place a piece of foil or wax paper under the wire rack where the bread has cooled. Note: the bread must be completely cool before glazing it or the glaze will drip off.

1/3 cup confectioners' sugar
1/4 teaspoon pure vanilla extract
1 to 2 teaspoons hot water

In a small bowl, combine all of the ingredients, whisking until smooth. Add a little more water if needed to adjust the consistency. The glaze should be thick yet pourable. Drizzle the glaze over the top of the cooled bread.

Cinnacrunch Muffins

Makes 1 dozen

Cinnamon lovers, this one is for you. The delicious crunch is baked right inside the muffins, not just on top. To make your next batch easier, make a double or triple batch of the crunch mixture. It stores well for up to 2 weeks if kept airtight.

CRUNCH:
1 cup packed light brown sugar
2/3 cup all-purpose flour
2 tablespoons ground cinnamon
6 tablespoons vegan margarine

MUFFINS:
1/2 cup canola oil
1 cup sugar
1/4 cup applesauce
1/4 cup soy milk
1/2 cup vegan sour cream
1 teaspoon pure vanilla extract
2 cups all-purpose flour
1 teaspoon baking powder
1/2 teaspoon baking soda
1 teaspoon salt
Pinch ground nutmeg

1. *Crunch:* Preheat the oven to 350°F. In a medium bowl, combine the brown sugar, flour, and cinnamon. Using a pastry cutter (or your fingers), crumble in the margarine until the mixture resembles pea-sized crumbs. Transfer the mixture to a baking sheet and bake for 7 to 8 minutes, until slightly golden. Remove from the oven and place the pan on a cooling rack for 2 hours, then break the crumb mixture apart so you have slightly larger than pea-sized crumbles. Set aside.

2. *Muffins:* Lightly oil a muffin tin. Preheat oven to 350°F. In a large bowl, combine the oil, sugar, applesauce, soy milk, sour cream, and vanilla. Whisk together until the sugar is dissolved and ingredients are combined.

3. In a medium bowl, whisk together the flour, baking powder, baking soda, salt, and nutmeg. Add the dry mixture to the wet ingredients. Add 1 1/4 cups of the crunch mixture. Stir gently to combine, but don't overmix. Transfer the batter to the muffin tin, filling the cups to almost full. Sprinkle 1 tablespoon of the remaining crunch mixture onto each muffin.

4. Bake 25 to 30 minutes, or until golden brown. Cool in the pan for 5 minutes, then transfer to a rack to finish cooling.

Around-the-Clock Coffee Cake

Serves 12

Not only is coffee cake great for breakfast, it's also wonderful with tea in the middle of the afternoon, or as a late-night snack. This is one of those cakes that you just keep slicing "one more piece" until, suddenly, it's all gone.

TOPPING:
1/4 cup all-purpose flour
1/2 cup packed light brown sugar
1 teaspoon ground cinnamon
1/4 teaspoon salt
1/4 cup vegan margarine, diced

CAKE:
1 tablespoon ground flaxseed
3 tablespoons hot water
1 cup sugar
1/2 cup vegan margarine, room temperature
1 teaspoon pure vanilla extract
2 cups all-purpose flour
1 teaspoon baking powder
1 teaspoon baking soda
1/2 teaspoon salt
1 cup vegan sour cream
1 to 2 tablespoons soy milk, if needed

1. *Topping:* In a medium bowl, combine the flour, brown sugar, cinnamon, and salt. Add the margarine, using your fingers to blend it in until it resembles peas. Set aside. Preheat the oven to 350°F. Lightly oil a 10-inch tube pan or a 9-inch square baking pan.

2. *Cake:* In a blender, combine the flaxseed and water and blend until frothy and thick. Set aside. In a medium bowl, combine the sugar and margarine. Use an electric mixer to cream them until fluffy. Add the flax mixture and vanilla. Mix to combine.

3. In a medium bowl, combine the flour, baking powder, baking soda, and salt. Mix well. Add half of the dry ingredients to the sugar mixture and mix until combined. Add the sour cream and the remaining dry ingredients. Mix well to combine. The batter should be thick but pourable. If it is too thick, add 1 to 2 tablespoons soy milk.

4. Spoon about two-thirds of the batter into the prepared pan, spreading evenly. Sprinkle with half of the topping. Spoon the remaining batter on top and spread as evenly as possible. Sprinkle with the remaining topping.

5. Bake for 40 to 45 minutes, or until a toothpick inserted in the center comes out clean. Let the cake cool in the pan on a wire rack. If using a tube pan, remove the cake from the pan once it has cooled. If using a square pan, serve the cake from the pan.

Darngood Donut Bites

Makes about 20

There's nothing like the wonderful aroma of fresh baked donuts, but vegan donuts can be hard to come by. These "bites" are quicker and easier than traditional donuts, and you don't have to get up at 4:00 A.M. to make them. Be sure to keep them close to 1-inch in diameter or the insides won't cook completely.

1/4 cup soy milk
1 teaspoon apple cider vinegar
2 tablespoons maple syrup
1 teaspoon pure vanilla extract
1/4 cup applesauce
1 1/3 cups all-purpose flour
3 tablespoons sugar, divided
1 teaspoon baking powder
1/2 teaspoon baking soda
1/2 teaspoon salt
1 1/2 teaspoons ground cinnamon
Canola oil, for frying

1. In a small bowl, combine the soy milk and vinegar. Let sit until curdled, about 3 minutes. Add the maple syrup, vanilla, and applesauce. Stir together and set aside.

2. In a medium bowl, combine the flour, 1 tablespoon of the sugar, baking powder, baking soda, and salt. Stir together. Add the liquid ingredients to the dry ingredients and mix together. The dough should be stiff, but easy to shape. Add 1 tablespoon extra soy milk or flour if needed.

3. Heat a 1/4-inch layer of oil in a large skillet over medium heat. Combine the remaining 2 tablespoons sugar and cinnamon on a plate. Set aside.

4. Shape the dough into 1-inch balls. Working in batches, fry the dough balls in the oil, turning often until all sides are golden brown, about 10 minutes. Remove and drain on paper towels. While still hot, roll the dough balls in the cinnamon sugar mixture. Serve immediately.

Chinatown Scramble

Serves 4

Enjoy the flavors of Chinatown in this fresh-tasting scramble. You can put it on the table in no time and enjoy it any time of day. If some of the people you feed like extra heat, serve some Sriracha chili sauce on the side.

1 pound extra-firm tofu, drained and
    pressed
1/2 teaspoon five-spice powder
1/2 teaspoon garlic powder
1/2 teaspoon turmeric
1/4 teaspoon ginger powder
1 teaspoon salt
1 tablespoon peanut oil
1/2 medium onion, chopped
1/2 red bell pepper, chopped
1 small hot chile, seeded and minced,
    optional
1 cup chopped shiitake mushroom caps
1/2 teaspoon chili oil, or to taste
3 tablespoons nutritional yeast
Juice of 1/2 lime
1 tablespoon soy sauce
1/4 cup scallions, sliced into 1/4-inch
    pieces, divided
1/2 cup bean sprouts, chopped into
    1-inch pieces
1/2 cup snow peas, trimmed, and cut
    into 1-inch pieces
1 teaspoon grated fresh ginger
2 cloves garlic, minced
2 cups bean sprouts, for plating
Toasted sesame seeds, optional garnish

1. Cut half of the tofu into 1/2-inch cubes and set aside. Crumble the remaining half of the tofu and set aside. In a small bowl, combine the five-spice powder, garlic powder, turmeric, ginger powder, and salt.

2. Heat 1 tablespoon oil in a large skillet over medium heat. Add the onion and cook 3 minutes. Add the bell pepper and chile, if using. Cook 2 minutes. Add the shiitakes and cook 3 to 5 minutes, or until the mushrooms are soft.

3. Add the reserved spice mixture to the skillet, then stir in the chili oil. Add the cubed and crumbled tofu. Cook, stirring occasionally, about 5 minutes, until the ingredients are combined and the tofu takes on some color.

4. Add the nutritional yeast, lime juice, and soy sauce. Cook, stirring occasionally, for 5 minutes. Add 2 tablespoons of the scallions, the chopped bean sprouts, snow peas, fresh ginger, and garlic. Cook until fragrant, about 2 minutes.

5. To serve, divide the whole bean sprouts among four plates, then spoon the scramble on top, dividing evenly. Top with the remaining scallions and sesame seeds, if using.

Mediterranean Scramble

Serves 4

This colorful scramble features the Mediterranean flavors of Little Italy for you to enjoy right in your own kitchen.

1 tablespoon olive oil
1/2 medium onion, chopped
1/2 medium red bell pepper, chopped
1 pound extra-firm tofu, drained,
   pressed, and crumbled
1 teaspoon dried parsley
1 teaspoon dried oregano
1 teaspoon dried basil
1/4 teaspoon turmeric
1 teaspoon salt
3 cloves roasted garlic (page 47)
Juice of 1/2 lemon
1/4 cup pitted black olives, chopped
1/2 cup ripe cherry tomatoes, halved
2 tablespoons nutritional yeast
2 cups tightly packed fresh baby spinach
Chopped fresh basil, for garnish

1. Heat the oil in a large skillet over medium heat. Add the onion and cook until almost translucent, about 5 minutes. Add the bell pepper and cook 2 to 3 minutes. Add the tofu and cook 3 to 5 minutes longer.

2. In a small bowl, combine dried herbs, turmeric, salt, roasted garlic, and the lemon juice and mix to a paste. Add the paste to the tofu mixture and continue to cook 3 to 4 minutes.

3. Add the olives, cherry tomatoes, and nutritional yeast. Cook, stirring, 5 minutes longer, then add the spinach and cook until just wilted, 3 to 5 minutes. Spoon the scramble onto plates and garnish with basil. Serve immediately.

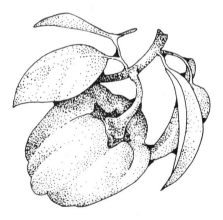

Tofu Rancheros

Serves 4

The Southwestern classic "Huevos Rancheros" is a popular feature on many breakfast menus. Now, with tofu taking the lead role, the dish is no longer off limits. Fire-roasted, diced tomatoes add a wonderful smoky flavor. Ordinary chili powder may be substituted for the chipotle chili powder. This dish may be a little spicy for some palates, so reduce the spices if you prefer.

SAUCE:

1 tablespoon olive oil
1/2 medium onion, chopped
2 cloves garlic, minced
1/2 small jalapeño, seeded and minced
1/2 medium red bell pepper, chopped
1 teaspoon ground cumin
1 teaspoon chipotle chili powder
1/2 teaspoon salt
1/2 teaspoon sugar
1 (14.5-ounce) can diced tomatoes, undrained

TOFU:

1 tablespoon olive oil
1/4 cup chopped scallions, divided
1/2 large poblano chile, seeded, and diced
2 cloves garlic, minced
1 teaspoon ground cumin
1 teaspoon salt
1/2 teaspoon smoked paprika
1/2 teaspoon dried oregano
1/2 teaspoon chili powder
1/2 teaspoon turmeric
1 pound extra-firm tofu, drained, pressed, and crumbled
1/4 cup nutritional yeast
1 1/2 cups cooked or 1 (15-ounce) can pinto beans, rinsed and drained
Juice of 1/2 lime
2 teaspoons canola oil, if using tortillas
4 corn tortillas for serving, optional

OPTIONAL TOPPINGS:

Vegan sour cream, shredded vegan cheese, chopped pitted green or black olives, chopped cilantro

1. *Sauce:* In a medium saucepan, heat the oil over medium heat. Add the onion and cook 3 to 5 minutes to soften. Add the garlic, jalapeño, and bell pepper. Cook for 2 minutes. Add the cumin, chili powder, salt, sugar, and tomatoes with juice. Bring to a boil then reduce to a simmer for 15 minutes. Keep warm.

2. *Tofu:* Heat the oil in a large skillet over medium heat. Add 2 tablespoons of the scallions and the poblano. Cook 3 minutes or until the poblano begins to soften. Add the garlic and cook 2 minutes. Add the cumin, salt, smoked paprika, oregano, chili powder, and turmeric. Stir for 1 minute. Add the crumbled tofu, nutritional yeast, pinto beans, and lime juice, and mix well. Cook, stirring occasionally for 12 to 15 minutes, until the tofu is golden brown. If the mixture is dry, add a tablespoon of water.

3. If serving with tortillas, heat the canola oil in a small skillet over medium heat. Cook each tortilla 3 to 5 minutes, until lightly browned. Turn and cook the other side, 1 to 2 minutes, until lightly browned. Arrange on plates. Spoon the tofu onto the tortillas, if using, or directly onto plates. Spoon the sauce on top of the tofu. Sprinkle with the remaining 2 tablespoons scallions and other toppings, as desired. Serve immediately.

Noodle Omelet

After cooking on the stove, the omelet is finished by baking it in the oven, similar to a frittata. The broiled top is a terrific way to accentuate the creamy noodle filling.

4 ounces capellini or other thin pasta
1 tablespoon plus 1 teaspoon olive oil, divided
1/4 cup minced red bell pepper
2 tablespoons finely minced onion
15 ounces extra-firm tofu, drained and crumbled
1/2 cup cooked chickpeas
1 tablespoon cornstarch
3 tablespoons nutritional yeast
1 tablespoon fresh lemon juice
1 cup vegetable broth
1/2 teaspoon garlic powder
1/2 teaspoon turmeric
1/2 teaspoon salt
1/4 teaspoon ground mustard
1/8 teaspoon ground white pepper
2 tablespoons minced fresh parsley

1. Cook the capellini in a pot of boiling salted water until al dente, 2 to 3 minutes. Drain, run under cold water, and drain again. Place the noodles in a large bowl and set aside. Preheat the oven to 375°F.

2. In a small skillet, heat 1 teaspoon oil over medium heat. Add the bell pepper and onion and cook 2 minutes to soften, then add to the bowl with the pasta. Set aside.

3. In a blender, combine the remaining ingredients except the parsley and remaining olive oil. Blend until smooth. Add the tofu mixture to the pasta and vegetables and mix well.

4. Heat a 10-inch ovenproof skillet over medium-high heat. Add the remaining tablespoon of oil and swirl to coat the bottom and sides of the skillet. Pour the mixture into the pan, spreading evenly. Reduce the heat to medium and cook 15 minutes, until the edges are dulled and golden brown. Transfer to the oven and bake 15 to 17 minutes, until the top surface is golden brown.

5. If desired, broil on high until nicely browned, about 3 additional minutes. Cut into quarters and serve garnished with parsley.

Western Omelet

Serves 4

Despite the old saying to the contrary, you really can make an omelet without breaking some eggs. This modern twist on the western omelet proves the point, and with fantastic flavor to boot.

OMELET:

15 ounces extra-firm tofu, drained and crumbled
1/2 cup cooked chickpeas
1/4 cup cornstarch
1/4 cup nutritional yeast
1 tablespoon plus 1 teaspoon red wine vinegar
2 teaspoons prepared mustard
1 teaspoon dried parsley
1 teaspoon All-American Spice Blend (page 13), or other spice blend
1/2 teaspoon salt
Pinch sugar
1 cup vegetable broth
2 tablespoons dry white wine, or more broth

FILLING:

1 tablespoon olive oil, plus more for cooking omelet
6 ounces Portobello mushroom caps, gills scraped out, thinly sliced
1/2 teaspoon liquid smoke (see note)
1/2 medium onion, thinly sliced
1 medium red bell pepper, thinly sliced
4 cups chopped Swiss chard
10 ounces Vegan Sausage Links (page 41) or store-bought, cut into 1/4-inch slices
2 cloves garlic, minced
1 teaspoon dried parsley
1/4 teaspoon smoked paprika
1/4 teaspoon red pepper flakes
1/2 teaspoon balsamic vinegar
Salt and black pepper
1/2 cup salsa, optional garnish
2 tablespoons chopped parsley

1. *Omelet:* Combine all the ingredients in a blender. Blend until very smooth, scraping the sides down as needed. Set aside.

2. *Filling:* Heat the 1 tablespoon oil in a large nonstick skillet over medium heat. Add the mushrooms and cook for 5 minutes, or until softened. Add the liquid smoke, then cook 1 more minute to blend flavors. Remove from the skillet and set aside. If any liquid remains in the skillet, that's okay.

3. In the same skillet over medium heat, add the onion and bell pepper and cook for 6 to 8 minutes, or until the onion begins to soften. Add the chard, sausage, garlic, parsley, paprika, red pepper flakes, and balsamic vinegar. Cook 4 to 5 minutes, or until the chard is wilted. Season with salt and pepper, to taste. Preheat the oven to 250°F.

4. Lightly oil a large nonstick skillet and heat it over medium heat. Ladle about 3/4 cup of the omelet batter into the hot skillet. Spread it gently with a spatula until it's about 7 inches across. Cook 5 to 7 minutes, or until the mixture is set and the top surface has darkened and the edges begin to curl. Sprinkle about one-fourth of the filling onto one half of the omelet and add one-fourth of the mushrooms. Fold the omelet and cook 2 more minutes. Repeat until all omelets are cooked. Keep the cooked omelets warm in the oven until all of them are cooked. Serve hot, garnished with the salsa, if using, and the parsley.

NOTE: Liquid smoke is a concentrated seasoning that gives a smoky flavor to food. Usually used in small amounts, it is sold in small bottles in the supermarket. It is typically vegan, but, as always, be sure to check the label.

Country Skillet

Serves 4

This homestyle favorite, made with potatoes, onions, peppers, and vegan sausage, makes a hearty brunch or dinner.

8 ounces small red potatoes, cut into 1-inch pieces
2 tablespoons olive oil, divided
1/2 medium onion, chopped
1/2 red or green bell pepper, chopped
6 ounces Vegan Sausage Links (page 41) or store-bought, cut into 1/4-inch slices
1 pound extra-firm tofu, drained, pressed, and cut into 1/2-inch dice
6 ounces Swiss chard, stemmed and chopped
2 cloves garlic, minced
1 cup sliced cremini mushrooms
3 tablespoons nutritional yeast
Juice of 1/2 lemon
1 teaspoon dried basil
1 teaspoon dried parsley
1 teaspoon dried thyme
1/2 teaspoon turmeric
1 teaspoon salt
Pinch ground cayenne

1. Steam the potatoes over a pot of boiling water until fork tender, 12 to 15 minutes. Heat 1 tablespoon oil in a large skillet over medium-high heat. Add the potatoes and cook 6 to 8 minutes, until they begin to turn to brown. Reduce the heat to medium if the potatoes get too dark, then transfer to a plate and set aside.

2. In the same skillet, heat the remaining 1 tablespoon oil over medium heat. Add the onion and cook for 2 minutes. Add the pepper and sausage and cook 2 minutes, or until the pepper starts to soften and the sausage begins to brown.

3. Add the tofu, chard, garlic, and mushrooms. Cook, stirring, for 5 minutes, or until the tofu begins to turn golden.

4. Add the yeast, lemon juice, herbs, salt, and cayenne. Cook for 5 minutes to allow the flavors to blend. If the mixture is dry, add a splash of water. Add the reserved potatoes to the tofu mixture and cook another 5 minutes. Serve immediately.

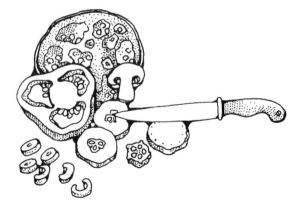

City Skillet

Serves 4

A dish that evokes the sounds and spices of a thousand sizzling skillets in city neighborhoods all over the Americas. Welcome to the neighborhood.

8 ounces small red potatoes, scrubbed and cut into 1-inch pieces
1/2 cup roasted red bell pepper (below) or store-bought
1 tablespoon tomato paste
1 tablespoon olive oil
2 medium shallots, sliced
1 cup sliced cremini mushrooms
2 cloves garlic, minced
1 pound extra-firm tofu, drained, pressed, and cut into 1-inch cubes
1 teaspoon dried *herbes de Provençe*
1/2 teaspoon All-American Spice Blend (page 13) or other spice blend
1/2 teaspoon ground ginger
1/2 teaspoon turmeric
1 teaspoon salt
3 tablespoons nutritional yeast
Juice of 1/2 lemon
3 tablespoons vegetable broth
1 tablespoon soy sauce
1 cup tightly packed fresh arugula
2 tablespoons chopped sun-dried tomatoes (oil-packed or reconstituted)

1. Steam potatoes over a pot of boiling water for 12 to 14 minutes or until just soft. Set aside.

2. In a blender or food processor, combine the roasted bell pepper and tomato paste and process until smooth. Set aside.

3. Heat the oil in a large skillet over medium heat. Add the potatoes. Cook 5 minutes, or until golden. Add the shallots and cook 5 minutes longer. Add the mushrooms and garlic, and cook another 3 minutes, or until the mushrooms begin to soften. Add the tofu, *herbes de Provençe*, spice blend, ginger, turmeric, and salt. Cook, stirring, for 1 minute, then add the yeast, lemon juice, broth, and soy sauce. Cook for 10 minutes, or until the tofu begins to turn golden.

4. Add the arugula and sun-dried tomatoes. Cook until the arugula starts to wilt, about 3 minutes. To serve, spoon the tofu mixture onto plates. Top each serving with the reserved sauce.

● ● ● ● ● ● ● ● ● ●

To Roast Bell Peppers and Chiles: Place the peppers on a small baking sheet and broil until blackened, turning every few minutes. Place the blackened peppers in a brown paper bag, then close the bag and set aside for 20 minutes. Remove and discard the skin and seeds. The peppers are now ready to use.

Southwestern Griddle

Serves 4

Discovering regional cuisines is one of my favorite reasons to visit mom and pop joints when traveling. To recall the deep, spicy flavors of the Southwest, I like to make this zesty dish that's great for breakfast, lunch, or dinner.

6 ounces small red potatoes, scrubbed, cut into 1-inch pieces
1 to 2 tablespoons canola oil
1/2 cup chopped red onion
1/2 cup chopped red bell pepper
1/2 jalapeño chile, seeded and minced
4 ounces Vegan Sausage Links (page 41) or store-bought, chopped
1 cup sliced cremini mushrooms
2 cloves garlic, minced
2 teaspoons ground cumin
1 1/4 teaspoons chili powder
1 teaspoon dried oregano
1 teaspoon salt
1 pound extra-firm tofu, drained, pressed, and crumbled
3 tablespoons nutritional yeast
2 tablespoons water
Juice of 1 lime, divided
1 teaspoon hot sauce
1 tablespoon chopped scallions
1 ripe Hass avocado, pitted, peeled, and cut into 1/2-inch dice
1 tablespoon chopped fresh cilantro
1/2 cup fresh cherry tomatoes, quartered
Black pepper

1. Steam the potatoes over a pot of boiling water for 12 to 14 minutes, or until just soft. Set aside.

2. Heat 1 tablespoon oil in large skillet over medium heat. Add the potatoes, tossing to coat with oil and cook 3 to 5 minutes, or until golden. Add the onion, bell pepper, chile, and sausage. If the mixture is sticking, add another tablespoon of oil. Cook 2 minutes, then add the mushrooms and garlic and cook 3 minutes, or until the mushrooms begin to soften. Add the cumin, chili powder, oregano, and salt. Stir to coat. The mixture will be dry. Add the tofu, yeast, water, half of the lime juice, and hot sauce. Stir to combine, then cook about 15 minutes to allow the flavors to combine, stirring occasionally.

3. While the mixture is cooking, make the topping. In a small bowl, combine the scallions, avocado, cilantro, remaining lime juice, and cherry tomatoes. Season with salt and pepper, to taste. To serve, spoon the tofu mixture onto plates and top each serving with the avocado mixture. Serve hot.

TIP

If the avocados at your market aren't at their peak, top this dish with some salsa instead. As always, adjust the spices to your own taste and pass the hot sauce at the table.

Cheezy Tofu Potato Skillet

Serves 4

This isn't one of those "ready in fifteen" type of breakfasts, but the preparation time is worth every minute. In a pinch, the tofu and vegetables can be prepared as a scramble and spread on the potato "crust" to save time.

8 ounces extra-firm tofu, drained,
    pressed, and cut into 1/2-inch cubes
1/2 teaspoon ground cumin
1/4 teaspoon garlic powder
1/4 teaspoon ground fennel
1 tablespoon nutritional yeast
1/2 teaspoon liquid smoke
2 tablespoons olive oil, divided
1/2 medium onion, diced
1/2 medium red bell pepper, diced
1/2 teaspoon dried basil
1/2 teaspoon dried oregano
1/4 teaspoon smoked paprika
2 cloves garlic, minced
1 recipe Classic Cafe Hash Browns
    (page 44)
1/2 cup chopped ripe cherry tomatoes
2 tablespoons minced pitted black
    olives, optional
1/2 recipe Quick-and-Easy Cheezy
    Sauce (recipe follows)

1. In a medium bowl, combine the tofu cubes with the cumin, garlic powder, fennel, yeast, and liquid smoke and toss to coat. Set aside.

2. In a small skillet, heat 1 tablespoon olive oil over medium heat. Add the onion, bell pepper, basil, oregano, and paprika. Cook for about 3 minutes. Add the garlic. Cook for 1 to 2 minutes, or until the garlic is fragrant. Transfer the vegetables to a plate and set aside.

3. To the same skillet, add the remaining 1 tablespoon olive oil over medium heat. Add the reserved tofu and cook until golden, about 10 minutes, turning as needed. Set aside. Preheat the broiler.

4. In an ovenproof skillet, top the hash browns with the onion mixture followed by the tofu mixture, leaving a 1/4-inch edge around the perimeter. Spread the tomatoes and olives, if using, over the tofu layer. Spoon the Cheezy Sauce over the top and place under the broiler for 3 to 4 minutes, or until the sauce starts to bubble. Cut into quarters and serve immediately.

Quick-and-Easy Cheezy Sauce

About 1 1/2 cups

This sauce is extremely versatile. Try it on baked potatoes, in other breakfast skillets, or over noodles for mac and cheeze in a snap.

1/4 cup olive oil
1/2 cup nutritional yeast
1 cup plus 1/4 cup soy milk, divided
1 teaspoon dried mustard
1 teaspoon salt
1 teaspoon garlic powder
1/2 teaspoon onion powder

1. Heat the oil in a small saucepan over medium heat. Whisk in the yeast, the 1 cup soy milk, mustard, salt, garlic powder, onion powder, basil, and thyme.

2. In a small bowl, combine the cornstarch with the remaining 1/4 cup soy milk, mixing until smooth. Add the cornstarch mixture to the saucepan, whisking constantly. Bring to a boil,

1/2 teaspoon dried basil
1/2 teaspoon dried thyme
2 tablespoons cornstarch
Salt and black pepper

then reduce the heat to low. Simmer gently to thicken. Season with salt and pepper to taste.

Sweet and Crunchy French Toast

Serves 4

"Order up" will get everyone's attention when this delightfully decadent French toast hits the plate. To add a touch of finesse, top with fresh berries.

1 1/2 cups vegan corn flakes
1 1/2 tablespoons sugar
3/4 teaspoon ground cinnamon
3/4 cup soy milk
3/4 cup vegan soy creamer or additional
   3/4 cup soy milk
1 1/2 tablespoons fresh orange juice
1 teaspoon pure vanilla extract
Pinch salt
1/4 cup all-purpose flour
2 tablespoons canola oil
8 (1-inch) slices day-old French bread
Vegan margarine and maple syrup, for
   serving

1. Place the corn flakes in a plastic bag and use a rolling pin to crush them into small pea-sized crumbs. Transfer the crumbs to a shallow pan, add the sugar and cinnamon and mix well. Set aside.

2. In a separate shallow pan, combine the soy milk, creamer, orange juice, vanilla, and salt. Mix together with a fork. Add the flour, stirring to combine. It's okay if the batter has a few lumps.

3. Heat the oil in a large skillet over medium heat. Preheat the oven to 250°F. Working in batches, dip the bread slices in the soy milk mixture, then dip them in the corn flake mixture, coating both sides. Place the coated bread in the hot skillet and cook for 5 minutes, or until golden brown. Turn to cook the other side for 3 to 4 minutes, or until golden.

4. Transfer the cooked French toast to an ovenproof platter and keep warm in the oven until all of it is cooked. Serve hot with margarine and maple syrup.

Any-Day French Toast with Sweet Spread

Serves 4

This is my take on a favorite French toast that my grandmother used to make. The key is in the amount of frying oil, which makes it taste so great. The Sweet Spread makes it extra special. Try the spread on any breakfast bread or even regular toast. Instead of using French bread, try other favorites, such as cinnamon bread or Very Vanilla Raisin Bread (page 18).

SWEET SPREAD:
1/4 cup vegan margarine, room temperature
1 to 2 tablespoons maple syrup
1/4 teaspoon ground cinnamon
Pinch salt

FRENCH TOAST:
1 1/2 cups soy milk
1 1/2 teaspoons pure vanilla extract
1/4 teaspoon salt
1 tablespoon sugar
1 teaspoon lemon or orange zest, optional
1 cup all-purpose flour
1 teaspoon ground cinnamon
8 (1-inch) slices day-old French bread
1/4 to 1/2 cup canola oil
Maple syrup, for serving

1. *Spread:* In a small bowl, combine the margarine, maple syrup, cinnamon, and salt. Whisk until smooth. Refrigerate until ready to serve.

2. *French toast:* In a shallow bowl, combine the soy milk and vanilla. Add the salt, sugar, and zest, if using. Add the flour and cinnamon, mixing together with a fork. The batter doesn't need to be smooth. Lumps are preferred. In a large skillet over medium heat, heat 1/4-inch canola oil. Preheat the oven to 250°F.

3. Dip each slice of bread in the batter until well coated. If the batter becomes too thick, mix in a little additional soy milk. Working in batches, place the coated bread in the skillet and cook for 5 minutes, or until golden brown. Turn to cook the other side for 3 minutes, or until golden brown.

4. Transfer the cooked French toast to an ovenproof platter and keep warm in the oven until all of it is cooked. Serve hot with Sweet Spread and maple syrup.

NOTE: If you don't have day-old bread, you can dry sliced fresh bread by baking it in a 200°F. oven for 5 to 7 minutes. As an alternative, you can slice it and leave it out to dry overnight.

Savory Stuffed French Toast with Mustard-Shallot Sauce

This recipe sounds more like a fancy bistro "Special" than a regular menu item, but it's so simple and quick to make, it's sure to be in regular rotation in your kitchen. For a delicious variation, substitute an apple for the pear and Seitan Breakfast Strips (page 42) for the "ham."

SAUCE:
3 tablespoons olive oil
1 shallot, minced
2 tablespoons sherry vinegar
3 tablespoons all-purpose flour
1 to 1 1/2 cups vegetable broth
1 1/2 tablespoons nutritional yeast
1 1/2 tablespoons Dijon mustard
1/4 teaspoon smoked paprika
1/4 teaspoon dried thyme

FRENCH TOAST:
8 (1 1/2-inch thick) slices day-old French bread
8 slices vegan ham, cut in half, or 1/2 recipe Diner Tempeh Breakfast Patties (page 43), halved
1 fresh ripe pear, cut into 1/4-inch slices
1/2 cup all-purpose flour
1/4 teaspoon dried sage
1/4 teaspoon turmeric
2 tablespoons nutritional yeast
1/4 teaspoon salt
Pinch black pepper
1 cup soy milk
Canola oil or nonstick spray, for cooking

1. *Sauce:* Heat the olive oil in a small saucepan over medium heat. Add the shallot and cook, stirring for 3 minutes, or until softened. Add the sherry and cook 2 minutes longer. Add the flour and stir until it forms a paste. Whisk in the broth, nutritional yeast, mustard, paprika, and thyme. Cook, stirring, until thickened, about 5 minutes. Remove from the heat and set aside.

2. *French toast:* Use a serrated knife to carefully cut pockets into the bread slices, leaving the slices intact. Do not cut all the way through the bread. Place one slice of ham or a patty into each bread pocket, along with 2 or 3 pear slices. Set aside.

3. In a shallow pan, combine the flour, sage, turmeric, nutritional yeast, salt, and pepper. Add the soy milk, stirring to combine. It's okay if some lumps remain in the batter. Heat a large skillet over medium heat with just enough oil (or cooking spray) to coat the bottom.

4. Dip the bread pockets into the batter, coating both sides, then transfer to the skillet. Cook until golden, about 5 minutes. Turn to cook the other side about 3 minutes, or until golden.

5. While the French toast is cooking, reheat the sauce, adding a little broth if needed to thin. To serve, divide the French toast among plates and top with sauce. Serve hot.

Mexican-Style 'Beans on Bread'

Serves 4

Beans-on-Bread, or B-O-B, was a dinner favorite of revolutionary America. Even then, it was the ultimate in colonial-style comfort food. My version transforms this dish into a fancy looking breakfast with a Mexican twist.

BEANS:

1 tablespoon olive oil
3/4 cup chopped red onion
2 cloves garlic, minced
3/4 cup chopped poblano chile
1 small jalapeño, seeded and minced
1 1/2 teaspoons ground cumin, divided
3/4 teaspoon dried oregano
1/8 teaspoon ground cayenne
1/4 cup plus 2 tablespoons corn, fresh or
    frozen, thawed
1 1/2 cups cooked or 1 (15.5-ounce) can
    black beans, rinsed and drained
1 cup canned diced tomatoes, with juice
Salt and black pepper

FRENCH TOAST:

1/4 cup finely ground cornmeal
1/2 cup all-purpose flour
1 tablespoon nutritional yeast
1/2 teaspoon ground cumin
1/4 teaspoon chili powder
1/2 teaspoon salt
1 1/4 cups soy milk
Canola oil, for cooking
8 (1-inch) slices day-old French bread
1 ripe Hass avocado, pitted, peeled, and
    cut into 1/2-inch wedges
Vegan sour cream and salsa, optional
    garnish

1. *Beans:* Heat the olive oil in a medium saucepan over medium heat. Add the onion, garlic, and chiles. Cook 5 minutes, or until the vegetables are softened. Add the cumin, oregano, and cayenne. Stir 2 minutes. Add the corn, beans, and tomatoes. Season with salt and pepper to taste. Bring to a boil then reduce to medium and simmer for 10 to 15 minutes. Keep warm.

2. *French toast:* In a shallow bowl, combine the cornmeal, flour, nutritional yeast, cumin, chili powder, and salt. Stir with a fork to mix. Add the soy milk and stir to combine. A few lumps in the batter are fine. Heat a large skillet over medium heat, with enough oil to cover the bottom. Preheat the oven to 250°F.

3. Working in batches, dip the bread slices in the batter, then add to the skillet and cook until golden, about 5 minutes. If the batter becomes too thick, add a little more soy milk to thin it. Turn to cook the other side until golden, about 3 minutes.

4. Transfer the cooked French toast to an ovenproof platter and keep warm in the oven until all of it is cooked. To serve, place the French toast on plates. Spoon the beans onto the French toast and arrange the avocado wedges around the toast. Top with sour cream and salsa, if using.

Spiced Sour Cream Waffles with Peaches

Serves 4

These rich waffles are spiced with cinnamon and ginger, then topped with peaches. They make a perfect cafe-style breakfast, any time of the day or night. Cooked waffles may be recrisped in a toaster for a quick breakfast.

2 cups all-purpose flour
1 tablespoon plus 1 teaspoon baking powder
2 teaspoons baking soda
2 teaspoons ground cinnamon
1 teaspoon ground ginger
1/2 teaspoon salt
1 cup soy milk
1 cup vegan sour cream
1/2 cup canola oil
1/4 cup maple syrup
1 teaspoon pure vanilla extract
1 quart fresh peaches, peeled, pitted, and sliced

1. Preheat the waffle iron. In a large bowl, combine the flour, baking powder, baking soda, cinnamon, ginger, and salt. Whisk together.

2. In a medium bowl, combine the soy milk, sour cream, oil, maple syrup, and vanilla. Whisk together. Add to the dry ingredients and mix well. If the mixture is too thick, add a little more soy milk as needed. Preheat the oven to 250°F.

3. Spray the waffle iron with nonstick cooking spray. Pour the waffle batter onto the waffle iron and cook according to the manufacturer's instructions. Transfer the cooked waffles to an ovenproof platter and keep warm in the oven until all of them are cooked. Serve the waffles topped with the sliced peaches.

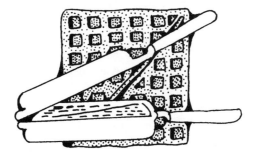

Summer Waffles
with Lemon Sauce

Serves 4

Diners have their own special language. For example, if these waffles were served in a diner, they might be called "Summer Checkerboard with a Twist."

3 cups soy milk
1/4 cup sugar
2 teaspoons active dry yeast
1/4 cup canola oil
3 1/2 cups all-purpose flour
2 teaspoons baking powder
1 teaspoon salt
1 teaspoon ground cinnamon
2 teaspoons pure vanilla extract
Lemon Sauce (recipe follows)
Fresh berries, for serving

1. Heat the soy milk to lukewarm then transfer to a large bowl. Stir in the sugar and yeast. Set aside to bubble and proof, about 5 minutes. Stir in the oil.

2. In a medium bowl, combine the flour, baking powder, salt, and cinnamon and mix well. Add the dry mixture to the wet mixture. Stir in the vanilla and mix well. Cover the batter with plastic wrap and let rise overnight in the refrigerator or for several hours at room temperature. **The longer the batter sits, the thicker it will be.**

3. Preheat the oven to 250°F. Spray the waffle iron with non-stick cooking spray. Preheat the waffle iron. Stir the batter. If it's too thick to spoon onto the waffle iron, stir in a little more soy milk until smooth. When the waffle iron is hot, cook the waffles according to the manufacturer's instructions.

4. Transfer the cooked waffles to an ovenproof platter and keep warm in the oven until all of them are cooked. To serve, drizzle with Lemon Sauce and top with berries.

Lemon Sauce

Makes 1 cup

1/4 cup fresh lemon juice
1/4 cup soy milk
3 1/2 to 4 cups confectioners' sugar, sifted
1 teaspoon fresh lemon zest
Pinch salt

Combine all the ingredients in a small bowl. Whisk together until well combined. Add a little more confectioners' sugar or soy milk until the mixture reaches the desired consistency.

Cinnamon Flapjacks

Serves 4

During the 1970s, pancake houses were all the rage with their multi-page menu choices – none of them vegan. Even if you could get vegan pancakes at a local eatery today, they still wouldn't be as delicious as the ones you make "to order" at home. Traditionally, flapjacks are a thinner pancake, but if you prefer them thicker, use less soy milk.

1 1/2 cups all-purpose flour
2 teaspoons baking powder
1 teaspoon baking soda
1/2 teaspoon ground cinnamon
1/2 teaspoon salt
1/2 cup vegan vanilla yogurt
2 tablespoons maple syrup
2 tablespoons canola oil, plus more for cooking
1/2 teaspoon pure vanilla extract
1 to 1 1/2 cups soy milk
Vegan margarine and maple syrup, for serving

VARIATION

Shredded apple is a great addition to these flapjacks and can be stirred into the batter just before pouring onto the skillet. For an extra wallop of cinnamon, top with Sweet Spread (page 32).

1. In a large mixing bowl, combine the flour, baking powder, baking soda, cinnamon, and salt. Whisk to combine. Set aside.

2. In a medium bowl, combine the yogurt, maple syrup, oil, and vanilla. Add 1 cup of the soy milk for thicker pancakes, or up to 1 1/2 cups for thinner ones. Stir well to combine.

3. Heat a large skillet over medium heat. Lightly oil the surface. The skillet is hot enough when you can flick water on it and the water sizzles. Preheat the oven to 250°F.

4. Pour the wet ingredients into the dry ingredients and stir until combined. Working in batches, use a measuring cup or ladle, to pour 1/4 to 1/3 cup of the pancake mixture onto the skillet for each pancake. Be sure to leave them room to spread.

5. Cook until the bottoms are golden brown, about 5 minutes. Turn to cook the other side until golden, about 3 minutes. Transfer the cooked pancakes to an ovenproof platter and keep warm in the oven until all the pancakes are cooked. Serve hot with margarine and maple syrup.

Blueberry-Oat Short Stack

Serves 4

In diner lingo, pancakes are sometimes called "blow-outs," because they look like blown-out tires. Whether you call them blow-outs, hotcakes, flapjacks, or pancakes, this "short stack" always hits the spot.

1 cup old-fashioned oats
1 cup all-purpose flour
2 tablespoons baking powder
2 teaspoons baking soda
1/2 teaspoon salt
Pinch nutmeg
1 cup vanilla vegan yogurt
1 cup soy milk
2 tablespoons agave nectar
2 tablespoons canola oil, plus more for cooking
1 teaspoon pure vanilla extract
Vegan margarine, maple syrup, and fresh blueberries, for serving

1. In a large bowl, combine the oats, flour, baking powder, baking soda, salt, and nutmeg. Whisk together.

2. In a medium bowl, combine the yogurt, soy milk, agave nectar, 2 tablespoons canola oil, and vanilla. Add the wet ingredients to the dry ingredients and whisk together to combine. It's fine if some lumps remain. Cover and refrigerate for at least 2 hours or overnight to soften the oats.

3. Heat a large skillet over medium heat. Lightly oil the skillet. Preheat the oven to 250°F. Working in batches, use a measuring cup or ladle to pour about 1/4 cup of batter into the skillet for each pancake. Cook until golden brown, about 3 to 5 minutes. Turn to cook the other side, until golden brown, about 3 minutes. Transfer the cooked pancakes to an ovenproof platter and keep warm in the oven until all of the pancakes are cooked.

4. Serve hot, topped with margarine, maple syrup, and blueberries.

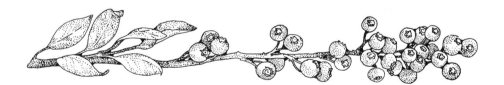

Yankee Cornbread with Blueberry Sauce

Serves 4

Northern cornbread tends to be sweeter and more cakey than its Southern cousin. Add the maple syrup and a bit of nutmeg, and you're talking Yankee all the way. If you omit the sauce, you've got a great stand-alone cornbread to serve for dinner, and you can enjoy the leftovers for breakfast the next day. It's best to make it the night before, because the cornbread must be completely cooled to cut well for grilling.

CORNBREAD:
1 1/2 cups soy milk
1 tablespoon apple cider vinegar
1 tablespoon ground flaxseed
3 tablespoons hot water
2 tablespoons canola oil
1/4 cup maple syrup
1 1/4 cups finely ground cornmeal
1 1/4 cup all-purpose flour
2 teaspoons baking powder
1/2 teaspoon baking soda
1/2 teaspoon salt
Pinch nutmeg
1 tablespoon sugar

SAUCE:
3 cups fresh blueberries
1/2 cup fresh orange juice
1/4 cup maple syrup
2 teaspoons pure vanilla extract
Pinch salt
1/4 cup vegan margarine, for cooking

TIP

For a thicker sauce, combine 1 tablespoon cornstarch with 2 tablespoons water and add to the berries. Cook until thickened.

1. *Cornbread:* Preheat the oven to 350°F. Lightly spray or oil an 8-inch square pan.

2. In a medium bowl, combine the soy milk and vinegar. Stir and set aside to curdle for 3 minutes.

3. In a small bowl, combine the flaxseed and water. Stir vigorously with a fork until the mixture begins to thicken. Add to the soy milk mixture. Stir in the oil and maple syrup and set aside.

4. In a large bowl, combine the cornmeal, flour, baking powder, baking soda, salt, and nutmeg. Whisk together. Make a well in the center and add the wet ingredients, gently stirring to combine. Do not overmix the batter. Pour the batter into the prepared pan and spread evenly. Sprinkle the sugar evenly over the top.

5. Bake for 35 to 40 minutes, or until slightly golden and the edges pull away from the sides. Cool completely. When the cornbread is cool, cut it into 4 large squares. Split the squares horizontally to make 8 thin squares. Set aside.

6. *Sauce:* In a medium saucepan, combine the blueberries, orange juice, maple syrup, vanilla, and salt. Bring to a boil over medium high heat, then reduce to medium and cook 7 to 9 minutes or until thickened. For a chunky texture, smash some of the berries with the back of your spoon. If using frozen berries, the cooking time will be slightly longer.

7. Heat a large skillet over medium high heat. Spread the margarine generously on both sides of the bread squares. When the skillet is hot, place the cornbread in the skillet and cook until golden brown, about 5 minutes. Turn to cook the other side until golden, about 3 minutes. To serve, arrange the cornbread on plates and top with the sauce. Serve hot.

Apple-Sausage Breakfast Quesadillas

Serves 4

Apples and sausage go together in a surprisingly delicious way in these tasty quesadillas. In addition to serving them for breakfast or brunch, they also make a terrific appetizer. You can substitute 8 ounces minced seitan, or minced Tempeh Breakfast Patties (page 43) for the sausage in this recipe.

1/3 cup vegan cream cheese, room
   temperature
1/3 cup plus 1/4 cup vegan sour cream,
   divided
1/4 cup Peppadew Relish (page 115)
1 tablespoon olive oil
8 ounces Vegan Sausage Links (page 41)
   or store-bought, minced
1/4 cup minced red onion
1 medium McIntosh, or other red apple,
   cored and diced, peeling optional
1 tablespoon fresh lemon juice, optional
4 (8-inch) flour tortillas
1/2 cup fresh blueberries, for garnish

VARIATION

Omit the relish and top with avocado chunks instead.

1. In a small bowl, combine the cream cheese and the 1/3 cup sour cream and set aside. In a separate bowl, combine the peppadew relish and the remaining 1/4 cup sour cream and set aside.

2. Heat the oil in a large skillet over medium heat. Add the sausage and onion and cook until the sausage is browned, 3 to 5 minutes. Set aside.

3. If not assembling right away, combine the diced apples with the lemon juice to prevent discoloration. Otherwise, omit the lemon juice.

4. Spread a thin layer of the cream cheese/sour cream mixture on each tortilla, dividing it evenly among them. Divide the sausage evenly on top. Spread the apple on top of the sausage.

5. Heat a large skillet over medium heat. Place one tortilla in the skillet and cook until golden brown and starting to crisp, 2 to 3 minutes. Fold in half and remove from the skillet. Repeat with the remaining tortillas.

6. To serve, cut the quesadillas into halves or quarters. Scatter a few blueberries on top and serve with a dollop of the reserved peppadew-sour cream mixture.

Vegan Sausage Links

Makes 6

These sausage links are great sliced alongside a scramble or used in the Apple Sausage Breakfast Quesadillas (page 40) or the Country Skillet (page 27). The spicy variation is especially good in recipes such as the Italian Big Bowl (page 137) or sandwiches such as the Diner Brats (page 119). **NOTE:** For sandwiches, make 12 smaller sausages instead of 6 large ones.

DRY INGREDIENTS:
2 cups vital wheat gluten
2 tablespoons instant tapioca
1/4 cup all-purpose flour
1 tablespoon smoked paprika
1 tablespoon ground fennel seed
1 tablespoon onion powder
1 tablespoon garlic powder
2 teaspoons dried oregano
1 1/2 teaspoons ground cumin
1 1/2 teaspoons salt
1/2 teaspoon ground black pepper

WET INGREDIENTS:
1/4 pound extra-firm tofu, drained
1/2 cup soy milk
2 tablespoons tomato paste
1 1/2 tablespoons canola oil
1 tablespoon soy sauce
1 tablespoon blackstrap molasses
1/2 tablespoon toasted sesame oil
2 teaspoons liquid smoke
1 teaspoon browning sauce
1 cup water

1. Prepare a steamer. Combine the dry ingredients in a large bowl. Whisk together and set aside.

2. Combine the wet ingredients in a blender. Blend until smooth and combined.

3. Pour the wet ingredients into the dry ingredients and mix with a fork, then use your hands to knead the mixture for 2 to 3 minutes. It will be slightly wet but should hold together. Add 1 to 2 tablespoons water, if needed, to form a loose dough.

4. Tear off six 12-inch pieces of foil for large sausages or twelve 8-inch pieces for smaller ones. Divide the mixture evenly among the foil pieces. Use the foil to shape the mixture into sausage links, about 5 to 6 inches long. Roll the foil around each sausage link, twisting the ends, but giving the sausage room to expand.

5. Place the links in the steamer. For large sausages, steam 1 hour and 15 minutes. For sandwich sausages, steam 1 hour, then remove from the steamer and unwrap to cool. When the sausages are cool, store them in an airtight container in the refrigerator for 1 week or freeze for up to 2 months.

VARIATION

For a spicy version: add 1 1/2 teaspoons chili powder and 3/4 teaspoon ground cayenne to the dry ingredients.

Seitan Breakfast Strips

About 2 pounds

Who needs bacon when you can serve these strips on the side for breakfast? They're also delicious in the B.L.T. Potato Salad (page 95) or sliced thicker and used in the Seitan Po' Boys (page 104). If you keep some unsliced in the refrigerator or freezer, you can slice it as needed. For the thinnest slices, freeze the seitan slightly and cut with a serrated knife. The seitan may be sliced and cooked, or refrigerated for up to 5 days, or frozen for up to two months.

SEITAN:

Dry Ingredients:

2 cups vital wheat gluten
2 tablespoons instant tapioca
2 tablespoons soy flour
2 teaspoons onion powder
2 teaspoons garlic powder
2 teaspoons smoked paprika
2 teaspoons ground cumin
2 teaspoons All-American Spice Blend (page 13) or other spice blend
1 teaspoon salt

Wet Ingredients:

3/4 cup vegan beer, such as Samuel Smith's Pure Brewed Lager
2 tablespoons soy sauce
1 tablespoon tomato paste
1/2 cup vegetable broth
1 teaspoon toasted sesame oil

COOKING BROTH:

1/2 cup vegan beer, such as Samuel Smith's Pure Brewed Lager
1/2 cup vegetable broth
2 tablespoons soy sauce
1 teaspoon liquid smoke

GLAZE:

1 tablespoon maple syrup
1 tablespoon prepared yellow mustard
1/2 teaspoon ground black pepper
1/2 teaspoon salt

1. *Seitan:* Combine the dry ingredients in a large bowl and mix well. Set aside.

2. Combine the wet ingredients in a medium bowl and mix well. Add the wet ingredients to the dry ingredients and knead together for a few minutes until smooth and cohesive.

3. Transfer the seitan dough to a work surface and shape it into a round, flat disk, about 1 1/2-inches thick. Lightly oil a 3-quart casserole dish that is at least 5 inches deep.

4. *Broth:* Combine the cooking broth ingredients in the casserole and set aside.

5. *Glaze:* Combine the glaze ingredients in a small bowl. Add the reserved seitan to the broth and use a spoon or your fingers to rub the glaze onto the top of the seitan.

6. Preheat the oven to 275°F. (or 250°F. if using a glass casserole dish). Cover the casserole tightly and bake for 1 hour and 15 minutes. Turn the oven off and leave the seitan in the oven 1 hour longer. Let cool completely before removing from the casserole.

7. Cut the cooked seitan into quarters, then use a serrated knife to cut each quarter into thin strips. Heat a large skillet over medium high heat, with just enough oil to cover the bottom. Cook for 3 to 5 minutes until browned, then turn and cook the other side for 3 minutes or until crisp.

● ● ● ● ● ● ● ● ● ●

VARIATION

Slow Cooker: To prepare in a slow cooker, proceed with the recipe using a 4-quart slow cooker instead of a casserole dish. Cook the seitan in the slow cooker on low for 8 hours. When done, allow the seitan to cool completely in the slow cooker before removing.

Diner Tempeh Breakfast Patties

Makes 4 patties

These tempeh patties are an easy breakfast side that also adds protein to your meal. They're equally terrific alongside a short stack or your favorite French toast. Full of flavor, they'll make your morning a breeze, especially if you let them marinate overnight. These can be kept in the refrigerator for up to a week. For an amazing spin on a BLT, try two patties on an English muffin with lettuce, tomato, and vegan mayo.

8 ounces tempeh
2 tablespoons maple syrup
1/4 cup vegetable broth
2 tablespoons balsamic vinegar
2 tablespoons ketchup
1 tablespoon olive oil
2 teaspoons ground cumin
1 teaspoon garlic powder
1 teaspoon smoked paprika
1/2 teaspoon salt
1/2 teaspoon white pepper
1 to 2 tablespoons canola oil

1. Use a serrated knife to cut the tempeh in half, then cut the pieces in half horizontally to make 4 thin patties. Simmer for 15 minutes (page 3) then set aside.

2. In a shallow glass baking pan, combine the remaining ingredients except the canola oil. Add the tempeh to the marinade and marinate for 1 hour or longer.

3. To cook, heat just enough oil to cover the bottom of a large skillet over medium heat. Add the tempeh and cook until golden brown, about 5 minutes. Turn to cook the other side for 3 to 5 minutes, or until browned.

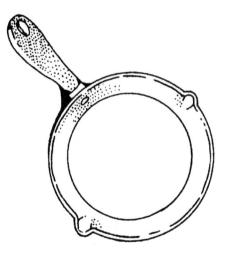

Classic Cafe Hash Browns

Serves 4

In additon to being great on their own, these hash browns and are also delicious in the Cheezy Tofu Potato Skillet (page 30).

1 pound russet potatoes
2 tablespoons minced onion
1/2 teaspoon salt
Pinch black pepper
2 tablespoons vegan margarine, divided

1. Shred the potatoes using a box grater or food processor. In a large bowl, combine the potatoes, onion, salt, and pepper. Toss to combine. Place the potatoes in the center of a clean dish towel and roll up. Twisting both ends, squeeze as much water from the potatoes as possible.

2. Heat a large skillet, preferably cast iron, over medium heat. Add 1 tablespoon margarine. Swirl the skillet so the margarine coats the bottom as it melts. Arrange the potatoes in a thin layer, covering the bottom of the pan. Cook for 10 to 12 minutes, pressing down with a spatula occasionally, gently checking for doneness by lifting one side. When the bottom is golden brown, place a plate on top of the skillet. Gently flip the mixture onto the plate.

3. Melt the remaining tablespoon of margarine in the skillet, then carefully slide the potatoes back into the skillet. Cook, pressing occasionally with the spatula, for 8 to 10 minutes, or until golden brown and crisp. Cut into quarters and serve.

Hubby's Home Fries

Serves 4

One of my husband's favorite sides, this easy breakfast dish would be as at home in any diner as it is in your kitchen.

2 pounds small yellow potatoes, such as
    Dutch Yellows, cut into 1/4-inch slices
2 tablespoons canola oil
Salt and black pepper
1/2 teaspoon sweet paprika, optional
Pinch ground cayenne, optional

1. Preheat the oven to 400°F. Place a large ovenproof skillet, preferably cast iron, over medium heat. Add the oil. When hot, add the potatoes. Season with salt and pepper to taste and add the paprika and cayenne, if using. Stir the potatoes to coat and cook 15 to 20 minutes, or until the potatoes begin to turn golden brown, stirring every 3 to 5 minutes so they don't burn.

2. Place the skillet in the oven and bake 15 to 20 minutes, stirring occasionally. Taste and adjust the seasonings and serve hot.

STARTERS

Whether served at a favorite bistro or your own kitchen table, appetizers are a good way to jump start the conversation as well as the taste buds. Whatever your mood, these "small plates" offer lots of exciting dishes to sample. For a taste of Chinatown, try the spicy Lettuce Wraps or the Two-Bite Eggless Rolls. Mexican starters include the robust Baked Poppers and Everybody's Favorite Taco Dip. Try regional favorites, such as St. Louis T-Ravs, Spicy Balsamic Maple Wingz (my updated version of the well-known Buffalo wings), or cook up some irresistible potato skins with a flourish of roasted garlic and asparagus. With this tasty selection of appetizers, you can make it a meal or make it a party.

Bistro Asparagus Twists

Makes 16

These tasty twists are a perfect late-night appetizer, with an added bonus: they're made with only a handful of ingredients. They also make an enticing start to a dinner or a side to a cup of soup. For convenience, make them ahead of time and bake them when your guests arrive.

DIPPING SAUCE:
2 tablespoons vegan mayonnaise
2 tablespoons vegan sour cream
1 tablespoon fresh lemon juice
1 clove garlic, minced
1/2 teaspoon prepared hot mustard

TWISTS:
16 asparagus spears, tough ends trimmed
1 sheet frozen vegan puff pastry, thawed
1 tablespoon prepared hot mustard

1. *Sauce:* In a small bowl, combine all the ingredients and mix until blended. Refrigerate until ready to serve.

2. *Twists:* Preheat the oven to 400°F. Steam the asparagus over a pot of boiling water for 5 minutes. Transfer immediately to a bowl of cold water to stop the cooking process. Pat dry.

3. Unroll the pastry sheet on a lightly floured work surface. Cut and remove one third of the pastry and rewrap and refrigerate the unused portion for another use. You should have a 6 x 9-inch pastry rectangle remaining.

4. Spread the mustard evenly over the puff pastry. Cut into 16 strips about 1/2-inch wide across the short side of the pastry.

5. Using one strip of pastry and one stalk of asparagus, beginning at the stem end, wrap the pastry diagonally around the asparagus, leaving space in between the pastry.

6. Arrange on the baking sheet and repeat, placing them about 1-inch apart, until the asparagus and pastry are used up. Bake 18 to 20 minutes, or until golden. Serve hot with dipping sauce on the side.

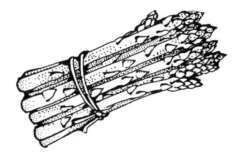

Roasted Garlic Pretzels

Makes 12

Mall food goes vegan! Do you remember eating fresh pretzels while sitting in the food court? These are even better! They can be served with mustard, Quick-and-Easy Cheezy Sauce (page 30), or vegan cream cheese, although we like them best as is. Leftover pretzels may be warmed in a 400°F. oven for about 3 minutes. When placing in the water bath, lift the pretzel by the two upper loops, letting gravity do its work, and the pretzel will be a more traditional shape.

3/4 to 1 cup warm water
1 tablespoon agave nectar
2 1/4 teaspoons active dry yeast
1 cup white whole wheat flour
1 cup all-purpose flour
1 1/2 teaspoons salt
4 to 6 cloves roasted garlic (see below), mashed
6 cups water, for simmering
2 tablespoons baking soda
3 tablespoons water, for glazing
1 tablespoon cornstarch
1 teaspoon garlic salt
2 teaspoons coarse salt
1 1/2 tablespoons olive oil

To Roast Garlic

Preheat the oven to 400°F. Cut the top off a head of garlic, exposing some of the cloves. Transfer the head of garlic to a 9-inch piece of foil. Drizzle with 1/2 tablespoon olive oil and season with salt and pepper. Shape the foil around the garlic, folding to close. Roast for 45 minutes.

Carefully remove the garlic head from the foil. Separate the individual garlic cloves from the papery skins. The garlic is now ready to use and can be stored in the refrigerator in an airtight container for up to 1 week.

1. In a small bowl, combine 3/4 cup warm water and the agave nectar. Add the yeast and stir to combine. Set aside to proof until bubbly, about 3 minutes.

2. In a large bowl, combine the flours and salt. Add the yeast mixture and mashed garlic. Stir to combine. Add more water, as needed, to make a cohesive dough. Transfer to a lightly floured work surface. Knead until smooth and elastic, about 8 to 10 minutes.

3. Shape the dough into a ball and place in a lightly oiled bowl, turning to coat with oil. Cover with a towel. Let rise 1 to 1 1/2 hours in a warm place, until doubled in bulk. Lightly oil 2 baking sheets, or cover them with parchment paper.

4. Transfer the dough to a lightly floured work surface. Flatten the dough and cut it into 12 equal pieces, then let rest for 10 minutes. Roll each piece into a 24-inch rope. To shape the pretzels, start to form a circle with a top end of the rope in each hand. Twist the ends together and fold down to meet the bottom of the circle. Repeat until all 12 pieces are shaped and place them on the baking sheets. Cover with towels and let rise for 30 minutes, or until nearly doubled.

5. During the last 10 minutes of the rising time, heat the 6 cups of water in a large saucepan and bring to a boil. Add the baking soda. The mixture will bubble. In a small bowl, combine 3 tablespoons water with the cornstarch and garlic salt. Set aside. Preheat the oven to 400°F.

6. Gently lift each pretzel, place it in the boiling water, and cook for 30 seconds. Remove the pretzels using a slotted spoon and arrange on the baking sheet. Brush with the cornstarch mixture and sprinkle with coarse salt. Bake 10 to 12 minutes, or until golden brown. Remove from the oven and brush with olive oil, then transfer to a wire rack. Serve hot.

Movie Night Potato Skins

Makes 24

Back in the 1970s and '80s, versions of potato skins were extremely popular in the bistro-style chain restaurants. This updated version is fantastic finger food with bolder flavors. Because they're so easy, we often make them for "movie nights," but they're also impressive for parties. For a pretty presentation, reserve some of the asparagus tips to top the potato skins.

12 small Yukon Gold potatoes, scrubbed
12 ounces asparagus, tough ends
    trimmed, cut into 1/4-inch pieces
3 tablespoons olive oil, divided
1/2 teaspoon soy sauce
1/2 teaspoon balsamic vinegar
1 1/2 tablespoons vegan margarine
1 teaspoon salt
1/4 teaspoon black pepper
1 1/2 tablespoons soy milk
1/4 to 1/2 teaspoon red pepper flakes
1 teaspoon Dijon mustard
4 to 6 cloves roasted garlic (page 47),
    mashed to a paste
1/4 teaspoon liquid smoke
 Paprika
Vegan sour cream, chopped chives,
    or Coconut 'Bacon Bits' (page 169),
    optional

1. Preheat the oven to 400°F. Pierce each potato twice with a fork, then arrange on a baking sheet. Bake for 45 minutes, or until tender.

2. Arrange the asparagus in a 9 x 13-inch baking pan. Add 1 tablespoon of the olive oil, soy sauce, and vinegar. Toss to coat the asparagus. Bake for 15 to 20 minutes, or until tender.

3. When the potatoes are cool enough to handle, cut them in half using a serrated knife. Using a spoon, gently remove the insides of each potato leaving 1/4-inch of outer skin intact. Place the potato insides in a medium mixing bowl. Add the margarine, salt, pepper, soy milk, red pepper flakes, mustard, and garlic. Mash together, then add the chopped asparagus. Taste and adjust the seasonings.

4. Combine the remaining 2 tablespoons olive oil with the liquid smoke and brush the oil mixture onto the inside of each potato. Divide the reserved filling among the potato skins and place on a baking sheet. Sprinkle with paprika. Bake for 15 minutes. Serve hot with sour cream, chives, or Coconut 'Bacon' Bits, if using.

● ● ● ● ● ● ● ● ● ● ● ●

VARIATION

Cafe Potato Skins: Omit the asparagus and roasted garlic from the recipe. To the potato filling ingredients, add: 1/4 cup vegan sour cream, 1 tablespoon minced chives, and 1/4 cup minced Seitan Breakfast Strips (page 42), Diner Tempeh Patties (page 43), or store-bought vegan bacon, then proceed with the recipe.

Spicy Balsamic Maple Wingz

Serves 4 to 6

Hot Wings are one of the best known appetizers of our time. This vegan version made with seitan is sure to please. If you don't want to serve them all at once, you can wrap the seitan airtight and refrigerate or freeze for later use. See Dredging Done Right (page 50) to make this recipe a snap.

SAUCE:
2 tablespoons balsamic vinegar
2 tablespoons maple syrup
1/3 cup plus 1 tablespoon hot sauce

SIMMERING BROTH:
6 to 8 cups chilled vegetable broth
1 tablespoon nutritional yeast
1/2 tablespoon chicken-flavored vegan
 bouillon paste
1/2 teaspoon dried rosemary
1/2 teaspoon dried thyme

WINGZ:
Dry Ingredients:
1 1/4 cups vital wheat gluten
1 tablespoon all-purpose flour
1 tablespoon whole wheat flour
1 tablespoon instant tapioca
3 tablespoons nutritional yeast
1 teaspoon onion powder
1/2 teaspoon garlic powder
1/2 teaspoon dried rosemary
1/2 teaspoon dried thyme
1/2 teaspoon salt
Wet Ingredients:
2 cloves garlic, minced
1 tablespoon olive oil
1 cup chilled vegetable broth
1/2 teaspoon browning sauce
1/2 teaspoon chicken-flavored vegan
 bouillon paste
Breading:
1/2 cup soy milk
1/3 cup all-purpose flour
1 cup panko crumbs
1 tablespoon smoked paprika
3/4 teaspoon dried thyme
3/4 teaspoon salt, divided
1/4 teaspoon black pepper
Canola oil, for frying

1. *Sauce:* In a small bowl, combine the vinegar, maple syrup, and hot sauce. Mix well and set aside.

2. *Broth:* Combine the ingredients for the simmering broth in a large saucepan and set aside.

3. *Wingz:* Combine the dry ingredients in a large bowl and mix well. Combine the wet ingredients in a medium bowl. Add the wet ingredients to the dry ingredients and mix with a fork. Transfer to a work surface and knead a few minutes until the dough forms a cohesive ball.

4. Shape the seitan into an 8 x 10-inch rectangle, then cut into 1-inch strips. Cut each strip into 3 pieces. Add the seitan pieces to the cold broth and bring to a simmer, but do not boil. Simmer gently in the broth for 1 hour 15 minutes, then let cool. At this point, the seitan may be packaged in airtight containers and refrigerated for up to 1 week or frozen for up to two months.

5. *Breading:* Pour the soy milk and 1/4 of the teaspoon salt into a shallow bowl. Line a baking sheet with paper towels or a brown bag for draining.

6. Combine the flour and 1/4 teaspoon of the salt in another bowl. In a separate shallow bowl, combine the panko, paprika, thyme, remaining 1/4 teaspoon salt, and the pepper.

7. Dip the seitan pieces in the soy milk, then dredge in the flour mixture. Dip in the soy milk again, then in the panko mixture, pressing some of the crumbs onto the seitan.

8. Heat 1/4-inch oil in a large skillet over medium heat. Add the wingz and cook for about 2 minutes per side, until golden brown. Drain on the prepared baking sheet. Toss with the sauce and serve hot.

NOTE: Panko crumbs are Japanese-style bread crumbs available in most supermarkets.

The easiest way to get the perfect crispy coating is with the two-handed technique. Begin by setting up the work station: Place the wet ingredients in a shallow bowl or pie plate. Place the dry ingredients in another. Place a baking sheet nearby for the coated food. If the dredging process in your particular recipe involves three layers of coating, you'll need an additional shallow bowl for the other ingredients.

If the food isn't wet to start with, the recipe instructions should tell you to dip it into a liquid. Using one hand, the "wet hand," place the food in the liquid. After it's coated, pick it up using the "wet hand" and place it in the breading mixture. Change hands and use the "dry hand" to cover the food with breading, picking up crumbs and coating it well. When it's coated, pick it up with the "dry hand," then transfer it to the baking sheet. The hardest part is keeping one hand wet and one hand dry.

If you have problems with breading sticking when you cook the food, refrigerate it on the baking sheet for 30 minutes to help set the crumbs.

Roasted Corn Avocado Salsa

About 3 cups

A colorful and delicious dip for chips, this salsa is also great as a topping for the Tex-Mex Taco Salad (page 101). Feel free to increase the hot pepper sauce if you like a little more zip.

2 ears roasted corn, cut from the cobs
2 tablespoons minced jalapeño
1/2 cup chopped scallions
2 tablespoons minced red bell pepper
2 cloves garlic, minced
2 tablespoons minced fresh cilantro
2 tablespoons fresh lime juice
1/2 teaspoon ground cumin
1/2 teaspoon hot pepper sauce
1/2 teaspoon agave nectar
1 ripe Hass avocado, pitted, peeled, and
   cut into 1/2-inch dice
1/8 teaspoon salt
Pinch black pepper

In a medium bowl, combine all the ingredients and mix well. Taste and adjust the seasonings and serve immediately.

Deli Reubenettes

Makes 24

The popular Reuben deli sandwich makes a special appearance as a vegan appetizer, all decked out in puff pastry. I often serve these for get-togethers since they are easy to assemble. You can prepare them ahead of time and refrigerate until needed. Just bake and serve when your guests arrive.

DIPPING SAUCE:
1/2 cup vegan mayonnaise
1/2 cup vegan sour cream
2 teaspoons prepared hot mustard
2 tablespoons ketchup
1/2 teaspoon ground cayenne

REUBENETTES:
1 tablespoon olive oil
6 ounces Savory Seitan (page 5), cut into
    1/8-inch dice
3 tablespoons minced onion
2 cloves garlic, minced
1 tablespoon capers
1 1/8 teaspoons ground coriander
1/8 teaspoon ground allspice
3/4 teaspoon ground caraway
1 tablespoon balsamic vinegar
3/4 teaspoon liquid smoke
1 3/4 cups sauerkraut, drained and lightly
    squeezed
1 to 2 tablespoons dry white wine or
    vegetable broth, if needed
2 sheets frozen vegan puff pastry, thawed

1. *Dipping Sauce:* In a small bowl, combine all the ingredients, stirring until smooth. Set aside. Refrigerate until serving time.

2. *Reubenettes:* Heat the oil in a large skillet over medium heat. Add the seitan, onion, and garlic. Cook, stirring, for 3 to 5 minutes, until the onion softens. Add the capers, coriander, allspice, caraway, vinegar, liquid smoke, and sauerkraut. Stir to combine and cook for about 5 minutes for the flavors to meld. Add a bit of wine or broth if the mixture is too dry.

3. Preheat the oven to 400°F. Spray 2 baking sheets with non-stick spray. Lightly flour a work surface. Roll a sheet of puff pastry out to a 12 x 16-inch rectangle, adding flour as needed. Cut the 12-inch side into thirds, then cut the 16-inch side across into quarters, making 12 (4-inch) squares.

4. Place a tablespoon of the filling on each square. Fold the two opposite points together to make a triangle. Pinch together to seal, wetting your fingers with water if needed. Transfer the triangles to a baking sheet. Bake 12 to 15 minutes or until golden. Serve hot with the dipping sauce.

Baked Poppers with Lime Cream

Makes 8

Spicy and sensational, these poppers are perfect with a margarita or an ice-cold vegan beer. This interpretation of a Mexican restaurant favorite may look like a lot of work, but it is actually quite easy to prepare. The filling is also delicious on crackers.

1/4 cup plus 2 tablespoons vegan sour cream
1 tablespoon plus 1 teaspoon fresh lime juice
1/4 cup chopped water chestnuts, or minced celery
2 teaspoons soy sauce
1/2 teaspoon liquid smoke
1/4 cup plus 2 tablespoons vegan cream cheese, room temperature
2 tablespoons nutritional yeast
1/2 teaspoon ground cumin
1/4 to 1/2 teaspoon ground cayenne
8 jalapeños, halved, seeded, stems removed
1/2 cup soy milk
2 tablespoons cornstarch
1/4 cup all-purpose flour
7-in-1 Seasoning (recipe follows)
1/2 cup panko crumbs
1/4 teaspoon salt
Olive oil

8 toothpicks

1. Combine the sour cream and lime juice in a small bowl. Cover and refrigerate until ready to serve.

2. Preheat the oven to 350°F. Lightly oil a baking sheet and set aside. In a small bowl, combine the water chestnuts, soy sauce, and liquid smoke, stirring to blend. Add the cream cheese, yeast, cumin, and cayenne. Mix together well.

3. Fill each jalapeño half with the cream cheese mixture until level. Pair the halves together and press the cheese sides together to form whole chiles.

4. Combine the soy milk with the cornstarch in a shallow bowl. Mix together until smooth. In another shallow bowl, combine the flour with half of the 7-in-1 Seasoning. In a third bowl, combine the panko with the remaining spice mixture and the salt.

5. Dip a jalapeño in the soy milk mixture, then in the flour, then in the soy milk mixture again. Dredge it in the panko mixture, pressing the crumbs to adhere. Stick a toothpick through the chile to secure the halves together and place it on the prepared baking sheet. Repeat with the remaining jalapeños.

6. Spray or brush the jalapeños lightly with oil. Bake for 40 minutes, or until golden, turning once half-way through, and spraying again with more oil. Serve hot with the reserved lime cream.

7-in-1 Seasoning

Besides being delicious in the Baked Poppers, this flavorful seasoning blend is great to keep on hand for any time you'd like a seasoned flour.

1 tablespoon olive oil
1/2 teaspoon dried thyme
1/2 teaspoon onion powder
1/2 teaspoon garlic powder
1/2 teaspoon white pepper
1/2 teaspoon oregano
1 teaspoon salt
1 teaspoon smoked or regular paprika

In a bowl, combine all the ingredients and mix well. Store in an airtight container at room temperature where it will keep for several months.

Fried Avocado Wedges

Serves 4

Peel and slice the avocados just before frying to prevent discoloration. For the cleanest cuts of avocado slices, store the ripe avocado in the refrigerator until ready to use.

3/4 cup all-purpose flour
1 1/2 teaspoons salt
1/2 teaspoon All-American Spice Blend (page 13) or other spice blend
Pinch black pepper
3/4 cup vegan Mexican-style beer, such as Corona
Juice of 1/2 lime
Canola oil, for frying (see page 67)
2 ripe Hass avocados, peeled, pitted and cut into 8 wedges
1/4 cup finely ground cornmeal
Tomato salsa, for serving

1. In a medium bowl, whisk together the flour, salt, spice blend, and pepper. Whisk in the beer and lime juice. Add additional beer or flour if needed for a dipping consistency that coats the avocado but isn't too heavy.

2. Heat the oil in a deep fryer or large skillet to 375°F. Line a baking sheet with paper towels or a brown bag for draining. Preheat the oven to 250°F.

3. Place the cornmeal on a plate. Coat the wedges in the cornmeal, then dip them in the batter. Working in batches, fry the avocados until golden, about 5 minutes. Drain on the baking sheet then transfer to an ovenproof platter and place in the oven to keep warm until the frying is complete. Serve immediately with a small bowl of salsa for dipping.

St. Louis T-Ravs

Serves 4

St. Louis is the home of this simple but delicious appetizer. T-Ravs are fried or "toasted" ravioli served with a marinara dipping sauce. For easier preparation, be sure to read Dredging Done Right (page 50).

1 (8-ounce) package frozen vegan ravioli
1/4 cup dry bread crumbs
1 tablespoon panko crumbs
1 tablespoon nutritional yeast
1/2 teaspoon dried basil
1/2 teaspoon dried parsley
1/4 teaspoon garlic powder
1/4 teaspoon salt
Pinch pepper
1/4 cup cold water
1 tablespoon cornstarch
2 tablespoons olive oil
Easy Marinara Sauce (recipe follows)

1. Cook the ravioli according to the package directions and drain well. Lightly spray a baking sheet with oil.

2. In a shallow bowl, combine the bread crumbs, panko, yeast, basil, parsley, garlic powder, salt, and pepper. In a small bowl, combine the water and cornstarch and mix well.

3. Dip a ravioli in the cornstarch slurry, then transfer to the crumb mixture. Coat the ravioli with the crumbs and transfer to the baking sheet. Repeat with the remaining ravioli.

4. Preheat the oven to 250°F. Heat the oil in a large skillet over medium heat. Working in batches, add the ravioli to the skillet and cook until golden, turning once, about 2 minutes per side. Transfer the ravioli to an ovenproof plate and keep warm in the oven. Continue until all the ravioli are fried, adding additional oil, if needed. Serve hot with the marinara sauce.

Easy Marinara Sauce

Makes 2 cups

1 tablespoon olive oil
1/4 cup minced onion
2 cloves garlic, minced
1 (15-ounce) can tomato sauce
1 teaspoon dried basil
1/2 teaspoon dried thyme
1/2 teaspoon dried oregano
Pinch sugar
1/4 teaspoon salt
1/8 teaspoon black pepper

Heat the oil in a medium saucepan over medium heat. Add the onion and garlic. Cook about 3 minutes, stirring. Add the remaining ingredients and simmer 15 to 20 minutes.

Lettuce Wraps

Serves 4

These wraps are even better than take-out because you make them "your way." For extra crunch, add a couple tablespoons of chopped peanuts to the mixture at the very end.

1 pound extra-firm tofu, drained, pressed, and cut into 1/4-inch dice
3 tablespoons soy sauce, divided
1 tablespoon chili oil
1 teaspoon toasted sesame oil
1 teaspoon five-spice powder, divided
1/2 teaspoon ground ginger
1 tablespoon peanut oil
1/2 cup chopped onion
5 ounces shiitake mushroom caps, chopped
1/2 cup shredded carrot
1 tablespoon grated fresh ginger
1 tablespoon minced garlic
1/4 cup chopped scallions
1/3 cup chopped water chestnuts
1 cup bean sprouts
1 tablespoon mirin
1 tablespoon ketchup
1 teaspoon Sriracha sauce
Salt and black pepper
8 to 10 lettuce leaves

1. Preheat the oven to 400°F. Lightly oil a baking sheet.

2. In a medium bowl, combine the tofu with 1 tablespoon of the soy sauce, the chili oil, sesame oil, 1/2 teaspoon of the five-spice powder, and the ground ginger. Toss to coat. Bake for 30 minutes, turning once. Set aside.

3. In a large skillet or wok, heat the peanut oil over medium heat. Add the onion and cook 2 minutes. Add the shiitakes, carrot, fresh ginger, garlic, scallions, and water chestnuts. Cook for 3 to 5 minutes, until the mushrooms are softened. Add the tofu mixture, bean sprouts, remaining 2 tablespoons soy sauce, mirin, ketchup, Sriracha, the remaining 1/2 teaspoon five-spice powder, and salt and pepper to taste. Mix well and cook until hot.

4. To serve, fill each lettuce leaf with a few tablespoons of the filling mixture and roll up.

Stick-to-Your-Ribs Pot-Stickers

Makes 24

Unless you live in a big city, you probably can't call your local Chinese restaurant and order vegan pot-stickers. But you'll be surprised how easy they are to make at home. This recipe complements the Two-Bite Eggless Rolls (page 58). So why not dig out your chopsticks and make a batch of each? For vegan wonton wrappers and eggroll wrappers check the freezer section of well-stocked supermarkets or Asian grocers.

5 ounces Savory Seitan (page 5), finely minced
3 tablespoons minced scallions
3 tablespoons minced shiitake mushroom caps
1 clove garlic, minced
1 teaspoon grated fresh ginger
1 tablespoon ketchup
1 1/2 teaspoons prepared yellow mustard
1 teaspoon blackstrap molasses
1/4 teaspoon ground cayenne
1/2 teaspoon red or barley miso paste
Juice of 1/2 lime
Salt and black pepper
24 vegan wonton wrappers
3 to 4 tablespoons peanut oil
3/4 to 1 cup vegetable broth
Pot-Sticker Dipping Sauce (recipe follows)

1. In a medium bowl, combine the seitan, scallions, shiitakes, garlic, ginger, ketchup, mustard, molasses, cayenne, miso, and lime juice in a medium bowl. Mix well and season with salt and pepper to taste.

2. Lightly dust 2 baking sheets with cornstarch or flour to prevent the pot-stickers from sticking. Fill a small bowl with a few tablespoons of cold water. Place 4 to 6 wrappers on a work surface. Fill each wrapper with about 1 teaspoon of filling in the center. Dip your fingers in the water and use them to wet the bottom two sides of the wrapper and fold the dry two sides against it to seal.

3. Place the filled wonton on the baking sheet and repeat until all the wrappers are used. If not using immediately, refrigerate the pot-stickers until needed. The pot-stickers may also be frozen on the baking sheets until firm then removed and packaged in airtight containers in the freezer until needed.

4. Preheat the oven to 250°F. Heat 2 tablespoons oil in a large skillet over medium heat. Add the pot-stickers in batches, keeping them separated. They will cook quickly, so turn over as they turn golden, about 2 minutes per side. When all the pot-stickers are golden, add about 1/4 cup broth to the skillet and cover to steam for about 2 minutes. Remove the lid and let any remaining broth cook off.

5. Transfer the pot-stickers to an ovenproof plate and keep warm in the oven while cooking the remaining batches. Wipe out the skillet and repeat, adding more oil and broth for each batch until all the pot-stickers are cooked. Serve hot with dipping sauce.

Pot-Sticker Dipping Sauce

Make 1/3 cup

1 tablespoon soy sauce
1 tablespoon rice vinegar
1 teaspoon blackstrap molasses
1/4 to 1/2 teaspoon chili oil, or to taste
Juice of1/2 lime

Mix all ingredients together in a small bowl. If not using right away, cover and refrigerate until needed.

Glorified Green Beans

Serves 4

Similar to vegetable tempura often served in Japanese restaurants, this recipe dresses up green beans and takes them into a comfort food zone. Umeboshi paste can be hard to find, but it's worth tracking down. Look in Asian stores or in the Asian aisle of a well-stocked grocery store.

1/4 cup soy sauce
2 tablespoons rice wine vinegar
1/2 teaspoon umeboshi paste
1/4 teaspoon Sriracha sauce
1 cup all-purpose flour
2 tablespoons cornstarch
1/4 teaspoon baking soda
1 teaspoon salt
2 teaspoons toasted sesame oil
1 cup club soda, chilled
Canola oil, for frying (see page 67)
8 ounces green beans, trimmed

1. In a small bowl, combine the soy sauce, vinegar, umeboshi paste, and Sriracha sauce. Mix well. Set aside until serving time.

2. In a shallow bowl, combine the flour, cornstarch, baking soda, and salt. Stir together with a fork. Add the sesame oil and club soda. The mixture will be slightly thick.

3. Heat the oil in a deep fryer to 375°F or in a large skillet over medium-high heat. Line a baking sheet with paper towels or a brown bag for draining and set it aside.

4. Working in batches, dip the beans in the batter. If the batter drips off, leaving bare spots on the beans, add a bit more flour. If it is too thick, add a bit more soda.

5. Gently place the beans into the fryer and fry 2 to 4 minutes, until nicely golden. Remove from the oil and drain on the baking sheet. Serve hot with the reserved sauce.

Two-Bite Eggless Rolls

Makes 32 to 36

These tasty bites are quick to make and quick to disappear. Be sure to finely chop the filling ingredients in order to get a little of everything in one bite. If you don't have Szechuan seasoning, substitute the same amount of Sriracha sauce or red pepper flakes. Vegan wonton wrappers can be hard to find. Check the frozen section of the grocery store or an Asian grocer.

1 tablespoon peanut oil
1/2 teaspoon chili oil
1/4 pound extra-firm tofu, drained, pressed, and cut into 1/8-inch dice
1/4 teaspoon Szechuan seasoning
1/4 teaspoon white pepper
1 tablespoon soy sauce
1 clove garlic, minced
1 teaspoon grated fresh ginger
1/2 cup snow peas, trimmed, and chopped into 1/8-inch pieces
3 tablespoons minced scallions
1 cup finely chopped napa cabbage
1/2 cup shredded carrot
1/2 cup bean sprouts, cut into 1/8-inch pieces
1 to 2 tablespoons vegetable broth, if needed
Salt and black pepper
32 to 36 vegan wonton wrappers
Canola oil, for brushing or spraying
Spicy Soy Dipping Sauce (recipe follows)

1. Heat the peanut and chili oils in a large skillet over medium heat. Add the tofu, Szechuan seasoning, and white pepper. Stir and cook for 2 to 3 minutes, or until very fragrant. Add the soy sauce, garlic, ginger, snow peas, scallions, cabbage, carrot, and bean sprouts. Continue to cook, stirring, for 3 to 5 minutes, until the tofu is lightly browned, but the vegetables are still crisp. Add a tablespoon or two of broth if the mixture sticks to the skillet. Add salt and pepper to taste. Remove from heat. Preheat the oven to 400°F. Lightly oil 2 baking sheets. Place a small bowl with cold water near a work surface.

2. Arrange 6 wrappers on the work surface with one of the points facing toward you. Spoon a scant tablespoon of filling near the center of the wrapper. Wet your fingers, and fold the point facing you up and over the filling. Tuck in the two opposite ends of the wrapper, then roll toward the last point. Wet your fingers as needed to seal the wrapper together. Place on the baking sheet and continue with remaining wrappers and filling.

3. Lightly brush or spray the rolls with oil. Bake for 6 to 8 minutes, or until golden brown. Carefully turn over with spatula and spray again. Return to the oven for an additional 4 to 5 minutes and bake until golden brown. Serve hot with the dipping sauce on the side.

Spicy Soy Dipping Sauce

Makes 1/3 cup

1/4 cup soy sauce
1 tablespoon rice vinegar
1 tablespoon minced scallions
1/2 teaspoon toasted sesame oil
1/4 teaspoon Sriracha sauce, or to taste

In a small bowl, combine the soy sauce, vinegar, scallions, sesame oil, and Sriracha to taste. Stir to combine.

Portobello Sticks

Serves 4

These crispy and delicious mushrooms are crunchy on the outside and juicy on the inside. They are especially addictive when paired with the spicy sauce. If the batter thickens as you get to the last mushrooms, add a splash of soy milk. For important information about deep frying, read Before You Deep Fry (page 67).

SAUCE

1/4 cup plus 2 tablespoons vegan
   mayonnaise
1 1/2 tablespoons ketchup
1 tablespoon minced shallot
1/4 teaspoon ground cayenne
1 tablespoon fresh lemon juice

MUSHROOMS

9 ounces Portobello mushroom caps,
   lightly rinsed, and patted dry
Canola oil, for frying (see page 67)
1 cup all-purpose flour plus 2
   tablespoons, divided
1 teaspoon salt, divided
Pinch black pepper
1 tablespoon finely ground cornmeal
1/2 teaspoon baking powder
1 teaspoon dried thyme
1/2 teaspoon ground cayenne
1 1/4 cups soy milk

1. *Sauce:* In a small bowl, combine the mayonnaise, ketchup, shallot, cayenne, and lemon juice. Mix well. Cover and refrigerate until serving.

2. *Mushrooms:* Use a teaspoon to gently remove the stems and gills from the mushrooms. Cut the caps in 1/4-inch slices. Heat the oil in a deep fryer to 375°F. If you don't have a deep fryer, a heavy bottomed skillet may be used instead. Spread a paper bag over a baking sheet for draining.

3. In a shallow bowl, combine 2 tablespoons flour with 1/2 teaspoon of the salt and the pepper. Set aside.

4. In a medium bowl, combine the remaining 1 cup flour, remaining 1/2 teaspoon salt, cornmeal, baking powder, thyme, and cayenne. Whisk together, then add the soy milk. Stir to combine.

5. Working in batches so that the deep fryer doesn't become crowded, dredge 4 mushroom slices in the flour mixture, then dip in the batter. Gently ease the mushrooms into the fryer and fry for 4 to 5 minutes, turning as needed, until golden brown. When done, carefully transfer to the baking sheet to drain. Repeat with the remaining mushroom slices until they are all cooked. Season with salt and pepper and serve hot with the reserved sauce on the side.

Tempting Tofu Dippers

Serves 4

These tofu sticks are sure to impress with their exotic flavor. What's better than take-out? Home-made take-out.

1 pound extra-firm tofu, cut into 8 slices, drained and pressed
1/2 cup soy milk
2 tablespoons cornstarch
1/4 cup plus 2 tablespoons panko crumbs
1/4 cup sesame seeds
1 tablespoon dried *herbes de Provençe*
1 tablespoon dried minced onion
1 teaspoon salt
Pineapple-Pomegranate Dipping Sauce (recipe follows)

1. Preheat the oven to 400°F. Lightly oil a baking sheet. Cut the tofu slices lengthwise in half to make 16 sticks.

2. In a shallow bowl, combine the soy milk with the cornstarch. In another shallow bowl, combine the panko, sesame seeds, *herbes de Provençe,* and dried onion. To help reduce clumping, reserve half of the crumb mixture on a sheet of waxed paper.

3. Dip the tofu into the soy milk mixture then into the crumbs, gently pressing the crumbs into the tofu. Place the coated tofu sticks on the baking sheet and repeat with the remaining tofu until they are all coated, adding the reserved crumb mixture as needed.

4. Spray the tofu sticks lightly with oil or nonstick cooking spray and bake for 30 minutes. Turn over, spray again, and bake another 10 minutes until light gold in color. Serve hot with dipping sauce.

Pineapple-Pomegranate Dipping Sauce

Makes 3/4 cup

1/2 cup pineapple juice
1/4 cup pomegranate juice
2 tablespoons soy sauce
2 tablespoons mirin
1 tablespoon agave nectar
1 teaspoon toasted sesame oil
2 cloves garlic, minced
2 teaspoons grated fresh ginger
1 tablespoon chopped scallions
1/2 teaspoon red pepper flakes

Combine all the ingredients in a small saucepan. Whisk together, then bring to a boil over medium-high heat. Reduce the heat to medium and simmer for 15 minutes or until the sauce has reduced by half.

Fried Dill Pickles

Makes 16

Not just a southern specialty, fried pickles are often featured in cafes and bistros in the Midwest. The best pickles for these are crisp, refrigerated dill pickles. We like them straight, but they could be served with any dipping sauce in this book. If you don't have a deep fryer, a heavy bottomed skillet may be used instead.

1/3 cup pickle juice
1/2 cup plus 1 tablespoon all-purpose
   flour, divided
1 tablespoon cornstarch
1 teaspoon prepared yellow mustard
1/2 teaspoon dried dill weed
1/4 teaspoon red pepper flakes
1/4 teaspoon salt, optional
Canola oil, for frying (see page 67)
4 refrigerated dill pickles, cut into 1/2-
   inch thick spears

1. In a shallow bowl, combine the pickle juice, the 1 tablespoon flour, cornstarch, and mustard. Stir together with a fork. In a second shallow bowl, combine the 1/2 cup flour, dill weed, red pepper flakes, and salt, if using. Stir together with a fork.

2. Heat the oil in a deep fryer or large skillet to 375°F. Line a baking sheet with paper towels or a brown bag for draining.

3. Dip a pickle spear into the flour mixture, then into the batter, then dip it in the flour again and back into the batter. Gently ease the pickle into the deep fryer. Repeat with the remaining pickle spears, working in batches so that the deep fryer doesn't get overcrowded. Fry 6 to 8 minutes, or until golden brown. Drain on the baking sheet. Serve hot.

Tomatillo Guacamole

Makes 1 1/2 cups

Like all dishes made with avocado, prepare this recipe close to serving time so it stays bright green in color. Serve it as a starter with tortilla chips, spread in a wrap, or with any Mexican dish.

2 ripe Hass avocados, pitted, peeled, cut
   into 1 to 2-inch chunks
1/2 cup Green Salsa (page 65) or store-
   bought
1 tablespoon fresh lime juice
Salt and black pepper

Place the avocados in a medium bowl and mash them with a fork. Add the salsa, lime juice, and salt and pepper to taste. Mix well and serve immediately.

Cashew Cheeze Stuffed Squash Blossoms

Makes 8

This Italian specialty is an elegant and unusual starter that looks much harder to make than it is. It's sure to have your friends and family *ooohing* and *aaahing* as they reach for seconds. Squash blossoms are seasonal and may be hard to find. The best bet is your local farmer's market in early summer or a well-stocked natural food store.

CHEEZE:
1/2 cup raw cashews, soaked in 1 cup cold water overnight, drained
1 tablespoon white miso paste
2 teaspoons nutritional yeast
1 tablespoon white vinegar
1 teaspoon capers plus 1 teaspoon caper juice

BLOSSOMS:
8 squash blossoms, gently rinsed
1/2 cup all-purpose flour
1/2 teaspoon salt
1/4 teaspoon dried thyme
1/4 teaspoon onion powder
Pinch sugar
1/2 cup chilled club soda
1/3 to 1/2 cup chilled water
Canola oil, for frying (see page 67)

1. *Cheeze:* Grind the cashews to a smooth paste in a blender or food processor. Add the remaining ingredients and process again until smooth. Set aside or refrigerate until needed.

2. *Blossoms:* Gently open the squash blossoms and fill with about 1 tablespoon of cheeze mixture. Lightly press the blossom closed, using the filling to hold them closed. Place on a baking sheet. Repeat with remaining blossoms. Set aside.

3. In a shallow bowl, combine the flour, salt, thyme, onion powder, and sugar. Mix together with a fork, then add the club soda and 1/3 cup cold water. The mixture should coat your finger and drip off, but not leave bare spots. If the mixture is too thick, add additional water.

4. Heat 1/8-inch of oil in a large skillet over medium heat. Cover a baking sheet with paper towels or a brown bag for draining.

5. Dip the blossoms in the batter, turning to coat them well. Transfer to the hot oil and fry until golden, 5 to 7 minutes, turning as needed until golden brown all over. Adjust the heat as needed to maintain the proper cooking temperature. Serve hot.

Three-Chile Hummus

Makes 2 cups

Hummus is a fixture in Greek and Middle Eastern restaurants. This version packs a spicy wallop with three kinds of chiles. Whether you serve it with corn chips, pita, or vegetable dippers, it will be one of the first things to vanish from the table. If you happen to have leftovers, it makes a great sandwich spread, too.

1 large poblano chile
1 1/2 cups cooked or 1 (15-ounce) can chickpeas, rinsed and drained
2 tablespoons tahini
1 1/2 tablespoons minced chipotle chile in adobo
1 tablespoon minced jalapeño
5 cloves roasted garlic (page 47)
1/2 teaspoon ground cumin
1/2 teaspoon smoked paprika
1/4 teaspoon chili powder
2 tablespoons fresh lime juice
3 tablespoons water, or more
1 tablespoon olive oil
1/2 teaspoon salt
Chopped scallions, optional garnish

1. Place the poblano chile on a small baking sheet and broil until blackened, turning it every few minutes. Place the blackened chile in a brown paper bag, then close the bag and set aside for 20 minutes. Remove and discard the skin and seeds and roughly chop the chile.

2. In a food processor, combine the poblano, chickpeas, tahini, chipotle, jalapeño, garlic, cumin, paprika, and chili powder. Process to a thick but smooth paste. Add the lime juice, water, olive oil, and salt. Process again, adding additional water, if needed, to reach the desired consistency. Taste and adjust the seasonings. Garnish with scallions, if using.

Everybody's Favorite Taco Dip

Serves 4 to 6

This dip is always on the table for our family get-togethers. It's great served with corn chips or cut raw vegetables.

2 tablespoons soy milk
1/2 cup vegan cream cheese
1/2 cup vegan sour cream
2 minced chipotle chiles in adobo
1 clove garlic, minced
1 teaspoon chili powder
1/2 teaspoon ground cumin
Pinch black pepper
2/3 cup cooked black beans
1 cup shredded lettuce
2 tablespoons chopped black olives
1/2 cup ripe chopped tomatoes
2 tablespoons chopped scallions
2 teaspoons minced pickled jalapeños

1. In a medium bowl, combine the soy milk, cream cheese, sour cream, chipotles, garlic, chili powder, cumin, and black pepper. Mix well until smooth and creamy, then spread the mixture evenly onto a dinner plate or serving platter.

2. Spread the remaining ingredients over the cream cheese mixture, layering them in the order given. Serve immediately or cover and refrigerate until needed.

Cafe Spinach Dip

Makes 1 1/2 cups

This is the classic café-style dip reimagined with vegan ingredients and Southwestern influences. It has a subtle heat that sneaks up on you, so add the hot sauce slowly and to taste. For dippers, go with sliced French bread or choose your favorite raw vegetables such as carrot and celery sticks, cauliflower florets, bell pepper strips, or ripe cherry tomatoes.

1/2 cup vegan sour cream
1/2 cup vegan mayonnaise
2 tablespoons Green Salsa (page 65) or
  store-bought
1 (10-ounce) package frozen chopped
  spinach, thawed and squeezed dry
1 tablespoon canned chopped green
  chiles
1 tablespoon pickled jalapeños, drained
  and finely chopped
3 tablespoons finely chopped celery
3 tablespoons finely chopped red bell
  pepper
3 tablespoons finely chopped red onion
1 tablespoon fresh lime juice
1/4 to 1 teaspoon hot pepper sauce
1/4 teaspoon ground cumin
1/4 teaspoon chili powder
1/2 teaspoon dried oregano
1/4 cup chopped black olives, for garnish

In a medium bowl, combine all the ingredients, except the black olives, and stir to combine. Refrigerate for 1 hour or longer to allow the flavors to meld. Serve topped with chopped black olives.

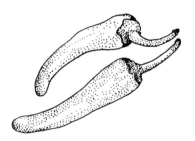

Green Salsa

Makes 1 cup

This unique green salsa made with roasted tomatillos is a delicious variation on the salsa you find on the tables of Mexican restaurants. It's great for dipping with chips or spooned onto the 21st Century Tacos (page 145).

1/2 dried ancho chile
12 ounces tomatillos
2 cloves garlic, minced
2 tablespoons minced onion
1 tablespoon chopped fresh cilantro
1 tablespoon chopped fresh parsley
1/2 tablespoon agave nectar
1 teaspoon adobo sauce (from canned chipotle chiles)
Salt

1. Heat a small skillet over medium heat. Add the ancho chile and cook, pressing it with a spatula, for about 1 minute per side, until fragrant. Remove from heat and place the chile in a small heatproof bowl with enough boiling water to cover. Place a fork on top of the chile to keep it submerged. Soak for 30 minutes, then drain and set aside. Preheat the broiler.

2. Remove and discard the papery husks from the tomatillos. Wash the tomatillos and arrange them on a baking sheet. Broil for 5 minutes, then turn and broil the other side until they are soft and have some black spots, 5 to 7 minutes longer.

3. Pour the tomatillos along with any juices and broken pieces into a food processor. Chop the reserved ancho chile and add to the processor along with the garlic, onion, cilantro, and parsley. Pulse to mix well.

4. Transfer the salsa to a bowl and stir in the agave nectar, adobo sauce, and salt to taste. Set aside to cool. The salsa may be served at room temperature or chilled. If not using right away, cover and refrigerate for up to 3 days.

Besto Pesto Dip

Serves 4 to 6

This dip looks restaurant perfect, but it couldn't be easier to put together. Serve this with a glass of vegan pinot grigio as a starter course for a wonderful homemade Italian meal. Instead of spreading the dip in a pie plate, you can use 2 (4-inch) springform pans.

2 tablespoons pine nuts
1/2 cup Besto Pesto (recipe follows)
8 ounces vegan cream cheese, room temperature
Salt and black pepper
2 tablespoons chopped oil-packed sun-dried tomatoes
1 loaf French bread, cut into 1/4-inch slices, for serving
Cauliflower florets, cherry tomatoes, bell pepper strips, or other vegetables, for serving

1. In a small skillet over medium heat, toast the pine nuts until golden, 3 to 5 minutes, stirring occasionally. Remove from the skillet and set aside to cool before proceeding.

2. In a medium bowl, combine the pesto, cream cheese, and salt and pepper to taste. Mix well.

3. Line a 7 or 8-inch pie plate with plastic wrap. Spread the pine nuts and sun-dried tomatoes in the bottom of the plate. Gently spread the pesto-cream cheese filling on top of the pine nuts and tomatoes, spreading evenly. Cover the dip with plastic wrap and refrigerate for at least one hour.

4. To serve, remove the plastic from the top of the pie plate. Place a plate on top of the dip and invert so that the pine nuts and tomatoes are on the top. Remove the plate and the plastic wrap liner. Serve with French bread and vegetables.

Besto Pesto

Make 1/2 cup

2 cloves garlic, minced
3 tablespoons pine nuts
2 cups tightly packed fresh basil
2 tablespoons nutritional yeast
2 tablespoons fresh lemon juice
1 tablespoon white miso paste
1/8 teaspoon salt
Pinch white pepper
3 tablespoons olive oil

In a food processor, combine the garlic and pine nuts and process until they are a rough paste. Add the basil, yeast, lemon juice, miso, salt, and pepper. Process until the mixture is a smooth paste. Drizzle in the olive oil and process until the mixture is emulsified, scraping down the sides as needed. The pesto is now ready to use in recipes or can be refrigerated or frozen in a tightly covered container.

Before You Deep Fry

Here are some important points to keep in mind whenever you deep fry at home:

The Basics:

- You can use either a deep fryer or a large heavy-bottomed skillet to deep fry foods.
- You will need to use enough oil to cover the ingredients you are deep frying.
- When using a skillet, it must be deep enough to fill it with at least 1-inch of oil, but since oil expands as it heats, be sure you have at least 3-inches of pan above the oil level.

The Oil:

- Canola oil or peanut oil are generally used for frying because of their neutral tastes, and higher smoke points.
- Never use olive oil for deep frying.
- Avoid frying sweet foods in the same oil after frying pungent foods, such as onions.

The Temperature:

- The ideal temperature for deep frying is between 350° and 375°F—hot enough to fry, but *not* at the smoking point.
- A candy thermometer is handy for checking the oil temperature, but if you don't have one, place a 1-inch cube of bread in the fryer. It should take 1 minute to turn golden brown at 365°F.
- Once the oil reaches the ideal temperature, fry a test piece of food. If the outside is golden brown and the inside is cooked, great. If the outside is golden, but the inside is not cooked, reduce the heat slightly.
- If the temperature is too low, the food will take too long to cook and will be too oily, so raise the heat slightly. Adjust the heat as needed.

The Frying:

- Be sure your ingredients are dry or coated before frying. If you need to fry wet ingredients (such as potatoes for French fries), pat them dry or coat them with flour or bread crumbs.
- Whenever you place food in the fryer, avoid splashing by placing the edge of the food closest to you in first, so that the far end will splash away from you.
- Fry in batches so the skillet or deep fryer doesn't get overcrowded. When you fry too many things at once, the temperature drops which causes the food to absorb more oil, making it greasy.
- When the food is cooked, drain on paper towels or brown bags and season immediately. Fried food absorbs the most flavor when it's hot. Keep fried foods warm in a 250°F oven until ready to serve.

SOUP OF THE DAY

There's something about a steaming bowl of soup that nourishes physically and emotionally. I remember soups my mother made me after I played in the snow or for a cozy lunch while watching a movie on a rainy afternoon. Soup is transporting. A pot of soup simmering on the stove seems to make the whole house smell delicious. On the local cafe or diner menu, the "soup of the day" evokes the taste of home. It's the hot bowl that warms both the weary traveler and the busy local. As with many foods that we now call American, incoming ethnic groups brought their soups with them and enriched our country's cuisine. This chapter is filled with delicious examples.

Great Gazpacho

Serves 6

Originating in Spain, Gazpacho is served in cafes and bistros all over the United States. It has many variations and this is my favorite version. Add the jalapeño and hot sauce to your taste.

2 (14.5-ounce) cans diced fire-roasted
   tomatoes, undrained
4 cups good quality tomato juice
1 celery rib, diced
1 medium green bell pepper, diced
1/2 small red onion, diced
1 seedless cucumber, peeled and diced
1 to 2 jalapeños, seeded and finely
   minced
1 tablespoon sugar
1/4 cup white vinegar
1 tablespoon chopped fresh basil
1 tablespoon chopped fresh parsley
3 tablespoons chopped fresh dill
1 tablespoon fresh lime juice
1 tablespoon olive oil
1 teaspoon hot sauce, or to taste
1/2 teaspoon liquid smoke
1/2 teaspoon salt
1/8 teaspoon black pepper
Balsamic vinegar, for drizzling
Minced fresh dill, parsley, or basil,
   optional garnish

1. In a large bowl, combine all the ingredients except the balsamic vinegar and the optional garnish. Stir together. Refrigerate 4 hours to allow the flavors to develop. Taste and adjust the seasonings.

2. To serve, ladle the soup into bowls and top with a drizzle of balsamic vinegar and the fresh herbs, if using.

Creamy Cold Avocado-Cucumber Soup

Serves 4

This refreshing summer soup is great on those days when you don't want to be stuck in the kitchen. It's rich, so serve it in cups, not bowls. Pickled jalapeños are usually sold near the pickles or condiments in grocery stores.

1 shallot, chopped
2 ripe Hass avocados, pitted, peeled, and cut into 1/2-inch dice
1 small cucumber, peeled and chopped
2 tablespoons pickled jalapeños, or to taste
1 cup vegetable broth
1/2 cup soy milk
Juice of 2 limes
1/2 teaspoon salt
1/4 teaspoon white pepper
1 tablespoon chopped fresh parsley
Chopped ripe tomato, optional garnish

1. In a food processor, combine the shallot, avocados, half of the cucumber, jalapeños, broth, soy milk, lime juice, salt, and pepper. Process until smooth.

2. Add the parsley and pulse to combine. Transfer to a medium bowl. Stir in the remaining cucumber. Cover and refrigerate at least 2 hours to allow the flavors to combine.

3. When ready to serve, taste and adjust the seasonings, then ladle into bowls and garnish with tomatoes, if using. This soup is best served on the day it is made.

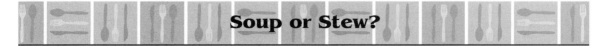

Soup or Stew?

The answer to this question can be confusing. Some people think stews are merely thick soups. However, soups are usually made with a thinner base and most often served in bowls. Stews are prepared with less liquid and are typically thicker in texture than soups. Also, stews are often made with more chunky ingredients. And yet, some soups are hearty and some stews may be a little thinner. Stews are sometimes served on a plate over noodles or a grain.

Another difference is in the cooking process. Although both may be made in a large pot, stews are sometimes cooked in the oven. As they are cooked at lower temperatures, stews generally take longer to cook, while soups are often cooked at higher temperatures for a shorter time.

A soup may be served as a starter course with a sandwich on the side, or as an entree, while a stew is served exclusively as an entree.

There is a good chance that your definitions of soups and stews are related to your mom's definition of them when you were growing up. However, rather than mince words, I'd rather mince vegetables.

Bistro French Onion Soup

Serves 4

French onion soup was made popular in the United States in the 1960s by Julia Child. With her television show and cookbooks, she led many of our moms down an exciting new road in cooking, and she changed our view of "comfort food" along the way. The optional vinegar brightens up the soup, but if your onions are at their peak, you probably won't need it.

1 tablespoon vegan margarine
1 tablespoon olive oil
2 medium shallots, sliced
4 large Vidalia or other sweet onions, sliced paper thin
1 leek, white part only, sliced
2 cloves garlic, minced
1/2 teaspoon sugar
1 teaspoon dried thyme
1 teaspoon smoked paprika
3/4 teaspoon chili powder
1 teaspoon salt
1/8 teaspoon black pepper
1/4 cup dry white wine
1/4 cup all-purpose flour
5 cups vegetable broth
1 tablespoon soy sauce
2 teaspoons white miso paste
1 tablespoon white vinegar, optional
2 sheets frozen vegan puff pastry, thawed

TIP

If you don't have ovenproof bowls, roll the pastry out and cut it into bowl-shaped rounds, then bake them on a baking sheet and place them on top of the soup to serve.

1. In a soup pot, combine the margarine and oil over medium low heat. Add the shallots, onions, leek, garlic, and sugar and cook, partially covered, for about 1 hour and 15 minutes, stirring occasionally, until the onions are brown and caramelized. Add the thyme, paprika, chili powder, salt, and pepper. Cook about 2 minutes longer.

2. Add the wine, scraping the bottom of the pot to deglaze. Add the flour and stir well. Cook about 2 minutes. Add the broth and soy sauce. Lower the heat to simmer and cook for 30 minutes. Taste to determine if the vinegar is needed and stir in the miso, then taste and adjust the seasonings.

3. Place the oven rack in the lower third of the oven to allow enough headroom for the puff pastry to expand as it bakes. Preheat the oven to 400°F.

4. On a lightly floured work surface, roll out the puff pastry. Place an ovenproof soup bowl upside down on the puff pastry. Cut the pastry about 1-inch larger than the rim of the bowl. Repeat to cut a total of 4 rounds, two from each sheet of pastry.

5. Ladle about 1/4 of the soup into each bowl, leaving 1/2 to 1-inch space at the top of each bowl. Wet your fingers and run them along the outer edge of a pastry round. Place the pastry on the top of the bowl tightly, sealing it with your fingers and not letting it touch the soup. Place the bowl on a baking sheet. Repeat with the other bowls. Bake for about 10 minutes, or until the pastry is puffed and golden. Serve immediately.

Mighty Miso Soup

Serves 4

I first became aware of miso when eating ramen noodles, a mainstay during my college years. However, miso is one of Japan's comfort foods, and it is always available in Japanese restaurants in the United States. Nutritionally, miso paste has 2 grams of protein per tablespoon and is a good source of vitamin B-12. In my version, quick-cooking orzo gives this soup extra body and texture. Be careful not to boil the soup once the miso paste has been added because boiling reduces miso's health benefits.

6 cups vegetable broth
1 cup chopped scallions
2 medium carrots, cut into 1/4-inch
   rounds
1/2 cup thinly sliced cremini or white
   button mushrooms
1 teaspoon chili oil
3 cloves garlic, minced
1 tablespoon minced fresh ginger
1 tablespoon soy sauce
1/2 teaspoon five-spice powder
Pinch white pepper
3/4 cup orzo, or other small pasta
1 cup shredded bok choy
1/3 cup dark miso paste

1. In a soup pot, combine the broth, scallions, carrots, mushrooms, chili oil, garlic, ginger, soy sauce, five-spice powder, and white pepper. Bring to a boil.

2. Add the orzo and reduce the heat to a low boil, not quite as low as a simmer. Cook for 5 minutes. Add the bok choy. Cook for 10 to 12 minutes, or until the pasta is tender, then remove from heat.

3. Remove about 1/2 cup of the broth and place it in a small bowl. Add the miso paste and stir until blended. Add the miso mixture back into the soup. Taste and adjust the seasonings. Serve hot.

Loaded Baked Potato Soup

Serves 4 to 6

I remember going with my family to steakhouses where salad and a baked potato were the only things I could eat. This soup is a homestyle homage to those times. While the roasted garlic gives this soup a delicious undercurrent, it may be omitted if you don't have any on hand.

2 pounds russet potatoes, scrubbed
7 cups vegetable broth, divided
2 tablespoons olive oil
1 large onion, chopped
1 cup cooked chickpeas
4 cloves garlic, minced
6 cloves roasted garlic (page 47),
   optional
1 teaspoon salt
1 teaspoon onion powder
1 teaspoon garlic powder
2 teaspoons dried chives
1/2 teaspoon celery salt
1/4 cup nutritional yeast
2 tablespoons soy sauce
2 tablespoons light miso paste
2 tablespoons dry white wine
3 cups small broccoli florets, cut into
   1-inch pieces

GARNISHES
1/2 cup vegan sour cream
2 tablespoons chopped fresh chives
1/4 cup chopped cooked Seitan
   Breakfast Strips (page 42), optional

1. Preheat the oven to 400°F. Using a fork, pierce each potato 2 or 3 times to allow steam to escape. Bake the potatoes for 1 hour, or until tender. Remove the potatoes from the oven and set aside until cool enough to handle. Cut 2 potatoes into 1 to 2-inch chunks and set them aside. Cut the remaining potatoes into 2-inch chunks and place them in a blender. Add 4 cups of the broth and blend until smooth, working in batches if necessary.

2. Heat the oil in a large pot over medium heat. Add the onion and cook 5 minutes, or until softened. Add the chickpeas, fresh garlic, and roasted garlic, if using. Cook 5 minutes longer.

3. Stir in the blended potato mixture and up to 3 cups of the remaining broth to reach the desired consistency. Add the reserved potato chunks. Add the remaining ingredients except broccoli and garnishes and bring to a simmer. Cook, partially covered, stirring occasionally, 15 minutes. Add the broccoli, partially cover, and simmer 15 minutes longer, or until the broccoli is tender. Ladle into bowls and garnish with a spoonful of sour cream, a sprinkling of chives, and Seitan Breakfast Strips, if using. Serve hot.

Smoky Cauliflower and Bean Soup

Serves 4 to 6

Low in fat and high in fiber, cauliflower is a superstar vegetable. It is especially good when partnered with beans, vegan sausage, and vegetables in this satisfying soup.

8 ounces rotini, or other bite-sized pasta
1 tablespoon olive oil
8 ounces Vegan Sausage Links (page 41) or store-bought, chopped
1 medium onion, chopped
3 cloves garlic, minced
4 cups small cauliflower florets
1 large carrot, chopped
2 teaspoons smoked paprika
1 teaspoon dried basil
1 teaspoon dried parsley
1/2 cup dry red wine
1 (14.5-ounce) can diced tomatoes, undrained
6 to 8 cups vegetable broth
1 1/2 cups cooked or 1 (15-ounce) can great northern beans, rinsed and drained
1 tablespoon soy sauce
Salt and black pepper
1/4 cup chopped fresh parsley

1. Cook the rotini in a pot of salted boiling water until al dente, 7 to 8 minutes. Drain and set aside.

2. Heat the oil in a large pot over medium heat. Add the sausage and cook about 10 minutes, or until browned. If the sausage sticks to the pot, stir in a splash of the broth. Remove the sausage from the pot and set aside.

3. To the same pot, add the onion and cook over medium heat for 5 minutes, or until translucent. Add the garlic, cauliflower, and carrot. Cook 2 to 3 minutes, or until the garlic is fragrant. Add the paprika, basil, dried parsley, and the reserved sausage. Cook for 2 to 3 minutes, then add the wine. Turn the heat to medium-high to deglaze the pot, scraping any bits off the bottom, and reduce the wine by half.

4. Add the tomatoes, 6 cups of broth, beans, and soy sauce. Season with salt and pepper, to taste. Add additional broth if desired. Bring to a boil and simmer 15 minutes. Stir in the fresh parsley. Taste and adjust the seasonings. Just before serving, add the cooked pasta. Serve hot.

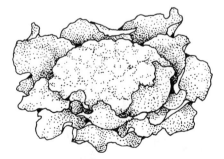

Mom's Noodle Soup 👍 🕐 ☺

Serves 4

This comforting soup is reminiscent of the chicken noodle soup many of us enjoyed as kids. In this version, a flavorful seitan replaces the chicken for a delicious soup that is oh-so-good for you – and a whole lot better for the chicken, too. Instead of using the Seitan Lite, you can substitute diced steamed tempeh in this recipe. I like to use the flower-shaped fiori pasta in this soup, but any kind of small pasta or short noodles will work.

1 1/2 cups fiori pasta or other small pasta or noodles
1 tablespoon olive oil
8 ounces Seitan Lite (page 6), cut into 1/2-inch dice
Salt and black pepper
1 large onion, chopped
1 celery rib, diced
2 medium carrots, chopped
4 cloves garlic, minced
1 teaspoon dried mustard
1 teaspoon dried thyme
1/2 teaspoon ground cumin
1/2 teaspoon ground coriander
1/2 teaspoon dried rosemary
1/2 teaspoon turmeric
2 tablespoons nutritional yeast
1/2 cup dry white wine
1/2 cup peas, fresh or frozen
1 cup chopped fresh spinach or Swiss chard
7 cups vegetable broth
3 tablespoons chopped fresh parsley

1. Cook the pasta in a pot of salted boiling water until al dente, 6 to 8 minutes. Drain and set aside.

2. Heat the oil in a large pot over medium heat. Add the seitan, season with salt and pepper, and cook until browned, about 5 minutes, stirring occasionally.

3. Add the onion, celery, and carrots, and cook for 5 minutes, or until softened. Add the garlic, mustard, dried herbs, and spices. Cook about 3 minutes, until fragrant. Add the yeast and wine. Stir to deglaze the pot, scraping any bits that are stuck to the bottom. Add the peas, spinach, and vegetable broth. Bring to a boil, then reduce heat to a simmer and cook 10 to 15 minutes or until the vegetables are tender and the flavors are combined. Taste and adjust the seasonings. When ready to serve, add the cooked pasta and the parsley. Serve hot.

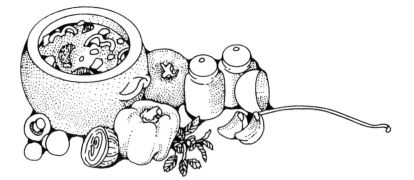

'Big Soup' Minestrone

Serves 4

Thank the Italian community for this classic vegetable soup that is often featured at diners, Italian eateries, and everywhere in between. The name actually means "big soup" and this recipe lives up to its name. Traditionally, it's made with whatever vegetables might be on hand in the kitchen, so feel free to adapt this to use other vegetables. Instead of tempeh, 1 1/2 cups of cooked white beans may be substituted.

1 cup ditalini, or other small pasta
8 ounces tempeh, steamed, and cut into 1/2-inch cubes
1 teaspoon onion powder
1 teaspoon garlic powder
1 teaspoon lemon pepper
2 to 3 tablespoons olive oil
1 medium onion, diced
2 celery ribs, diced
3 carrots, cut into 1/4-inch slices
3 cloves garlic, minced
1 teaspoon dried basil
1 teaspoon dried parsley
1 teaspoon *herbes de Provençe*
1 teaspoon dried thyme
1 teaspoon smoked paprika
1/2 cup dry red wine, or additional broth
2 tablespoons soy sauce
6 to 8 cups vegetable broth
1/2 to 1 teaspoon hot sauce
1 (14.5-ounce) can diced tomatoes, undrained
1 cup fresh green beans, trimmed, and cut into 1-inch pieces
1/2 cup fresh or frozen green peas
Salt and black pepper
Vegan Parmesan (page 137) or store-bought, optional garnish

1. Cook the ditalini in a pot of boiling salted water until al dente, 5 to 7 minutes. Drain and set aside.

2. In a small bowl, combine the tempeh with the onion powder, garlic powder, and lemon pepper. Toss to coat. (If using beans instead of tempeh, omit this step and add the onion powder, garlic powder and lemon pepper to the soup pot with the onion, celery, and carrots.)

3. Heat 2 tablespoons of oil in a large pot over medium heat. Add the tempeh and cook until golden brown, about 7 to 10 minutes, stirring occasionally. Add the additional oil, if needed. Remove the tempeh from the pot and set aside.

4. To the same pot, add the onion, celery, and carrots. Cook about 10 minutes. Add the garlic and herbs. Cook another 4 to 5 minutes. Add the red wine, soy sauce, 6 cups of broth, hot sauce, tomatoes, green beans, peas, and reserved tempeh. For a thinner soup, add another 1 to 2 cups of vegetable broth. Bring to a boil, then simmer about 45 minutes. Season with salt and pepper to taste. Add the cooked pasta and serve hot with Parmesan on the side, if using.

Chase-the-Chill Chili

Order chili at a diner, and you might hear the server call out a "bowl of red." I prefer the chili I make in my own kitchen, since I can season it just the way I like. It's especially good served with a side of Yankee Cornbread (page 39). Like all soups and stews, this chili tastes better the next day. It also freezes well. The seitan can be minced by hand or in the food processor for more of a "ground" texture.

1 tablespoon olive oil
1 large onion, chopped
1 medium red bell pepper, chopped
1/2 medium green bell pepper, chopped
1 jalapeño, seeded and minced
4 cloves garlic, minced
1 pound Savory Seitan (page 5), cut into
   1/2-inch dice
2 tablespoons chili powder
1 tablespoon ground cumin
1 teaspoon dried oregano
1 cup vegan beer, such as Sam Smith's
   Lager
1 (28-ounce) can whole plum tomatoes,
   undrained
1 (15-ounce) can fire-roasted tomatoes
   with chiles, undrained
1 1/2 cups or 1 (15-ounce) can black
   beans, rinsed and drained
1 1/2 cups or 1 (15-ounce) can red
   kidney beans, rinsed and drained
1 tablespoon minced chipotle chile in
   adobo
1 tablespoon blackstrap molasses
1 tablespoon unsweetened cocoa
   powder
Salt and black pepper
1 to 2 cups vegetable broth

1. Heat the oil in a large pot over medium heat. Add the onion, bell peppers and jalapeño. Cook, stirring, for 5 minutes, or until softened. Add the garlic, seitan, and spices. Cook until the seitan is browned, about 5 minutes. Add the beer and stir to deglaze the pot, scraping any bits off the bottom.

2. While the plum tomatoes are still in the can, use a knife to cut through them a little to break them up a bit. To the seitan mixture, add the tomatoes, beans, chipotle, molasses, cocoa powder. Season with salt and pepper to taste. Stir to combine, then add the broth to desired consistency. Bring to a boil then reduce to simmer for 30 minutes or longer to blend the flavors. Serve hot.

Black Bean Soup

Serves 4 to 6

This hearty soup is popular in Mexican-American eateries, as well as almost any restaurant that features a "soup of the day." Sometimes called turtle beans, black beans are a great source of protein and go back at least 7,000 years. NOTE: For a thicker soup, use an immersion blender or blender to puree some of the soup.

1 tablespoon olive oil
1 large onion, chopped
3 cloves garlic, sliced
6 ounces Yukon gold potatoes, scrubbed, and minced
3 medium carrots, cut into 1/4-inch rounds
1 1/2 celery ribs, diced
1/2 medium jalapeño, seeded and minced
1 tablespoon ground cumin
1 1/2 teaspoons dried oregano
1 1/2 teaspoons ground chipotle chili powder
1 1/2 teaspoons smoked paprika
1/2 teaspoon black pepper
1 teaspoon salt
4 1/2 cups cooked or 3 (15-ounce) cans black beans, rinsed and drained
4 1/2 cups vegetable broth
3 tablespoons ketchup
1 tablespoon liquid smoke
1/2 to 1 teaspoon hot sauce
Juice of 1 lime
Salt and black pepper
Vegan sour cream, optional garnish

1. Heat the oil in a large pot over medium heat. Add the onion, garlic, potatoes, carrots, celery, and jalapeño. Cook 5 minutes to soften. Add the cumin, oregano, chili powder, smoked paprika, pepper, and salt. Cook, stirring for 2 minutes. Stir in the beans, broth, ketchup, liquid smoke, and hot sauce. Bring to a boil then reduce to a simmer and cook for 45 minutes.

2. Just before serving, add the lime juice. Season to taste with salt and pepper. Serve hot with additional hot sauce and a dollop of sour cream, if using.

Corn and Bean Chowder

Serves 4 to 6

In New England, chowders are typically made with clams and are offered in nearly every restaurant. Most likely, the name derives from the old English word "jowter," which refered to someone selling fish. There's no seafood here, but a few vegan oyster crackers go well with this satisfying chowder.

1 tablespoon olive oil
1 large onion, minced
2 large carrots, minced
1 celery rib, minced
12 ounces Yukon Gold potatoes, cut into
　1/2-inch dice
3 cloves garlic, minced
1 teaspoon salt
1 cup fresh or frozen corn kernels
4 cups vegetable broth, divided
1 tablespoon minced chipotle chile in
　adobo
1 1/2 cups cooked or 1(15-ounce) can
　great northern beans, drained and rinsed
1 1/2 cups cooked or 1 (15-ounce) can
　cannelini beans, drained and rinsed
1 tablespoon nutritional yeast
1 teaspoon All-American Spice Blend
　(page 13) or other spice blend
1 teaspoon ground cumin
1 teaspoon smoked paprika
1/2 teaspoon dried mustard
1/2 teaspoon celery seed
1/8 teaspoon black pepper
Juice of 1/2 lemon
1/4 cup chopped fresh parsley

1. Heat the oil in a large pot over medium heat. Add the onion, carrots, celery, and potatoes. Cook 5 minutes, stirring occasionally, until the onion is translucent. Add the garlic and salt. Cook for 2 minutes, or until the garlic becomes fragrant.

2. In a blender, combine the corn, 1 cup of the broth, and the chipotle and blend until smooth. Add the corn mixture to the pot along with the remaining 3 cups of broth, beans, yeast, and spices. Bring to a boil. Reduce the heat and simmer, partially covered, for 30 minutes, or until the vegetables are tender. Adjust the seasonings. Just before serving, stir in the lemon juice and parsley. Serve hot.

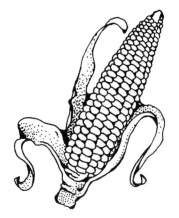

Pasta and Bean Soup

This is a distant cousin of the more traditional pasta fagioli. This soups is more brothy, but just as substantial. First popularized in the United States after World War II, this hearty soup can be found on menus everywhere, not just in Italian restaurants. One taste and you'll know why.

12 ounces ditalini, or other small pasta
1 tablespoon olive oil
1 bunch scallions, chopped
6 to 8 cloves garlic, minced
3/4 cup minced fresh parsley
1 teaspoon dried basil
1 teaspoon All-American Spice Blend
  (page 13) or other spice blend
1/2 to 1 teaspoon red pepper flakes
1 1/2 cups cooked or 1 (15-ounce) can
  chickpeas, drained and rinsed
1 1/2 cups cooked or 1 (15-ounce) can
  navy beans, drained and rinsed
1 1/2 cups cooked or 1 (15-ounce) can
  cannellini beans, drained and rinsed
1/4 cup dry red wine
6 to 8 cups vegetable broth
1/4 cup tomato paste
1 tablespoon soy sauce
1/2 to 1 teaspoon hot sauce
1/2 teaspoon salt
1/8 teaspoon black pepper

1. Cook the ditalini in a pot of boiling salted water until al dente, 5 to 7 minutes. Drain and set aside.

2. Heat the oil in a large pot over medium heat. Add the scallions, garlic, parsley, basil, and spices. Cook 5 minutes, then add the beans. Cook 5 minutes longer. Add the remaining ingredients, except the pasta. Bring to a boil, then reduce to simmer and cook for 30 minutes.

3. Just before serving, add the reserved pasta, then taste and adjust the seasonings. Serve hot.

Mushroom Barley Stew

Serves 4 to 6

This slightly smoky stew has a deep flavor and a wonderful texture. It makes a hearty meal when served with a side salad. Instead of using diced tempeh patties, you can substitute Seitan Breakfast Strips (page 42).

2 tablespoons olive oil
3 ounces Diner Tempeh Breakfast Patties (page 43), diced
1 medium onion, finely chopped
1/2 celery rib, finely chopped
4 cloves garlic, minced
12 ounces cremini mushrooms, cut into quarters
1 teaspoon dried thyme
1 teaspoon dried tarragon
1 teaspoon All-American Spice Blend (page 13) or other spice blend
1/2 teaspoon smoked paprika
1/2 cup dry white wine
1 cup pearl barley
1 tablespoon soy sauce
6 to 8 cups vegetable broth
Salt and black pepper
Vegan sour cream and chopped fresh parsley, optional garnishes

1. Heat the oil in a large pot over medium heat. Add the tempeh and cook until browned, about 5 minutes. Remove from the pot and set aside.

2. To the same pot, add the onion and cook over medium heat until softened, about 5 minutes. Add the celery and garlic and cook 2 minutes, or until the garlic is fragrant. Add the mushrooms, herbs, and spices. Cook 3 to 5 minutes, or until the mushrooms begin to soften. Add the reserved tempeh. Increase the heat to medium-high and add the wine to deglaze, scraping any bits off the bottom of the pot.

3. When the liquid reduces to one half, add the barley, soy sauce, and broth. Season with salt and pepper to taste. Bring to a boil, then reduce to a simmer. Cook 50 to 60 minutes, or until the barley is tender, adding more broth if needed. Taste and adjust the seasonings. Serve hot, garnished with sour cream and parsley, if using.

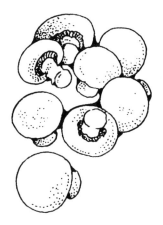

Seitan Brew Stew

My ancestors ran a "Bread and Beer" in Cambridge, Massachusetts back in the 1600s. I like to think that they served a full-bodied stew like this one, using their own homemade brew.

1 tablespoon olive oil
1 medium onion, cut into 1-inch dice
1 celery rib, cut into 1/2-inch dice
3 medium carrots, cut into 1/2-inch dice
3 tablespoons all-purpose flour
1/2 teaspoon salt
1/8 teaspoon black pepper
1 pound Savory Seitan (page 5), cut into
    1-inch dice
2 cloves garlic, minced
1 pound baby white potatoes, scrubbed,
    and cut into 1-inch dice
1 tablespoon dried parsley
2 teaspoons dried thyme
1 teaspoon dried rosemary
1/8 teaspoon red pepper flakes
1 dried bay leaf
1 1/2 cups vegan beer, such as Magic Hat
    Mother Lager
1 teaspoon vegan Worcestershire sauce
1/4 teaspoon liquid smoke
2 (15-ounce) cans diced tomatoes,
    undrained
1/2 cup vegetable broth, if needed

1. Heat the oil in a large pot over medium heat. Add the onion, celery, and carrots and cook 5 minutes.

2. In a medium bowl, combine the flour, salt, and pepper. Add the seitan and toss to coat. Transfer the seitan and any remaining flour to the pot. Add the garlic and potatoes. Stir and cook 5 minutes. Stir in the herbs and spices and cook 2 minutes longer. The mixture may stick a little.

3. Add the beer, stirring to deglaze, and scrape any bits off the bottom of the pot. Add the Worcestershire sauce, liquid smoke, and tomatoes. Add just enough broth, if needed, to cover the ingredients. Partially cover and simmer 1 hour, or until the potatoes are tender. Taste and adjust the seasonings. Remove bay leaf. Serve hot.

SALAD BAR

These tasty salads are a far cry from those "iceberg only" salads of years ago, referred to in diner lingo as "rabbit food." Some of the "big bowl" salads in this chapter, such as the Midtown Greek Salad and the Spicy Tofu Noodle Salad, can be served as satisfying meals in themselves. This chapter also contains a selection of all-American side salads, including macaroni salads, coleslaw, and potato salads. Many feature new takes on familiar favorites. For the perfect accompaniment to barbeque or burgers, be sure to try the bright-tasting Farmhouse Coleslaw or the flavor-packed Mustard Mac Slaw, a perfect potluck dish or anytime side.

Midtown Greek Salad

Serves 4

Greek salad is featured on almost every diner and cafe menu, but rarely is it vegan. Thanks to easy-to-make faux feta, now you can enjoy this salad at home.

DRESSING:

1/4 cup plus 2 tablespoons red wine vinegar
2 cloves garlic, minced
1 1/2 teaspoons dried oregano
1/4 teaspoon dried basil
1/4 teaspoon dried rosemary
1/4 teaspoon dried thyme
1/4 teaspoon salt
1/8 teaspoon ground white pepper
Pinch sugar
1/4 cup plus 2 tablespoons olive oil

SALAD:

8 cups chopped romaine lettuce
1 medium red onion, thinly sliced
1 cucumber, peeled and chopped
1 large ripe tomato, chopped
1 medium red bell pepper, cut into 1/4-inch slices
1/2 medium green bell pepper, cut into 1/4-inch slices
3/4 cup small cauliflower florets
3/4 cup halved pitted kalamata olives
1/2 cup chopped sun-dried tomatoes (oil-packed or reconstituted)
Faux Feta (recipe follows)

1. *Dressing:* In a small bowl, combine all the ingredients except the oil. Set aside for 30 minutes to soften the dried herbs, then whisk in the olive oil. Refrigerate until serving. Whisk again just before using.

2. *Salad:* Combine all the salad ingredients in a large bowl. Add the faux feta and the reserved dressing. Toss to coat. Serve immediately.

Faux Feta

Makes 2 cups

12 ounces extra-firm tofu, drained and pressed
1 1/2 tablespoons nutritional yeast
3/4 teaspoon dried oregano
3/4 teaspoon dried parsley
3/4 teaspoon salt
1/4 teaspoon lemon pepper
1 1/2 tablespoons fresh lemon juice
1 1/2 tablespoons olive oil

In a small bowl, crumble the tofu into 1/2-inch pieces. Add the remaining ingredients and gently stir to combine. Cover and refrigerate until needed. This is best if made a few hours ahead of time or up to a day in advance.

Bistro Chopped Salad

Serves 4

The key to a chopped salad is chopping all ingredients the same size. Begin with the tomatoes and use them as a size guide for the remaining vegetables. This refreshing salad is paired with a flavorful French dressing, but also goes well with the Creamy Garlic Basil Dressing (below). For a main dish, add 1 1/2 cups or 1 (15-ounce) can of white beans.

FRENCH DRESSING:
3 tablespoons ketchup
1/4 cup apple cider vinegar
2 tablespoons agave nectar
3 tablespoons canola oil
1/2 teaspoon vegan Worcestershire sauce
1/2 teaspoon onion powder
1/4 teaspoon paprika
1/4 teaspoon celery salt
Salt and black pepper

SALAD:
1 cup ripe cherry tomatoes, quartered
8 cups chopped romaine lettuce
1 cup chopped cauliflower florets
1/2 cup chopped celery
1/2 cup chopped carrots
1/2 cucumber, peeled, seeded, and chopped
1/4 cup chopped pitted green olives

1. *Dressing:* In a small bowl, combine the ketchup, vinegar, agave nectar, canola oil, Worcestershire sauce, onion powder, paprika, and celery salt. Salt and pepper to taste. Mix together well with a fork and set aside.

2. *Salad:* In a large bowl, combine all the chopped salad ingredients and toss to combine. Add the reserved dressing and toss to combine. Serve immediately.

Creamy Garlic Basil Dressing

Makes 1/2 cup

1 clove garlic, minced
1 tablespoon olive oil
1/2 cup raw cashews
2 tablespoons dry white wine
2 tablespoons fresh basil
1/4 cup plus 2 tablespoons water
1/4 teaspoon dry mustard
1/2 teaspoon salt
Pinch black pepper

1. In a small saucepan, heat the oil over medium heat. Add the garlic and cook 1 minute, until just fragrant. Set aside.

2. In a blender, process the cashews until they are powdered. Add the remaining ingredients and the reserved oil mixture. Process until creamy and well blended. Add additional water to this, if desired. Taste and adjust the seasonings. If not using right away, transfer to a bowl, cover tightly, and refrigerate until needed. This dressing is best if used on the same day it is made.

Italian Deli Pasta Salad

Serves 4

Save a trip to the Italian deli and make this delicious salad yourself. If you won't be eating it immediately, add the tomatoes just before serving, so they don't lose their flavor in the refrigerator.

8 ounces rotini or other pasta
1 teaspoon chili oil
2 teaspoons capers
2 tablespoons chopped pitted kalamata olives
1 cup ripe cherry tomatoes, cut into quarters
1 cup tightly packed fresh baby spinach, finely chopped
1/2 cup chopped red bell pepper
1/4 teaspoon dried oregano
2 tablespoons minced scallions
3 tablespoons vegan mayonnaise
1 tablespoon apple cider vinegar
1 tablespoon olive oil
2 tablespoons chopped fresh basil, divided
1/2 teaspoon fresh thyme
2 cloves roasted garlic (page 47)
Salt and black pepper

1. Cook the pasta in a pot of boiling salted water for 7 minutes, or according to package directions. Drain, run under cold water, and drain again. Place in a medium bowl. Toss with the chili oil. Add the capers, olives, tomatoes, spinach, bell pepper, oregano, scallions, and 1 tablespoon chopped basil.

2. In a blender, combine the mayonnaise, vinegar, olive oil, remaining 1 tablespoon basil, thyme, roasted garlic. Season with salt and pepper to taste. Blend until smooth. Pour over the pasta and toss to combine. Taste and adjust the seasonings. Cover and refrigerate until ready to serve.

Best Macaroni and Pasta Salads

Follow these simple tips to make your macaroni and pasta salads shine:

- Avoid undercooking the pasta, or it will be too chewy. Don't overcook the pasta, or it will turn to mush. The pasta should be cooked al dente.

- Use extra salt when cooking the noodles for best flavor (about 2 tablespoons per pound in a gallon of cooking water).

- When the noodles are cooked, rinse them under cold water immediately. This keeps them from clinging to each other and stops the cooking process. Drain well so no hidden water makes the dressing runny.

- Chill thoroughly and season again right before serving.

Homestyle Macaroni Salad

Serves 4

This creamy, crunchy macaroni salad is popular picnic fare and a great side on a burger or sandwich platter. Add other favorite vegetables to make it your own. As always, adjust the seasonings to your personal taste.

8 ounces elbow macaroni
1/3 cup minced onion
1/4 cup chopped celery
1/4 cup chopped red bell pepper
1/4 cup chopped carrot
1/4 cup chopped pitted kalamata olives
1/4 cup chopped dill pickle
1/2 cup vegan mayonnaise
Juice of 1/2 lemon
2 tablespoons chopped fresh parsley
1/4 teaspoon garlic salt
1/8 teaspoon celery salt
1/8 teaspoon salt
Pinch black pepper

1. Cook the pasta in a pot of boiling salted water for 7 minutes, or until just tender. Drain, run under cold water, and drain again. Transfer to a large bowl.

2. Add the remaining ingredients to the macaroni. Mix well to combine, then taste and adjust the seasonings. Refrigerate until serving. When ready to serve, add a tablespoon or two of additional mayonnaise, if needed, to moisten.

Cafe Broccoli Salad

Serves 4

Broccoli doesn't always have to be hot to be delicious. This light and flavorful salad is a throwback to the café salads of the 1970s. This version preserves the delicious crunch.

1 tablespoon pine nuts
1/2 head broccoli, cut into 1-inch florets
10 seedless red grapes, halved
1/2 cup chopped celery
2 tablespoons minced red onion
2 tablespoons dried unsweetened cherries
1/4 cup vegan mayonnaise
1 tablespoon agave nectar
1 tablespoon apple cider vinegar
1/2 teaspoon fresh tarragon or 1/4 teaspoon dried

1. Toast the pine nuts in a small dry skillet over medium heat for 5 minutes, stirring often, until golden. Remove from the skillet immediately to prevent over-browning. Set aside.

2. Steam the broccoli until just tender, but still quite crisp, about 3 minutes. Run under cold water to stop the cooking. Drain and place in a medium bowl. Add the grapes, celery, onion, cherries, and reserved pine nuts. Set aside.

3. In a small bowl, combine the mayonnaise, agave nectar, vinegar, and tarragon. Stir to mix well, then pour over the salad and toss to coat. Serve immediately, or cover and refrigerate until needed.

Poblano Macaroni Salad

Serves 4

This unique interpretation of macaroni salad is a great summer side dish for entertaining at home. Make a big bowl of it for your next potluck or cookout. To turn it into a main dish, add 1 1/2 cups cooked or 1 (15-ounce) can black beans, rinsed and drained, to the pasta.

8 ounces rotini pasta
1/4 cup minced onion
1/2 cup chopped red bell pepper
2 poblano chiles, roasted (page 28) and
  chopped
1/4 cup chopped celery
1/4 cup corn kernels, fresh or frozen,
  thawed
1/4 cup grated carrot
1/4 cup minced scallions
1/3 cup vegan mayonnaise
1 clove garlic, minced
1 chipotle chile in adobo, minced
1 tablespoon prepared barbeque sauce
1 tablespoon white vinegar
2 tablespoons fresh lime juice
2 tablespoons chopped fresh parsley or
  cilantro
1/2 teaspoon ground cumin
1/2 teaspoon dried oregano
1/4 teaspoon chipotle chile powder, or
  more
Pinch sugar
1/4 teaspoon salt
Pinch black pepper

1. Cook the pasta in a pot of boiling salted water for 8 minutes, or until just tender. Drain, run under cold water, and drain again. Transfer to a large bowl. Add the onion, bell pepper, chiles, celery, corn, carrot, and scallions.

2. In a small bowl, combine the remaining ingredients and mix well. Pour the dressing over the rotini and vegetables. Mix well to combine. Taste and adjust the seasonings. Refrigerate for at least one hour before serving to allow flavors to blend. When ready to serve, add a tablespoon or two of additional mayonnaise, if needed, to moisten.

Fried Corn Salad

Serves 4

This Midwestern homestyle favorite is one of the best uses for leftover corn on the cob. Thawed frozen corn kernels may be used if fresh corn is unavailable. This salad can be served either cold or at room temperature.

1 tablespoon vegan margarine
2 cups cooked corn kernels
1/4 cup chopped red bell pepper
1/4 cup chopped celery
1/4 cup chopped peeled cucumber
2 tablespoons chopped scallions
1/2 small jalapeño, seeded and minced, optional
1 tablespoon minced fresh dill weed
1/2 teaspoon ground cumin
Juice of 1/2 lemon
2 tablespoons red wine vinegar
2 teaspoons olive oil
Salt and black pepper

1. Heat the margarine in a medium skillet over medium-high heat. Add the corn, stirring to coat with the margarine. Cook, stirring occasionally, 10 to 12 minutes, or until golden brown. Remove from the heat and transfer the corn to a medium bowl. Add the bell pepper, celery, cucumber, scallions, and jalapeño, if using. Toss to combine.

2. In a small bowl, combine the dill, cumin, lemon juice, vinegar, olive oil, and salt and pepper to taste. Mix well, then pour over the vegetables and toss to combine. Taste and adjust the seasonings. Serve warm or cold.

Farmhouse Tomato Salad

Serves 4

If you don't grow your own flavorful heirloom tomatoes, hopefully, you live near a farmer's market where you can buy them. Without fresh ripe tomatoes, this salad just isn't the same. For the cleanest tomato slices, use a serrated knife. This salad is especially good served with Southern Fried Seitan (page 151).

1 tablespoon finely chopped shallots
1/4 cucumber, peeled, seeded, and finely chopped
2 tablespoons chopped fresh basil
1/2 tablespoon agave nectar
1 tablespoon white vinegar
1 tablespoon olive oil
4 ripe heirloom tomatoes, cut into 1/2-inch slices
Salt and black pepper

1. In a small bowl, combine the shallots, cucumber, basil, agave nectar, vinegar, and oil, and mix until well blended. Set aside.

2. Arrange the tomato slices on a serving platter. Drizzle the dressing over the tomatoes. Season with salt and pepper to taste. Serve immediately.

Asian-Style Salad Bowl

Serves 4

There's something about chunks of spicy baked tofu over a cold and refreshing salad that wakes up the taste buds. Serve this dazzling bistro salad with some chopped peanuts on top for extra crunch.

1/4 cup soy sauce
2 tablespoons mirin
1 tablespoon Sriracha sauce
1 tablespoon blackstrap molasses
1/4 cup nutritional yeast
3 cloves garlic, minced
1 tablespoon grated fresh ginger
16 ounces extra-firm tofu, drained, pressed, and cut into 3/4-inch dice
1 1/2 cups small broccoli florets
1 1/2 cups sugar snap peas, cut in half
1/2 cucumber, peeled, halved, and thinly sliced
1 large carrot, thinly sliced
6 cups chopped romaine lettuce
1 1/2 cups shredded napa or Chinese cabbage
1/2 medium red bell pepper, cut lengthwise into 1/4-inch strips
1 tablespoon peanut oil
2 tablespoons fresh lime juice
1 tablespoon smooth peanut butter
1/2 teaspoon red pepper flakes, or to taste
1 cup bean sprouts
1/2 cup chopped scallions

1. In an 8-inch baking pan, combine the soy sauce, mirin, Sriracha, molasses, nutritional yeast, garlic, and ginger. Add the tofu and toss to coat. Refrigerate for one hour or longer to marinate, stirring occasionally.

2. Fill a medium saucepan halfway with water and bring to a boil. Add the broccoli and cook for 1 minute. Add the sugar snap peas and cook 1 minute longer. Immediately drain and run under cold water. Transfer the vegetables to a large bowl. Add the cucumber, carrot, romaine, cabbage, and bell pepper. Stir to combine. Set aside or refrigerate while cooking the tofu.

3. Heat the peanut oil in a large skillet over medium heat. Use a slotted spoon to transfer the tofu to the skillet. Reserve the marinade. Cook the tofu 10 to 15 minutes, until browned, stirring as needed.

4. Transfer the reserved marinade to a small bowl. Add the lime juice, peanut butter, and red pepper flakes. Mix well. To serve, arrange the salad mixture on plates. Top each plate with 1/4 cup bean sprouts and 2 tablespoons scallions followed by one quarter of the tofu. Drizzle the dressing over the salad. Serve with extra Sriracha on the side.

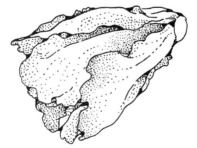

Not-So-Niçoise Salad

Serves 4

This is my version of the classy Niçoise salad found on café and bistro menus, with grilled smoked tofu taking the place of tuna. Smoked tofu is available in the refrigerated section of natural food stores and well-stocked supermarkets. If unavailable, use 8 ounces drained and pressed extra-firm tofu, marinated for 1 hour in 1 tablespoon soy sauce and 1 teaspoon liquid smoke.

6 ounces small red potatoes, scrubbed, cut into 1-inch pieces
1 1/2 tablespoons fresh lemon juice, divided
Salt and black pepper
4 ounces green beans, cut into 1-inch pieces
1 tablespoon Dijon mustard
3 tablespoons vegan mayonnaise
1 teaspoon capers
Pinch ground cayenne
1/8 teaspoon garlic powder
3 tablespoons soy milk
1/4 teaspoon sugar
1 (8-ounce) package smoked tofu
4 cups chopped romaine lettuce
1 cup shredded radicchio
1/2 cup chopped celery
1/2 cup medium red onion, thinly sliced
1/2 cucumber, peeled, seeded and chopped
1/2 cup ripe cherry tomatoes
1/4 cup chopped pitted black olives

1. Steam the potatoes over a pot of boiling water for 12 to 15 minutes, or until fork tender. Transfer the potatoes to a large bowl, toss with 1 tablespoon lemon juice, and season with salt and pepper to taste. Set aside.

2. Steam the green beans for 3 to 4 minutes, until just softening, but still crisp. Run under cold water, then drain well and add to the bowl with the potatoes. Set aside.

3. In a blender or food processor, combine the mustard, remaining 1/2 tablespoon lemon juice, mayonnaise, capers, cayenne, garlic powder, soy milk, sugar, 1/4 teaspoon salt, and pepper to taste. Blend until well combined. Set aside.

4. Grill the tofu over medium heat on a well-oiled grill pan for 5 to 7 minutes or until grill marks appear. Turn to grill the other side, about 5 minutes, or until grill marks appear.

5. Add the remaining vegetables and olives to the bowl with the potatoes and green beans. Add the reserved dressing and toss to combine. Arrange the salad on plates, top with the tofu, and serve immediately.

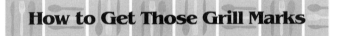

How to Get Those Grill Marks

To get perfect grill marks on the tofu, be sure the grill pan is hot. After placing the tofu on it, don't move it until you can see slight imprints on the edge of the tofu slice, which will let you know it's cooked. For cross-hatch marks, turn the cooked tofu ninety degrees and cook again until marked.

Three-Bean Salad

Serves 6 to 8

Few activities honor the summer season like cookouts. Whether your big family get-togethers are Memorial Day, the Fourth of July, or Labor Day, this easy salad is the perfect side to whatever you are grilling. Green beans bring a lively, fresh taste to this salad, but any combination of canned beans support them well. Either oil-packed or dehydrated sun-dried tomatoes will work in this recipe.

9 ounces fresh green beans, trimmed and cut into 1-inch pieces (about 1 1/2 cups)
1 1/2 cups cooked or 1 (15-ounce) can chickpeas, drained and rinsed
1 1/2 cups cooked or 1 (15-ounce) can red kidney beans, drained and rinsed
1/2 small red onion, chopped
1/2 medium red bell pepper, chopped
1/2 cup chopped celery
1/4 cup sun-dried tomatoes, (see note), chopped
2 tablespoons minced fresh parsley
2 tablespoons minced fresh dill
1/4 cup olive oil
2 cloves garlic, minced
2 teaspoons lemon zest
3 tablespoons fresh lemon juice
2 tablespoons white vinegar
1 teaspoon prepared yellow mustard
Pinch sugar
Salt and black pepper

1. In a medium saucepan, cook the green beans in boiling water for 2 minutes. Drain and run under cold water immediately to stop cooking. Transfer to a large bowl. Add the chickpeas, kidney beans, onion, bell pepper, celery, sun-dried tomatoes, parsley, and dill. Set aside.

2. In a small saucepan, heat the oil over medium-low heat. Add the garlic and lemon zest. Cook for 2 minutes, until just fragrant. Remove from heat. Use a fork to mix in the lemon juice, vinegar, mustard, and sugar. Pour the dressing over the reserved salad. Season with salt and pepper. Cover and refrigerate for one hour for flavors to blend before serving.

To rehydrate dried tomatoes, soak them in a bowl with enough hot water to cover until softened, about 20 minutes. Some varieties do not need to be rehydrated, so read the package to be sure.

B.L.T. Potato Salad

Serves 4

The deli-style sandwich goes salad. Add the seitan strips just before serving so they stay crisp. For best flavor, wait until you're ready to serve before adding the tomatoes.

1 pound small red potatoes, scrubbed
2 tablespoons red wine vinegar
Salt and black pepper
4 ounces Seitan Breakfast Strips (page 42), thinly sliced
2 tablespoons chopped red onion
3 tablespoons chopped dill pickles
2 tablespoons chopped celery
2 tablespoons chopped red bell pepper
1 tablespoon chopped fresh parsley
1 cup packed chopped fresh baby spinach
1/4 cup vegan mayonnaise
1/8 teaspoon ground cayenne
1 teaspoon prepared yellow mustard
1/2 cup ripe cherry tomatoes, halved

1. In a medium saucepan, combine the potatoes with enough water to cover by 1-inch. Bring to a boil, then reduce heat to a simmer and cook for 15 to 20 minutes, or until fork tender. Drain well. When cool enough to handle, use a serrated knife to cut the potatoes into 1-inch pieces and transfer to a large bowl. Add the red wine vinegar, and salt and pepper to taste. Toss to combine, then set aside to cool.

2. Preheat the broiler. Place the breakfast strips on a lightly oiled baking sheet. Broil about 5 minutes or until crisp. Set aside.

3. When the potatoes have cooled, add the onion, pickles, celery, bell pepper, parsley, and spinach. Set aside.

4. In a small bowl, combine the mayonnaise, cayenne, and mustard. Mix well and add to the salad, stirring to combine. Just before serving, chop the seitan and add it to the salad, along with the cherry tomatoes. Mix well. Taste and adjust seasonings, then serve immediately.

Best Potato Salads

Here are a few tricks to help keep your potato salads on track:

- Use small red potatoes, boiled whole. They retain their shape and texture the best.

- To keep them looking good, cut cooked potatoes while still warm. Use a serrated knife so the skins don't tear.

- Season cooked potatoes with vinegar, salt, and pepper while still warm for best flavor.

Deli Potato Salad

Serves 4

The Ranch Dressing for this salad is so flavorful, you'll want to make extra to use on salads or to serve with the Spicy Balsamic Maple Wingz (page 49).

2 pounds small red potatoes, scrubbed
1 teaspoon apple cider vinegar
Salt and black pepper
1/4 cup chopped celery
1/4 cup chopped scallions
2 tablespoons chopped radishes
1 tablespoon sweet pickle relish
Ranch Dressing, (recipe follows)

1. In a medium saucepan, combine the potatoes with enough water to cover by 1-inch. Bring to a boil, then reduce heat to a simmer and cook for 15 to 20 minutes, or until fork tender. Drain well.

2. When cool enough to handle, use a serrated knife to cut the potatoes into 1-inch pieces and transfer to a large bowl. Add the vinegar and season with salt and pepper, to taste. Toss to combine. Refrigerate for 30 minutes.

3. To the cooled potatoes, add the celery, scallions, radishes, and pickle relish. Add about 1/2 cup of the dressing and stir to combine. Taste and adjust the seasonings, adding more dressing if needed. Serve immediately or cover and refrigerate until needed.

Ranch Dressing

Makes 3/4 cup

1/2 cup vegan mayonnaise
1/4 cup vegan sour cream
1 tablespoon minced fresh chives
1 tablespoon plus 1 teaspoon minced fresh parsley
2 teaspoons minced fresh dill
2 teaspoons minced fresh thyme
2 tablespoons minced celery leaves
1 clove garlic, minced
1 teaspoon onion powder
1 teaspoon apple cider vinegar
1 teaspoon prepared Dijon mustard

In a small bowl, combine all the ingredients. Mix well, then cover and refrigerate for one hour before using to allow flavors to blend. Properly stored, the dressing will keep for 3 days.

Asian Slaw

Serves 4

Bistros are known for serving creative and cutting edge dishes in a comfortable setting. With its exciting Asian flavors, this is the type of slaw that might be served in a metropolitan bistro. This colorful side dish is especially good used in the San Fran Seitan Wraps (page 107).

6 cups shredded napa cabbage
3/4 cup snow peas, chopped into 1/2-inch pieces
3/4 cup chopped red bell pepper
1/3 cup chopped scallions
1 cup shredded carrot
1/4 cup plus 2 tablespoons rice vinegar
1 1/2 tablespoons soy sauce
3 tablespoons smooth peanut butter
1 1/2 tablespoons agave nectar
Juice of 1 lime
1 1/2 tablespoons minced jalapeño, seeded
1 1/2 teaspoons grated fresh ginger

1. In a large bowl, combine the cabbage, snow peas, bell pepper, scallions, and carrot. Set aside.

2. In a small bowl, combine the vinegar, soy sauce, peanut butter, agave nectar, lime juice, jalapeño, and ginger. Stir vigorously to blend well. Pour the dressing over the vegetables, tossing to coat. Cover and refrigerate for 30 minutes before serving to allow the flavors to blend.

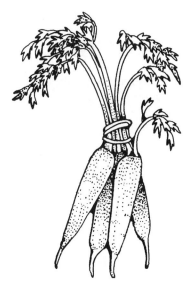

Sweet-and-Sour Slaw

Serves 4

Fresh and crunchy, this bistro-style slaw combines crisp vegetables with colorful fruit for a dazzling and delicious side salad. If your blueberries are too dry, try soaking them in a cup of hot water for 10 minutes to soften them, then drain before using. Sweetened dried cranberries may be substituted for the blueberries. If you have fresh or canned pineapple on hand, consider adding a few table-spoons, finely chopped.

2 tablespoons minced onion
3 cups shredded green cabbage
3 cups shredded red cabbage
2 tablespoons shredded carrot
2 tablespoons dried blueberries
3 tablespoons pineapple juice
1 tablespoon agave nectar
2 tablespoons olive oil
2 tablespoons umeboshi vinegar or
   white vinegar
1/8 teaspoon celery salt
1/4 teaspoon salt

1. In a large bowl, combine the onion, green cabbage, red cabbage, carrot, and blueberries. Set aside.

2. In a small bowl, combine the pineapple juice, agave, olive oil, vinegar, celery salt, and salt. Mix with a fork to lightly emulsify. Pour the dressing over vegetables, tossing to coat. Serve at once, or cover and refrigerate until needed.

Midwest Vinegar Slaw

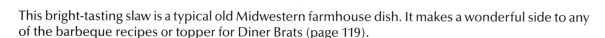

Serves 4

This bright-tasting slaw is a typical old Midwestern farmhouse dish. It makes a wonderful side to any of the barbeque recipes or topper for Diner Brats (page 119).

1/2 medium head green cabbage,
   shredded (6 cups)
1/2 green bell pepper, diced
1 medium carrot, shredded
2 tablespoons finely grated onion
2 teaspoons agave nectar
1 1/2 teaspoons Dijon mustard
1/4 cup white vinegar
1/2 teaspoon dried marjoram
2 tablespoons olive oil
Salt and black pepper

1. In a large bowl, combine the cabbage, bell pepper, carrot, and onion. Set aside.

2. In a small bowl, combine the agave nectar, mustard, vinegar, and marjoram and mix well. Add the olive oil and salt and pepper to taste. Stir well to emulsify. Pour the dressing over the vegetables and toss to coat. Serve at once, or cover and refrigerate until needed.

Mustard Mac Slaw

Serves 6 to 8

Sometimes you want coleslaw, and sometimes you want macaroni salad, but there are other times when you want both. With big, bold flavors, this slaw really delivers. Serve with extra hot sauce on the side for those who like to spice things up.

4 ounces small shell pasta
4 cups finely shredded green cabbage
1/2 medium red bell pepper, chopped
1/2 cup chopped celery
1 medium carrot, grated
1/4 cup chopped red onion
1 teaspoon celery seed
Juice of 1 lemon
Salt and black pepper
1/4 cup sugar
2 tablespoons agave nectar
1/2 cup prepared yellow mustard
1/8 cup apple cider vinegar
1 tablespoon hot sauce, optional

1. Cook the pasta in a pot of boiling salted water for 5 minutes, or until just tender. Drain, run under cold water, and drain again.

2. In a large bowl, combine the cabbage, bell pepper, celery, carrot, onion, and celery seed. Add the reserved pasta and the lemon juice. Stir to mix, then season with salt and pepper to taste.

3. In a small bowl, combine the sugar, agave nectar, mustard, vinegar and hot sauce, if using. Mix well. Pour over the slaw mixture. Stir to coat, then cover and refrigerate 1 hour before serving to allow the flavors to blend.

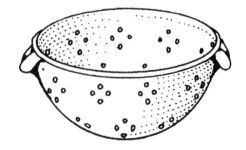

Spicy Tofu Noodle Salad

Serves 4

This flavorful noodle salad is hearty enough to make a meal. If Szechuan seasoning is unavailable, substitute red pepper flakes, or omit it entirely, if you prefer your salad less spicy. Various brands of Szechuan seasoning are available at well-stocked supermarkets.

1 pound cappelini, or other long pasta
3 tablespoons chili oil, divided
2 tablespoons toasted sesame oil
1/8 teaspoon Szechuan seasoning, or to taste
2 tablespoons grated fresh ginger
4 cloves garlic, minced
1/3 cup plus 2 tablespoons soy sauce, divided
2 tablespoons fresh lemon juice
2 tablespoons rice vinegar
1/4 cup agave nectar
1/2 teaspoon salt
4 cups shredded bok choy or napa cabbage
1 1/2 cups chopped scallions
1 medium red bell pepper, halved lengthwise and cut into 1/8-inch slices
1 cucumber, peeled, seeded, and chopped
1/4 cup chopped fresh cilantro
1 pound extra-firm tofu, drained, pressed, and cut into 8 slices
1 tablespoon mirin, dry white wine, or dry sherry
2 tablespoons toasted sesame seeds
1/2 cup chopped peanuts, optional

1. Cook the pasta in a large pot of boiling salted water for 2 to 3 minutes, or until just tender. Drain, run under cold water, and drain again. Transfer to a large bowl.

2. In a small saucepan, combine 2 tablespoons of the chili oil, the sesame oil, Szechuan seasoning, ginger, and garlic. Cook over medium heat for 2 minutes, or until fragrant. Remove from the heat. Whisk in the 1/3 cup soy sauce, the lemon juice, rice vinegar, agave nectar, and salt. Pour the sauce over the noodles.

3. Add the bok choy, scallions, bell pepper, cucumber, and cilantro to the noodles. Toss to combine. Set aside or refrigerate until ready to serve.

4. Cut the tofu slices in half lengthwise to make 16 pieces. In a large skillet, heat the remaining 1 tablespoon chili oil over medium heat. Add the tofu and cook 5 minutes, or until golden. Turn to cook the other side, 3 to 5 minutes. Add the remaining 2 tablespoons soy sauce and the mirin, stirring to coat. Cook until the liquids are absorbed.

5. To serve, divide the noodle salad among four plates. Top each serving with one-fourth of the tofu and a sprinkling of sesame seeds. Top with the peanuts, if using. Serve immediately.

Mom's Noodle Soup (variation), page 76

Cherry Chocolate Bread Pudding with Vanilla Sauce, page 196

New York-Style Cheesecake, page 192

All-American Incrediburger, page 122; Fifty/Fifty Burger Bun, page 128; Midway French Fries, page 166.

Mom's Apple Pie, page 178

Eggplant Parm with Tomato Basil Sauce, page 139

Summer Waffles with Lemon Sauce, page 36

Margherita Pizza with Roasted Red Pepper Sauce, page 157

Seitan Katsu with Tonkatsu Sauce, page 143

Seitan Brew Stew, page 83

Rosemary Carrots, page 170

Country Skillet, page 27

Sweet Garlicky Ribz, page 150

Taters and Strings, page 165

Veggie Fried Rice, page 173

Spicy Balsamic Maple Wingz, page 49

Route 66 Seitan Sandwich with Peppadew Relish, page 114; Handcut Potato Chips, page 168; and Midwest Vinegar Slaw, page 98

Beer-Battered Onion Rings, page 162

Midtown Greek Salad with Faux Feta, page 86

Wet Bean Burritos, page 146

Apricot Cream Cheese Cookies, page 194

Any-Day French Toast, page 32

Seitan Goulash with Kraut, page 148

Southern-Style Rice and Red Beans, page 172

Banana Split Cake, page 190

Western Omelet, page 26;
Hubby's Home Fries, page 44

Fried Avocado Wedges, page 53

Tex-Mex Taco Salad

Serves 6

Despite its many steps, this salad comes together quickly and makes a delicious and satisfying main dish. The various components (except the avocado), can be made ahead of time for quick assembly when ready to serve. Serve it topped with Roasted Corn Avocado Salsa (page 50) and a bowl of tortilla chips and vegan sour cream or salsa.

TOPPING:

1 pound Savory Seitan (page 5), cut into 1/2-inch dice
1 tablespoon plus 1 teaspoon ground cumin
2 teaspoons chili powder
1 teaspoon salt
1/4 teaspoon white pepper
1 tablespoon olive oil
1 medium onion, chopped
2 medium red bell peppers, chopped
2 tablespoons minced jalapeño
4 cloves garlic, minced
2 chipotle chiles in adobo, minced
1/2 teaspoon liquid smoke
2 tablespoons water
2 tablespoons ketchup
2 tablespoons fresh lime juice

DRESSING:

1/2 cup vegan mayonnaise
2 chipotle chile peppers in adobo
1/4 cup plus 2 tablespoons soy milk
2 cloves garlic, minced
2 tablespoons nutritional yeast
1/4 cup vegan sour cream
1 teaspoon smoked paprika
1/2 teaspoon salt
2 teaspoons fresh lime juice

SALAD:

8 cups chopped romaine lettuce
1/2 cup chopped scallions
2 large ripe tomatoes, chopped and seeded
2 medium carrots, sliced
1 ripe Hass avocado, pitted, peeled, and cut into 1/2-inch dice

1. *Topping:* Combine the seitan with the cumin, chili powder, salt, and pepper. Rub the spices into the seitan. Set aside.

2. Heat the oil in a large skillet over medium-high heat. Add the onion, bell peppers, jalapeño, garlic, and seasoned seitan. Cook 10 minutes, or until the onion is translucent. Add the chipotles, liquid smoke, water, ketchup, and lime juice. Stir together and simmer 15 minutes, to allow the flavors to blend. Add a little more water if the mixture is too dry. Taste and adjust the seasonings.

3. *Dressing:* Combine all the ingredients in a blender and blend until smooth. Add a little more soy milk, if the mixture is too thick. It should be pourable. Refrigerate until serving.

4. *Salad:* Combine the lettuce, scallions, tomatoes, and carrots in a large bowl. Toss to mix. Just before serving, add the avocado.

5. Divide the salad mixture among six plates. Top each with a spoonful of the hot seitan mixture, dividing evenly. Drizzle with the dressing and serve immediately.

SANDWICH BOARD

Ask anyone to name their favorite sandwich, and you'll get a wide range of answers. Whether it's the peanut butter and jelly sandwich that Mom packed in our school lunch box, or the burgers we enjoyed at a favorite fast-food restaurant, sandwiches hold a special place in our hearts. Although Americans share a common affection for sandwiches, many longstanding favorites go by a variety of names. Take the submarine sandwich: in the Midwest and New England, it's called a grinder; in New York, a wedge or hero; and in Philadelphia, it's a hoagie. Another version of the sub is found in New Orleans, and you'll find them all here. You know the old expression, "It's the best thing since sliced bread." Well, if we're talking about the sandwiches in this chapter, it's true.

Seitan Po' Boys

Serves 4

The innovative po' boy sandwich first earned its placed in the heart of New Orleans. It was created at the Martin Brothers' Coffee Stand and Restaurant in 1929 to feed local streetcar workers during a strike. Its popularity spread across the country from there.

1 pound Seitan Breakfast Strips (page 42)
  or 1 pound Savory Seitan (page 5)
4 cups shredded green cabbage
1 cup shredded red cabbage
2 tablespoons minced onion
1/2 cup shredded carrot
1/4 cup vegan mayonnaise
1 1/2 tablespoons fresh lime juice
1/2 teaspoon ground coriander
1/2 teaspoon dried tarragon
1/2 teaspoon caraway seeds
1 teaspoon Dijon mustard
Pinch sugar
Salt and black pepper
1 tablespoon olive oil
1 French bread loaf, sliced in half
  horizontally, lightly toasted
Dijon mustard, for serving
Sliced pickles and tomato, optional

1. Cut the seitan into 1/4-inch thick slices. Set aside.

2. In a medium bowl, combine the green cabbage, red cabbage, onion, and carrot and set aside.

3. In a small bowl, combine the mayonnaise, lime juice, coriander, tarragon, caraway seeds, mustard, and sugar. Stir to mix. Pour the dressing over the cabbage mixture and stir to combine. Season with salt and pepper, to taste.

4. Heat the oil in a large skillet over medium heat. Add the seitan slices and cook until hot, turning occasionally, about 5 minutes.

5. To serve, spread the mustard on the cut sides of the French bread loaf. Top with the seitan strips, pickle and tomato slices, if using. Top with the coleslaw. Cut the sandwich into four equal parts and serve immediately.

TIP

To get the thinnest seitan slices, use partially thawed frozen seitan and slice with a serrated knife.

Sloppy Joes

Serves 4

The Sloppy Joe was originally served at Sloppy Joe's Bar in Key West, a favorite hang-out of Ernest Hemingway. My mom made a version that I've loved since I was a kid, because of her secret ingredient – pickles. Try it, and it'll be our secret. These Sloppy Joes are especially good served on the Fifty/Fifty Burger Buns (page 128).

1 1/2 cups texturized vegetable protein granules or 12 ounces tempeh, steamed and crumbled, or 12 ounces Savory Seitan (page 5), minced
1 1/3 cups hot water
1 tablespoon olive oil
1/2 medium onion, chopped
1/2 medium green bell pepper, chopped
1 (15-ounce) can tomato sauce
1/4 cup chopped dill pickle
1 tablespoon dark brown sugar
1 tablespoon soy sauce
1 teaspoon browning sauce
1 teaspoon vegan Worcestershire sauce
1 teaspoon prepared yellow mustard
1 teaspoon garlic powder
1 teaspoon onion powder
1 teaspoon chili powder
1 teaspoon smoked paprika
1/4 teaspoon salt
Pinch black pepper
4 burger buns, sliced and toasted

1. Rehydrate the texturized vegetable protein in the hot water for about 10 minutes, until softened. If using tempeh or seitan, omit this step.

2. Heat the oil in a large skillet over medium heat. Add the rehydrated texturized vegetable protein, onion, and bell pepper. Cook, stirring occasionally, about 10 minutes, until the onion begins to soften.

3. Add the remaining ingredients (except the buns) and stir to combine. Bring to a boil. Reduce the heat to medium and simmer 15 minutes to allow the flavors to blend. If the mixture is too thick, add a bit of water or vegetable broth. Adjust the seasonings. To serve, divide the filling among the four buns.

● ● ● ● ● ● ● ● ● ● ●
VARIATION

Sloppy Josés: Prepare as above but substitute a chopped poblano chile for the green bell pepper. Add 1 minced jalapeño when adding the poblano. Increase the chili powder to 1 tablespoon. Add 1 teaspoon ground cumin with the other spices. Add 1 teaspoon hot pepper sauce or more to taste.

Fork-and-Knife Reubens

Serves 4

The popular Reuben deli sandwich is notoriously messy to eat, so my version is served with a fork and knife – you'll probably still need extra napkins. For quick assembly, the seitan can marinate overnight and the dressing can be made ahead of time.

2 tablespoons ketchup
1/4 cup dill pickle juice
2 tablespoons soy sauce
1 tablespoon ground coriander
1/4 teaspoon ground allspice
2 teaspoons blackstrap molasses
1/2 cup vegetable broth
1/3 cup dry red wine, or additional broth
2 tablespoons finely minced onion
2 cloves garlic, minced
1 teaspoon dried mustard
1/2 teaspoon black pepper
1 to 2 tablespoons canola oil
1 pound Savory Seitan, (page 5), thinly sliced
8 slices rye bread, toasted
2 tablespoons Dijon mustard
2 cups sauerkraut, drained
Reuben Dressing (recipe follows)

1. In a 9 x 13-inch glass baking dish, combine the ketchup, pickle juice, soy sauce, coriander, allspice, molasses, broth, wine, onion, garlic, mustard, and pepper. Stir to combine. Add the seitan and refrigerate for 1 hour or longer to marinate.

2. Heat the oil in a large skillet over medium heat. Use a slotted spoon to transfer the seitan into the skillet. Reserve the marinade. Cook the seitan for 5 to 7 minutes, turning occasionally, until hot. Add the reserved marinade and cook until it is evaporated.

3. In a small saucepan, heat the sauerkraut over medium heat, stirring occasionally, for 5 minutes.

4. To serve, place 1 piece of toast on each plate. Spread with mustard. Top with one quarter of the seitan mixture and one quarter of the kraut. Top with the remaining piece of toast and drizzle the outside of the sandwich with dressing.

Reuben Dressing

Makes 1 cup

In addition to serving with the Fork-and-Knife Reubens, this dressing makes a great sauce for burgers.

1/3 cup raw cashews
1 1/2 tablespoons chopped dill pickle
1/4 cup soy milk
1/4 cup white vinegar
3 tablespoons dill pickle juice
1 1/2 tablespoons ketchup
1 1/2 teaspoons Dijon mustard
1/4 teaspoon white pepper
1/4 teaspoon ground coriander
1/4 teaspoon salt

Combine all the ingredients in a blender. Blend thoroughly, until the dressing is smooth and creamy. If the mixture seems too thin, add a few more cashews and blend until smooth. Transfer to a small bowl and use immediately, or cover and refrigerate until needed, up to three days.

San Fran Seitan Wraps

Serves 4

Colorful slaw combines with skillet-crisped seitan to make this Asian influenced cafe-style wrap.

3 tablespoons soy sauce
1 1/2 tablespoons toasted sesame oil
1 1/2 tablespoons red wine vinegar
2 teaspoons blackstrap molasses
2 teaspoons ground ginger
3/4 teaspoon garlic powder
1/2 teaspoon five-spice powder
12 ounces Savory Seitan (page 5), thinly
  sliced
1 tablespoon canola oil
4 (7-inch) flour tortillas
Asian Slaw (page 97)

1. In a shallow pan, combine the soy sauce, sesame oil, vinegar, molasses, ginger, garlic, and five-spice powder. Add the seitan into the marinade and refrigerate for 30 minutes or longer.

2. Heat the oil in a large skillet over medium heat. Use a slotted spoon to transfer the seitan from the marinade into the skillet. Cook until lightly browned and the edges are just beginning to crisp, 5 to 7 minutes. Turn to cook the other side, 3 to 5 minutes.

3. To serve, arrange the tortillas on a flat work surface and fill the center of each tortilla with one-fourth of the seitan and one-fourth of the slaw. Fold the ends in, then roll up the sandwiches. Serve immediately.

A Brief History of the Reuben Sandwich

Some food historians believe the Reuben was invented in the 1920s at the Blackstone Hotel in Omaha, Nebraska.

A group of men who regularly played poker there would make sandwiches from cold cuts. One of the players, Reuben Kulakofsky, was said to have made the best sandwiches. The Reuben sandwich was so loved that it earned a place on the Blackstone menu.

The second story claims that a NYC deli, owned by Arnold Reuben, was the home of the first Reuben. In this version, one of Charlie Chaplin's leading ladies, Annette Seelos, came into the deli late one night in 1914 and requested a "combo" sandwich. Reuben's creation included ham, turkey, Swiss cheese, coleslaw and Russian dressing. Seelos loved it and asked that the sandwich be named after her. However, Reuben opted to name it after himself.

According to Arnold Reuben's son, his father's chef had tired of seeing him eat hamburgers and first made him a Reuben in the form we know today, made with corned beef, sauerkraut, Swiss cheese, and Russian dressing on rye bread.

Ultimate Tempeh Salad Sandwiches

Serves 4

Chicken salad is a cafe standby, and this vegan version will wake up your taste buds with its delightful flavors. The avocado really takes this sandwich to the next level, but it can be made without it, if you prefer. Instead of using it in a sandwich, the filling is also delicious served on a bed of lettuce.

1 teaspoon ground cumin
1 teaspoon ground coriander
1 teaspoon ground garlic
1 teaspoon ground ginger
1/2 teaspoon salt
1/2 teaspoon white pepper
8 ounces tempeh (page 3), steamed, cut into 1/2-inch dice
1 tablespoon canola oil
1/4 cup chopped green bell pepper
1/2 medium jalapeño, seeded and minced
1/4 cup chopped dill pickle
1/4 cup chopped red onion
1/2 cup vegan mayonnaise
1 tablespoon minced fresh parsley
1/2 teaspoon celery seed
Salt and black pepper
1 ripe Hass avocado
4 lettuce leaves
4 slices ripe tomato
8 slices sandwich bread, toasted

1. In a medium bowl, combine the cumin, coriander, garlic, ginger, salt, and white pepper. Add the hot steamed tempeh and toss to coat.

2. Heat the oil in a large skillet over medium heat. Add the tempeh and cook until golden brown, 6 to 8 minutes, stirring occasionally. Return the tempeh to the bowl. Add the bell pepper, chile, pickle, onion, mayonnaise, parsley, celery seed. Season with salt and pepper to taste. Stir to coat, then taste and adjust the seasonings.

3. Halve, pit, and peel the avocado. In a small bowl, mash one half of the avocado until smooth, then mix it into the tempeh salad. Slice the remaining avocado half into thin slices and set aside. Arrange a lettuce leaf and tomato slice on a piece of toast. Top with one quarter of the tempeh salad mixture and a quarter of the avocado slices. Place a second piece of toast on top. Repeat with the remaining ingredients and serve at once.

Chickanini Sandwiches

Serves 4

Panini sandwiches have become popular fare at bistros and cafes, known for featuring creative, delicious sandwiches. No panini pan? No grill? No problem. Just wrap a brick with foil and use it as a top weight for the sandwiches. The Sandwich Bread (page 127) works great for these paninis.

2 cups packed fresh baby spinach, divided
1/4 cup plus 2 tablespoons vegan mayonnaise
2 cloves garlic, minced
2 teaspoons capers
2 to 3 tablespoons vegan margarine, room temperature
8 slices sandwich bread
4 cutlets Seitan Lite (page 6)
1 ripe tomato, cut into 1/4-inch slices
1/2 red or yellow bell pepper, cut into 1/4-inch slices
1 tablespoon plus 1 teaspoon minced red onion

1. In a blender or food processor, combine 1 cup of the spinach, mayonnaise, garlic, and capers. Blend until smooth. Set aside or refrigerate until ready to use.

2. Heat a large skillet, preferably cast iron, over medium-high heat or preheat a panini grill.

3. Spread the margarine on the outside of each slice of bread. On the unbuttered side of four of the bread slices, arrange a cutlet, a tomato slice, one fourth of the bell pepper, one fourth of the onion, and one quarter cup of the remaining spinach. On the unbuttered side of the remaining bread slices, spread about one fourth of the reserved mayonnaise mixture and place on top of the sandwiches.

4. Place the sandwiches in the skillet (or grill) and place a brick on top, if using. Reduce heat to medium. Grill 5 to 7 minutes, or until golden. Turn to grill the other side and cook until golden, 4 to 5 minutes. Serve immediately.

Deli-Style Cutlet Sandwiches

Serves 4

A cousin to the famous Philly cheese steak, this recipe features seitan cutlets instead of chipped steak. What's not to love about crusty rolls slathered with a cheezy mustard mayo, then stuffed with sautéed vegetables and seitan? Bursting with flavor, this palate-pleaser is definitely a two-handed sandwich.

MARINADE:
1/4 cup vegetable broth
2 tablespoons fresh lemon juice
1 teaspoon hot sauce
2 tablespoons soy sauce
1/2 teaspoon salt
Pinch pepper
4 cutlets Seitan Lite (page 6)

CHEEZY MUSTARD MAYO:
2 tablespoons nutritional yeast
1/3 cup vegan mayonnaise
2 tablespoons prepared yellow mustard

SANDWICHES:
1 tablespoon olive oil, or more
1/2 medium onion, thinly sliced
1 small red bell pepper, thinly sliced
2 cups sliced cremini or button
    mushrooms
Salt and black pepper
4 ciabatta rolls, sliced in half, toasted
2 ripe tomatoes, sliced
1/2 small head lettuce, shredded

1. *Marinade:* In a shallow glass pan, combine the broth, lemon juice, hot sauce, soy sauce, salt, and pepper. Add the seitan and refrigerate for 1 hour or longer to marinate.

2. *Cheezy Mustard Mayo:* In a blender or spice grinder grind the nutritional yeast to a powder then transfer it to a small bowl. Add the mayonnaise and mustard and mix well. Set aside or refrigerate until ready to use.

3. *Sandwiches:* In a medium skillet, heat the olive oil over medium heat. Add the onion and bell pepper and cook for 5 minutes, or until the onion is translucent. Add the mushrooms. Cook 3 to 4 minutes, or until just softened. Remove from the heat, and season with salt and pepper to taste. Remove the vegetables and place them on a plate.

4. Using the same skillet in which you cooked the vegetables, add 1 tablespoon of oil if the skillet is dry. Add the cutlets and cook for 5 minutes, or until golden. Turn to cook the other side 4 to 5 minutes, or until golden. Spoon 1 tablespoon of the marinade over each cutlet while cooking.

5. Spread the rolls with the reserved mayo. Place a cutlet on the bottom of each roll. Divide the tomato slices among the four sandwiches. Top with the cooked vegetables and the shredded lettuce. Place the top of each roll onto the sandwiches and serve immediately.

VARIATION

To grill the cutlets: Heat a grill pan over medium heat. Grill the cutlets, 5 to 8 minutes, or until marked. Turn to grill the other side, about 5 minutes, or until marked. While grilling, spoon a tablespoon or so of the marinade over the cutlets.

Tex-Mex Stackers with Salsa Spread

Serves 4

Stacked sandwiches became famous in the 1930s when the cartoon character Dagwood would raid the refrigerator at night and make towering, impossible-to-eat, deli sandwiches. Combining wonderful Mexican flavors with American ingenuity, this sandwich is definitely homestyle. It's also spicy, so adjust the heat according to your own tastes.

SALSA SPREAD:
1/4 cup vegan mayonnaise
1 tablespoon prepared salsa
1/4 teaspoon ground cayenne

STACKERS:
1/4 cup vegetable broth, plus 1/4 cup, as needed
1 tablespoon soy
1 tablespoon min
adobo, or 1 te
powder
Juice of 1/2 l
reserved
2 teaspoor
1 teaspoo
Pinch suga
1 loaf Frer
1 tablespc
1/2 mediu
1/2 mediu
2 tablespc
jalapeñ
3 cloves g
12 ounces
sliced
Salt and b
1/4 small
2 ripe toma

1. *Salsa Spread:* In a small bowl, combine all the ingredients. Mix well and set aside or refrigerate until using.

2. *Stackers:* Combine 1/4 cup broth, soy sauce, chipotle, lime umin, 1/2 teaspoon chili powder, and sugar. Set aside. the broiler.

read in half and remove some of the insides so the fit better. Broil the bread cut side up about 3 min- til lightly browned. Set aside.

il in a large skillet over medium heat. Add the cook until nearly translucent, about 5 minutes. pepper, jalapeños if using, garlic, remaining chili seitan. Cook for 3 minutes to lightly brown the e broth mixture and cook until the liquid has out 5 minutes. Add the additional broth, up to mixture is dry. Parts of the seitan may break kay. Season with salt and pepper to taste.

mixture evenly on the cut sides of the bread. and tomatoes evenly onto the bottom of the seitan and vegetables over the tomatoes. ining lime half over the seitan. Place the ut the sandwich into 4 pieces and serve.

Handitos

Serves 4

Similar to take-out food available at taco stands out West, this Tex-Mex wrap is quick to make any night of the week. It sure beats take-out. As always, adjust the seasonings to suit your own taste.

2 teaspoons ground cumin
1 teaspoon chili powder
16 ounces Seitan Lite (page 6), cut into
    1/4 x 1-inch strips
1 tablespoon canola oil
1 medium onion, thinly sliced
1 cup chopped green or red bell pepper
1 jalapeño, seeded and minced, optional
3/4 cup minced Vegan Sausage Links
    (page 41) or store-bought, crumbled
2 cloves garlic, minced
1 1/4 cups sliced cremini mushrooms
1 tablespoon minced fresh cilantro
1 1/2 tablespoon adobo sauce from
    canned chipotle chiles
1 1/2 tablespoons soy sauce
Juice of 1/2 lime
Salt and black pepper
4 (7-inch) flour tortillas
1/2 small head lettuce, shredded
2 ripe medium tomatoes, seeded and
    chopped
Vegan sour cream, salsa, or guacamole,
    optional toppings

1. Combine the cumin and chili powder in a shallow pan. Add the seitan and toss to coat. Set aside.

2. Heat the oil in a large skillet over medium heat. Add the seitan and cook 5 to 7 minutes, or until browned. Remove the seitan from skillet and set aside.

3. In the same skillet, add the onion, bell pepper, jalapeño, if using, and sausage. Cook over medium heat 5 to 8 minutes, until softened. Add the garlic, mushrooms, and cilantro. Cook 3 to 5 minutes, or until tender. If mixture is too dry, add one to two tablespoons of water. Add the seitan back into the skillet.

4. In a small bowl, combine the adobo sauce with the soy sauce and lime juice. Season with salt and pepper to taste. Add to the mixture in the skillet and cook, stirring 2 to 3 minutes. Taste and adjust the seasonings. To serve, spoon the mixture into tortillas and add lettuce, tomato, and other toppings, if using. Fold both ends in, then roll the tortilla around the filling.

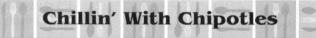

Chillin' With Chipotles

Chipotle chiles in adobo are packed with flavor, but most recipes only call for one or two, leaving us with lots of left-over chiles. The good news is that the chiles can be frozen for later use. It's best to freeze them in small amounts so you can thaw as needed for use in recipes. To do this, cut 4-inch squares of parchment paper and place them on a baking sheet. Place two peppers and a bit of sauce on each square, then transfer the baking sheet to the freezer. When frozen, wrap the peppers closed and place in an airtight container.

Seitan on a Shingle

Serves 4

The "S.O.S." sandwich was originally made with chipped beef, a readily available World War II GI ration. Creative military cooks dressed the beef in a creamy sauce. When the soldiers returned home, they brought the sandwich idea with them and soon it was in demand at diners everywhere. With a green salad on the side, this vegan version will be in demand at your house, too. Although it's great as an open-faced sandwich on toast, the filling also tops a baked potato in style.

1 to 2 tablespoons olive oil
16 ounces Portobello mushrooms, stems
 and gills removed, chopped
1 large shallot, minced
2 tablespoons all-purpose flour
1/4 teaspoon salt
Pinch black pepper
8 ounces Savory Seitan (page 5), cut into
 1/2-inch dice
2 tablespoons dry red wine
3/4 cup vegetable broth
1 tablespoon soy sauce
1 tablespoon tomato paste
1 teaspoon minced fresh thyme
4 slices bread, toasted

1. Heat 1 tablespoon oil in a large skillet over medium heat. Add the mushrooms and shallot and cook 3 to 5 minutes, or until softened. Remove from the heat and spoon the mushroom mixture into a bowl and set aside.

2. In a shallow bowl, combine the flour with the salt and pepper. Add the seitan and toss to coat.

3. Return the skillet to the heat. Add the additional 1 tablespoon oil, if needed. Add the seitan and cook, stirring occasionally, 5 to 10 minutes, until browned.

4. Return the mushrooms and shallot to the skillet. Add the wine. Turn the heat to medium-high to deglaze the pan, scraping any bits off the bottom of the skillet. When the wine has reduced by half, reduce the heat to medium.

5. Add the broth, soy sauce, tomato paste, thyme, and salt and pepper to taste. Cook, stirring until thickened, 5 to 10 minutes. Arrange the toast on plates and spoon the seitan mixture on top. Serve immediately.

Route 66 Seitan Sandwiches

Serves 4

Mom-and-pop eateries thrived along Route 66, a highway that took travelers from Chicago to Barstow, California. This recipe is a vegan version of a hearty sandwich that was often on the menu at such establishments. I love these sandwiches with Peppadew Relish, but they're also good slathered with Cheezy Mayo (page 121). Try these made with the 50/50 Burger Buns (page 130).

1 1/4 cups vital wheat gluten
2 tablespoons nutritional yeast
2 tablespoons soy flour
2 tablespoons soy sauce
2 tablespoons dry red wine
2 tablespoons olive oil, divided
1 tablespoon ketchup or barbeque sauce
2 cloves garlic, minced
1/8 teaspoon black pepper
1/2 teaspoon browning sauce, optional
  (see Tip below)
5 to 7 cups chilled vegetable broth,
  divided
1/4 cup vegan mayonnaise
4 burger buns, sliced and toasted
Lettuce leaves, ripe tomato slices,
  pickles, optional
Peppadew Relish (recipe follows)

TIP

Browning sauce products add color and flavor to recipes. They come in various brands, such as Kitchen Bouquet and Gravy Master and are available in most supermarkets.

1. In a medium bowl, combine the vital wheat gluten, nutritional yeast, and soy flour.

2. In a small bowl, combine the soy sauce, wine, 1 tablespoon of the oil, ketchup, garlic, black pepper, browning sauce, if using, and 1/2 cup of the broth. Stir to combine.

3. Stir the wet ingredients into the dry ingredients. Knead to combine, adding up to 1/4 cup more broth, as needed, to form a cohesive dough. Roll into a log about 3 inches across. Set aside for 15 minutes.

4. Cut 1/2-inch slices off the seitan and flatten it between 2 pieces of parchment paper, making it slightly larger than you want your finished cutlet to be. It should be about 1/4-inch thick and about 4-inches across. Continue to roll out all the seitan, adjusting the size of the cuts as needed to get the desired size. Preheat the oven to 300°F. Lightly oil a 9 x 13-inch pan.

5. Heat the remaining 1 tablespoon of oil in a large skillet over medium heat. Add the cutlets and cook 4 to 5 minutes, until lightly browned. Turn to brown the other side, 3 to 4 minutes. Place the cutlets in the prepared pan and add as much of the broth as needed to cover the seitan. Cover tightly with foil and bake for 1 hour, turning once about halfway through. Cool the cutlets in the broth and refrigerate before using.

6. When ready to serve, lightly oil a large skillet over medium heat or spray it with nonstick cooking spray. Add the cutlets and cook 4 to 6 minutes until lightly browned. Turn and cook the other side, 3 to 5 minutes.

7. Spread mayonnaise on the toasted buns, place the cutlets on top, then top with lettuce, tomato, pickles, if using, and the relish.

Peppadew Relish

Makes 2 cups

This relish is made with peppadews, the small, sweet, and slightly hot peppers from South Africa. These vibrantly red-colored pickled peppers are increasingly found in the olive bar in natural food stores or in jars in the condiment aisle. The relish is ideal on the Route 66 Seitan Sandwiches and also delicious on the Apple Sausage Breakfast Quesadillas (page 40).

1 cup peppadew pickled peppers, drained and chopped
1/2 cup ripe tomato, seeded and chopped
1/4 cup chopped red bell pepper
1/4 cup minced onion
2 tablespoons minced fresh parsley
1 tablespoon apple cider vinegar
1/8 teaspoon salt
Pinch black pepper

In a small bowl, combine all the ingredients and mix well. Let sit 1 hour to allow the flavors to blend.

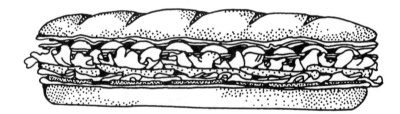

Peanutty Tofu Kale Pockets

Serves 4

This unique sandwich is an example of international comfort food. Middle Eastern pita bread combines with Ethiopian and Asian flavors to make a satisfying sandwich.

1 tablespoon olive oil
1/2 cup plus 2 tablespoons vegetable broth, divided
2 tablespoons All-American Spice Blend (page 13) or other spice blend
2 tablespoons soy sauce
2 tablespoons dry white wine
Black pepper
2 pounds extra-firm tofu, drained, pressed, and cut into 1/4-inch slices
1 medium cucumber, peeled, seeded, and chopped
1/2 cup shredded carrot
1/4 cup chopped fresh Thai basil or cilantro
6 cups chopped kale, tough stems removed
4 (7-inch) whole wheat pitas, halved
Peanut Sauce (recipe follows)

1. In a 9 x 13-inch baking pan, combine the oil, the 1/2 cup of broth, spice blend, soy sauce, wine, and black pepper to taste. Place the tofu in the pan to marinate and refrigerate for 1 hour or longer. Turn the tofu occasionally.

2. In a small bowl, combine the cucumber, carrot, and basil. Toss to combine and set aside.

3. Preheat the oven to 400°F. Lightly oil a baking sheet. Transfer the marinated tofu to the baking sheet and bake for 40 minutes, turning once about halfway through.

4. In a large skillet, combine the kale with the remaining 2 tablespoons broth over medium heat. Cook, stirring occasionally, until softened, 10 to 15 minutes. Add more broth if the kale is crisping, but it should not be too wet or it will soak through the pita.

5. To serve, arrange 2 slices of tofu in each pocket. Add the kale and the cucumber mixture, dividing evenly among the pita pockets. Top each sandwich with 2 tablespoons of peanut sauce. Serve extra peanut sauce on the side.

Peanut Sauce

Makes 3 cups

In addition to using this sauce with the Peanutty Tofu Kale Pockets above, it's also wonderful when thinned slightly with broth and tossed with cooked noodles and steamed broccoli.

3 tablespoons peanut oil
1 1/2 teaspoons chili oil
3 cloves garlic, minced
1 tablespoon minced fresh ginger
1 1/2 to 2 cups vegetable broth
3/4 cup smooth peanut butter
3 tablespoons agave nectar
2 teaspoons umeboshi paste
1/4 cup plus 2 tablespoons rice vinegar
3 tablespoons soy sauce
1 to 2 teaspoons red pepper flakes
3 tablespoons fresh lime juice

1. In a small saucepan, combine the peanut oil and chili oil over medium heat. Add the garlic and ginger and cook for 3 minutes.

2. Reduce the heat to medium low. Add 1 1/2 cups of the broth, the peanut butter, agave nectar, umeboshi, rice vinegar, soy sauce, and red pepper flakes, to taste. Whisk to combine. Add the additional broth, as needed, for desired consistency. Stirring occasionally, cook for 8 to 10 minutes to blend the flavors. Stir in the lime juice. Taste and adjust the seasonings.

Smokin' BBQ Portobello Sandwiches

Serves 4

The spicy sauce in this recipe is just as delicious paired with seitan instead of mushrooms.

1 tablespoon olive oil
24 ounces Portobello mushrooms, gills removed, cut into 1/4-inch slices
Salt and black pepper
Smokin' Chipotle BBQ Sauce (below)
1/4 cup vegan mayonnaise, for serving
4 burger buns, sliced and toasted

1. Heat the oil in a large skillet over medium heat. Add the mushrooms, and season with salt and pepper to taste. Cook, stirring occasionally, 5 to 7 minutes, or until softened. Turn the heat off and add the barbecue sauce to the mushrooms, stirring to coat.

2. To serve, spread 1 tablespoon of the mayo on each toasted bun. Spoon the mushroom mixture evenly onto the buns and serve immediately.

● ● ● ● ● ● ● ● ● ● ● ●

VARIATION

Use the seitan from the Route 66 Seitan Sandwiches (page 114) in place of the mushrooms. Cut the seitan into 1/4 to 1/2-inch slices and proceed with the recipe.

Smokin' Chipotle BBQ Sauce

Makes 1 cup

Increase the chipotle chili powder if you're feeling dangerous. Or use a little less, if you prefer.

1 tablespoon olive oil
1/4 cup finely minced onion
2 cloves garlic, minced
2/3 cup ketchup
2 tablespoons minced chipotle chiles in adobo
3/4 teaspoon chipotle chili powder
1 1/2 tablespoons apple cider vinegar
1 1/2 tablespoons blackstrap molasses
1 teaspoon liquid smoke
3/4 teaspoon vegan Worcestershire sauce

Heat the oil in a medium saucepan over medium heat. Add the onion and garlic. Cook about 5 minutes, or until the onion has softened. Add the ketchup, chipotles, chili powder, vinegar, molasses, liquid smoke, and Worcestershire sauce. Bring to a boil then immediately reduce to simmer. Simmer 15 minutes, stirring occasionally. Taste and adjust the seasonings.

Portobello Popeye Club Sandwiches

Serves 4

In diner lingo, anything spinach is called "Popeye," hence the name for this variation on the classic club sandwich. Although we often see club sandwiches with a third slice of bread, they were originally made with two slices. Some people believe the name came from the club cars, which date back to the late 1800s.

1/2 cup port wine, dry red wine, or vegetable broth
3 tablespoons soy sauce
1 1/2 teaspoons dried rosemary
1 1/2 teaspoons dried parsley
1 1/2 teaspoons dried thyme
3 cloves garlic, minced
2 tablespoons ketchup
1/3 cup olive oil, divided
Salt and black pepper
4 large Portobello mushroom caps, gills removed, lightly rinsed, and patted dry
2 medium zucchini, trimmed and cut lengthwise into 1/4-inch thick slices
1 (12-inch) loaf ciabatta bread, or 4 individual ciabatta rolls
2 large red bell peppers, cut into quarters
1 medium onion, cut into 1/4-inch thick slices
1 cup Besto Pesto (page 66)
3 cups packed fresh baby spinach

1. In a 9 x 13-inch pan, combine the wine, soy sauce, dried herbs, garlic, ketchup, 1 tablespoon of the olive oil. Season with salt and pepper, to taste. Add the mushrooms and zucchini slices and marinate for 15 minutes.

2. Heat the grill to medium high. Cut the bread in half horizontally, removing some of the insides to create more room for the filling. Brush the cut sides with 2 to 3 tablespoons olive oil. Transfer to the grill, cut-side down. Grill until just turning golden brown, about 2 to 3 minutes. Remove and set aside.

3. Grill the mushrooms, zucchini, bell peppers, and onion, brushing with remaining olive oil as needed, so the vegetables do not dry out. The time will vary, but should take about 5 minutes per side. Remove the vegetables as they are done cooking.

4. To prepare the sandwiches, spread the cut sides of the bread with pesto. Layer the vegetables evenly over the sandwich starting with the mushrooms, then the zucchini, bell peppers, and onion. Layer with the fresh spinach, then add the top of the loaf. To serve, press down on the sandwich while cutting, using a serrated knife. Cut into four sections and serve immediately.

TIP

To remove the gills on the mushrooms, gently break the stem off with your thumb. Use a spoon to scrape the inside of the mushroom cap and remove the gills.

Diner Brats

Serves 4

These brats make a quick-and-easy lunch or dinner, especially with a tasty relish that really dresses them up. For other topping ideas, see Brats and Slathers below. The sausage roll variation of the Fifty/Fifty Burger Buns (page 128) is great for these brats.

DINER BRAT RELISH:
2 tablespoons minced red onion
1/4 cup minced dill pickle
1 medium ripe tomato, seeded and chopped
2 tablespoons chopped pickled jalapeños
2 tablespoons prepared yellow mustard
1 teaspoon white vinegar
Pinch sugar

BRATS:
4 (4-ounce) Vegan Sausage Links (page 41), spicy or regular
4 sausage rolls
2 tablespoons vegan mayonnaise

1. *Relish:* In a small bowl, combine the onion, pickle, tomato, jalapeños, mustard, vinegar, and sugar. Stir to combine. Set aside.

2. *Brats:* Preheat a grill or grill pan to medium. Place the sausages on the grill. Cook for 5 minutes or until nicely marked. Turn over to grill the other side, about 3 minutes.

3. Slice the buns in half and toast in the oven (or on the grill), if desired. Set aside.

4. To serve, spread the mayonnaise on the inside of the buns, then arrange a sausage in each bun. Add the reserved relish and serve immediately.

Brats and Slathers

The relish served on the Diner Brats tastes great, but other toppings, such as the Peppadew Relish (page 115) or the Cheezy Mustard Mayo (page 110), can make your sausage sandwich a standout, too. Here are some additional topping ideas to try. NOTE: the quantities are scaled for a single sandwich, so increase the amounts as needed.

- 1/4 cup sauerkraut, squeezed dry, mixed with 1 teaspoon prepared spicy mustard

- 1 tablespoon sweet relish mixed with 1/4 teaspoon Sriracha sauce

- 1 tablespoon vegan sour cream mixed with 2 tablespoons chopped tomatoes and 1/2 tablespoon Coconut 'Bacon' Bits (page 169)

- 1 tablespoon vegan mayonnaise mixed with 1 teaspoon Dijon mustard and 1/8 teaspoon chili powder

- 1/4 cup sauerkraut, squeezed dry, mixed with 2 teaspoons sweet pickle relish and a pinch of caraway seeds

- 1 tablespoon chopped onion mixed with 1/2 tablespoon minced jalapeño

- 2 tablespoons barbeque sauce mixed with 1 tablespoon vegan mayonnaise

No-Tuna Melt Paninis

Serves 4

The soy curls in this recipe give the filling a flaked texture, similar to tuna. If soy curls are unavailable, substitute 2 cups of cooked chickpeas (mash them with a fork) and begin with 1/4 cup of the mayonnaise, mixing in a bowl instead of the food processor. A panini press makes these sandwiches a cinch. If you don't have one, use a foil-covered brick or a cast iron skillet to press the sandwich down.

4 cups water
1 tablespoon soy sauce
2 cups soy curls (see sidebar)
1/3 cup minced red onion
1/3 cup minced celery
1 tablespoon capers
1 tablespoon sweet relish
1 tablespoon apple cider vinegar
1 tablespoon minced fresh tarragon
1/4 cup to 1/3 cup vegan mayonnaise
Salt and black pepper
Pinch kelp granules or powder, optional
Cheezy Mayo (page 121)
8 slices sandwich bread
1 large ripe tomato, cut into 8 slices
2 tablespoons vegan margarine

1. In a medium saucepan, bring the water to a boil. Remove from the heat and add the soy sauce and soy curls. Set aside for 15 minutes. Drain in a colander and squeeze the soy curls dry. Transfer to a food processor and pulse a few times until they are a chunky consistency, then transfer to a large bowl. Add the onion, celery, capers, relish, vinegar, and tarragon. Stir together. Add just enough mayo for the mixture to hold together. Season with salt and pepper to taste. Add kelp, if using. Set aside.

2. Heat a large skillet over medium high heat or preheat a panini grill. Spread the margarine on the outside of each slice of bread. Place one quarter of the filling mixture (about 1/2 cup) on the unbuttered side of 4 slices of bread. Place 2 tomato slices on top of the filling mixture. Spread about one quarter of the Cheezy Mayo on the inside of each of the remaining bread slices, then place the bread on top of the sandwiches.

3. Working in batches, place the sandwiches in the skillet or on the grill, buttered sides out, and place a sandwich press or foil-covered brick on top, if using. Reduce the heat to medium and cook 5 to 7 minutes, then turn to cook the other side, about 5 minutes, or until golden. Serve immediately.

Soy Curls

Soy Curls are a product made from cooked soybeans that are then texturized and dried. A good source of protein, fiber, and amino acids, they must be reconstituted for use in recipes. To do this, soak the soy curls in a large bowl of hot water for 10 to 15 minutes, then drain well and use your hands to squeeze the remaining liquid from them. Soy Curls are made by Butler Foods and are available in well-stocked supermarkets or natural food stores, or may be purchased online. They should be stored in an airtight container at a cool temperature or in the freezer to prevent rancidity.

Cheezy Mayo

Makes 1/3 cup

In addition to using on the No-Tuna Melt Paninis this flavorful condiment is a stand-out on burgers and sandwiches, so you may want to double the recipe and refrigerate the rest for future sandwiches. Also see the Cheezy Mustard Mayo variation (page 110).

1/4 cup nutritional yeast
1 tablespoon Dijon mustard
1 teaspoon white miso paste
1/4 cup vegan mayonnaise

Combine all the ingredients in a small bowl. Mix well. Cover and refrigerate until needed. Properly stored, it will it keep for up to 5 days.

Almost-Philly Cheese Steak Sandwiches

Serves 4

It is said that you can't get a real Philly cheese steak sandwich outside of Philadelphia. Still, as you feast on this sandwich, you might want to do the "Philadelphia lean": roll up your sleeves, bend forward to avoid drips, and enjoy.

1 tablespoon olive oil
1 large onion, chopped
1 medium red bell pepper, chopped
12 ounces Savory Seitan (page 5), thinly sliced
1 1/2 cups chopped cremini mushrooms
1 1/2 tablespoons all-purpose flour
1/2 cup vegetable broth
1 1/2 tablespoons soy sauce
Salt and black pepper
1 loaf French bread
1 cup shredded vegan cheese
1/4 cup vegan mayonnaise
2 cups shredded iceberg lettuce
1 large ripe tomato, sliced
2 dill pickles, sliced
1/2 medium cucumber, peeled and sliced

1. Heat the oil in a large skillet over medium heat. Add the onion and cook for 4 minutes, or until the onion begins to soften. Add the bell pepper and cook 2 minutes. Add the seitan and mushrooms. Cook 3 to 5 minutes longer, or until the vegetables are tender.

2. In a small bowl, combine the flour, broth, and soy sauce. Mix well, then add to the skillet. Cook, stirring, 1 to 2 minutes, or until the sauce is thick and lightly coats the seitan and vegetables. Season with salt and pepper to taste. Sprinkle the shredded cheese evenly over top, cover, and keep warm.

3. Cut the French bread in half horizontally. Spread with mayonnaise. Spoon the seitan mixture over the bottom part of loaf.

4. Add the lettuce, tomatoes, pickles, and cucumbers. Place the top on the bread, secure with toothpicks if desired, and slice the sandwich into quarters.

All-American Incrediburgers

Everyone will want to try one of these burgers right off the grill. The minced onion, which steams into the burgers, give these a wonderful old-fashioned diner taste. For a cheesy burger, spread the buns with Cheezy Mayo (page 121) or top with your favorite vegan cheese. With these burgers, you really can have it "your way."

1 1/3 cups hot water
1 cup texturized vegetable protein
   granules (page 7)
1/4 cup finely minced onion
1 tablespoon garlic powder
1 tablespoon onion powder
1 tablespoon All-American Spice Blend
   (page 13) or other spice blend
2 teaspoons instant tapioca
1 1/2 teaspoons smoked paprika
1/2 teaspoon salt
1/2 teaspoon white pepper
1/4 teaspoon black pepper
2 tablespoons tomato paste
1 tablespoon plus 1 teaspoon vegan
   Worcestershire sauce
1 tablespoon plus 1 teaspoon toasted
   sesame oil
1 tablespoon liquid smoke
1 1/2 cups vital wheat gluten
1/4 cup plus 2 tablespoons vegetable
   broth
2 tablespoons olive oil
6 burger buns, sliced and toasted
Toppings: lettuce, tomato slices, pickles,
   condiments

1. In a large bowl, combine the hot water with the texturized vegetable protein to rehydrate, about 10 minutes. Prepare a steamer and tear off six (12-inch) squares of foil.

2. When the texturized vegetable protein is rehydrated, add the ingredients in the order given, down to and including the vital wheat gluten. Mix well, and knead for about 4 minutes to make sure the mixture is combined and the gluten is activated. Squeeze the mixture together to work the ingredients throughout.

3. Divide the mixture into 6 equal pieces. Shape each piece into a burger, about 4 inches across, and place in the center of a piece of foil. Fold the foil over each burger to make a packet. The foil should not be tight against the burger, to allow for expansion. Transfer to the steamer and steam 1 hour. Remove from the steamer and unwrap carefully. Transfer the burgers to a plate and refrigerate for 1 hour.

4. To grill: Preheat the grill. Brush the burgers with olive oil and place on the grill. Grill about 5 minutes, or until brown. Brush the top with oil and turn over to cook the other side, about 5 minutes. Serve on buns with toppings of choice.

● ● ● ● ● ● ● ● ● ● ●

VARIATIONS

To panfry: Heat 1 tablespoon of oil in a large skillet over medium-high heat. Add the burgers and cook until browned on both sides, turning once, about 10 minutes total.

To bake: Arrange the burgers on a lightly oiled baking sheet and brush lightly with oil. Bake for 20 minutes at 375°F, turning once halfway through, or until browned.

Old-Fashioned Tempeh Burgers

Serves 4

Back in the 1980s, tempeh burgers were one of the best items on the menu in natural food cafes. This recipe uses tempeh that is sliced in half to make thinner burgers so they absorb even more of the flavor-packed marinade. You can keep these marinating in the refrigerator for up to a week, for a fast and delicious meal in minutes. For a real treat, make your own burger buns (page 128).

16 ounces tempeh
1/4 cup apple cider vinegar
1/4 cup soy sauce
1/4 cup red miso paste
1/2 cup dry red wine
1/4 cup tomato paste
2 tablespoons toasted sesame oil
1 teaspoon liquid smoke
2 cloves garlic, minced
1/2 teaspoon red pepper flakes
1 tablespoon olive oil
Burger Sauce (recipe follows)
4 burger buns, sliced and toasted
Toppings: Lettuce, tomato slices, pickles, vegan cheese

1. If the tempeh is in 8-ounce packages, cut it in half vertically, then cut in half again horizontally to make 4 patties. Repeat with the second package. If the tempeh is not rectangular, cut it to fit the buns as well as you can, then steam the tempeh (page 7).

2. In a 9 x 13-inch pan, combine the vinegar, soy sauce, miso paste, wine, tomato paste, sesame oil, liquid smoke, garlic, and red pepper flakes. Add the burgers to the marinade and refrigerate for 1 hour or longer, turning occasionally. For maximum flavor, marinate overnight.

3. To cook, heat a large skillet over medium heat. Add the oil. Transfer the burgers to the skillet and cook 4 to 5 minutes until lightly browned. Turn to cook the other side, 3 to 5 minutes, or until browned.

4. Spread the sauce on the buns. Arrange 2 patties on each bun. Top with lettuce, tomatoes, pickles, and cheese, as desired.

Burger Sauce

Makes 3/4 cup

This yummy sauce goes great on the tempeh burgers above, as well as the All-American Incrediburgers (page 122).

1/4 cup vegan mayonnaise
2 tablespoons Dijon mustard
1/4 cup finely minced onion
2 tablespoons minced fresh parsley

In a small bowl, combine all the ingredients. Cover and refrigerate for 30 minutes to allow the flavors to develop. Properly stored, the sauce will keep for up to 2 days.

Greek Town Gyros

Serves 4

By the late 1950s, Greek-Americans owned more than six-hundred diners in the Northeast alone, and the meat-centered gyro sandwich was a prominent menu item. Enhanced by a yogurt-based sauce, the popular sandwiches are often served at street fairs as well. My version is made with seitan.

GYRO SEITAN:

Dry Ingredients:
1 1/2 cups vital wheat gluten
1/4 cup tapioca flour
2 tablespoons chickpea flour
2 tablespoons nutritional yeast
1 teaspoon onion powder
1 teaspoon garlic powder
1/2 teaspoon dried rosemary
1/2 teaspoon dried parsley
1/2 teaspoon dried oregano
1/2 teaspoon sugar
1/2 teaspoon salt
1/4 teaspoon white pepper

Wet Ingredients:
1 cup chilled vegetable broth
1 1/2 tablespoons tahini
1 tablespoon dry white wine, or
   additional broth
1/2 tablespoon olive oil
1 clove garlic, minced

MARINADE:
1/4 cup dry white wine
1/4 cup vegetable broth
1/2 teaspoon dried oregano
1/2 teaspoon salt
1/4 teaspoon white pepper

TO SERVE:
4 (7-inch) pita loaves
1 tablespoon olive oil
1/3 cup chopped red onion
1 medium cucumber, peeled, seeded
   and chopped
2/3 cup chopped ripe tomato
1/4 head iceberg lettuce, shredded
Tzatzika Sauce (recipe follows)

1. *Gyro Seitan:* Prepare a steamer. In a large bowl, combine the dry ingredients and mix with a fork.

2. In a medium bowl, combine the wet ingredients and mix well. Add the wet ingredients to the dry ingredients. Mix well with a fork, then knead with your hands for a few minutes. If the mixture is too dry, add a little broth. If it's too wet, add a little vital wheat gluten to make a cohesive dough.

3. On an 18-inch sheet of foil, shape the seitan into a 4 x 7-inch rectangle. Fold the foil to enclose the seitan, making a packet. Do not seal it tightly. Place the seitan packet in the steamer and steam for 55 minutes, then let cool. Refrigerate until needed.

4. *Marinade:* In a shallow pan, combine the marinade ingredients. Use a serrated knife to cut the seitan as thinly as possible, then add it to the marinade and set aside for 30 minutes or longer.

5. *To serve:* Preheat the oven to 350°F. Wrap the pitas in foil and bake for 5 minutes to heat and soften.

6. Heat the oil in a large skillet over medium heat. Add the seitan slices, along with any remaining marinade, and heat until hot, about 5 minutes. If mixture appears dry, add a splash of broth.

7. In a medium bowl, combine the onion, cucumber, tomato, and lettuce and stir to combine.

8. Spoon one fourth of the seitan onto each pita. Top with one fourth of the vegetable mixture, and a spoonful of the Tzazika Sauce. Fold the pita in half, like a taco, and serve.

Tzatzika Sauce

Makes 1 cup

This cool and creamy sauce is a must-have on a gyro.

1/2 cup vegan mayonnaise or vegan
   yogurt, or a blend
3/4 teaspoon Dijon mustard
1 1/2 tablespoons fresh lemon juice
1 clove garlic, minced
1/3 cup finely chopped, peeled and
   seeded, cucumbers
2 tablespoons minced fresh parsley
2 scallions, minced
1/2 teaspoon paprika
1/2 teaspoon dried dill
Pinch ground cayenne
1/8 teaspoon salt
Pinch black pepper

In a small bowl, combine all the ingredients and mix well. Cover and refrigerate for 30 minutes or longer to allow the flavors to blend.

Bread Basics

Although it may seem intimidating to bake bread for the first time, a few basic tips apply to most bread recipes. These bread basics will help to make the magic happen in your own kitchen.

Be sure to use the type of yeast specified in the recipe. The water for active dry yeast should feel lukewarm to the touch, about 110° to 115°F. If the water is too hot, the yeast won't activate. If it's too cool, the process will take much longer.

Dough can be kneaded by hand, by using a dough hook on a stand mixer, or in a bread machine set on manual. Because the kneading methods vary, keep an eye on the dough, adding a bit more flour if the mixture seems too sticky. If the dough seems too dry, add a bit more water, a teaspoon at a time.

Letting the bread rise in a warm, draft-free place is important. If the house is cold, place the bowl of dough in the oven turned to the lowest setting. As soon as the oven starts to heat up, turn the oven off and let the dough rise inside.

The first rise usually takes an hour to an hour and a half. Be sure to use a large bowl because the bread usually doubles in size. It's done rising when you can poke it with a finger up to the first knuckle and the dough doesn't fill in right away. Bakers call this the "finger test." Typically, the second rise takes about half as long as the first, and the bread will again double in size.

The bread is done baking when the bottom sounds hollow after taking it from the pan and thumping it with your knuckles.

To get the neatest slices, let the loaf cool completely before cutting.

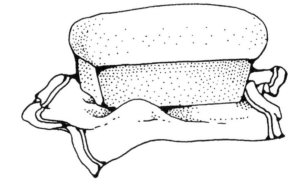

Sandwich Bread

Makes 2 loaves

This easy-to-bake bread is wonderful for novice bread bakers. It's versatile and makes great sandwiches. The dough can also be shaped into two rustic free-form loaves. This bread can be used for any recipes calling for sandwich bread.

1 1/2 cups warm water
1 tablespoon active dry yeast
2 tablespoons sugar, divided
3 cups all-purpose flour
2 cups bread flour
1 teaspoon salt
2 tablespoons canola oil

1. Combine the water with yeast and 1 tablespoon of the sugar. Stir to combine, then set aside for 5 minutes. Lightly oil 2 (8 x 4-inch) bread pans or spray with nonstick spray.

2. Combine the remaining 1 tablespoon sugar, flours and salt in a large mixing bowl. Stir to combine, then add the yeast mixture and oil. Stir to mix, adding 1 tablespoon additional water if needed to make a workable dough. The dough should not be sticky, but slightly stiff. Transfer to a lightly floured work surface and knead about 10 minutes, until the dough is smooth.

3. Transfer the dough to a lightly oiled bowl. Turn the dough over so the top is oiled and cover with a towel. Let rise in a warm, draft-free place until doubled in size, about 1 1/2 hours. You should be able to stick a finger (up to the first knuckle) into the dough without the hole filling in. When the dough reaches that stage, transfer again to the lightly floured work surface.

4. Press to flatten. Cut the dough into two equal parts. Fold the ends under and roll the sides together to create a loaf. Transfer to the loaf pan. Repeat for the second loaf. Cover the loaves with a clean towel and let rise in a warm, draft-free place about 45 minutes, or until your finger leaves no indentation.

5. Preheat the oven to 400°F. Bake the loaves for about 20 minutes. You'll know it's done when the loaves sound hollow when tapped on the bottom. Remove from the pans and place on a rack to cool. For the neatest slices, let the bread cool completely and slice with a serrated knife. The sliced bread may also be wrapped airtight and frozen for up to two months.

Fifty/Fifty Burger Buns

Makes 6

Many restaurants used to make their own breads and it's rewarding to make your own at home, too. These delicious buns are made with fifty-percent whole wheat flour and fifty-percent all-purpose flour. The dough can be used to make six burger buns or four sausage rolls, or you can make some of each. Keep in mind that the sausage rolls take a little more dough, so you'll get fewer than the burger buns. Use these buns in any recipe calling for burger buns or sausage rolls.

3/4 cup soy milk, warmed, but not hot
1 tablespoon agave nectar
2 1/4 teaspoons active dry yeast
1/4 cup warm water
1 tablespoon ground flax seed
1 1/2 cups all-purpose flour
1 1/2 cups white whole wheat flour
1 1/2 teaspoons salt
3 tablespoons canola oil
1 1/2 tablespoons sesame seeds, optional
1 tablespoon vegan margarine, optional (see Tip)

TIP

If you're not adding sesame seeds, a little margarine rubbed on the top of these buns after baking makes a wonderful soft crust.

1. In a small bowl, combine the soy milk, agave nectar, and yeast. Stir together and let sit about 5 minutes until it begins to bubble.

2. In a small bowl, combine the water and flaxseed and blend well with a fork.

3. In a large bowl, combine the flours and salt, and mix with a wooden spoon. Add the yeast mixture, the flax mixture, and the oil. Stir to mix well. When combined, knead on a lightly floured work surface for about 10 minutes. It will be a soft dough, but add a bit more flour or water if needed to make it manageable. The dough should be smooth and elastic. Shape into a ball.

4. Lightly oil a large bowl. Place the dough in the bowl, turning once so that the top is covered with oil. Cover with a clean towel and place in a warm, draft-free place for 1 to 1 1/2 hours, until nearly doubled in size.

5. Lightly oil a baking sheet. Divide the dough into 6 pieces for burger buns or 4 for sausage rolls. For burger buns, shape into balls, flatten slightly, then arrange on baking sheet. Cover with a towel and let rest for 10 minutes. Gently flatten again. Brush with water and sprinkle with sesame seeds or margarine, if using. For sausage rolls, roll into a rope-like shape, tucking the ends under. Place on the baking sheet. Continue until all the rolls are shaped. Cover with a towel and let rise in a warm, draft-free place until doubled in size, about 1 hour.

6. Preheat the oven to 375°F. Bake 14 to 17 minutes, until golden. They should sound hollow if you tap them on the bottom with your knuckles. Remove from the baking sheet and let cool on a rack. When completely cool, store in an airtight bag or container at room temperature. The buns can also be wrapped individually in plastic wrap, then in foil, and frozen in an airtight container.

menu

MAIN DISHES

This chapter is brimming with vegan versions of American comfort food classics such as the Tuna-free Noodle Casserole, Seitan and Herb Dumplings, Salisbury Seitan Steak with Mushrooms, as well as the fun and savory Brewpub Tater-Tot Pie. There's also a fair share of our favorite Italian comfort food dishes, pasta and pizza. For a taste of nostalgia, you can create your own blue plate specials by paring main dishes with the sides in the next chapter. Need help? See the Blue Plate Specials list of suggestions beginning on the next page.

Try Our Blue Plate Specials

The term "blue plate special" was coined in American cafes and diners during the 1920s, and it's still seen today in retro restaurants. Typically, the inexpensive special was served on a partitioned plate and consisted of a main dish and two sides. The specials changed daily, and no substitutions were allowed to keep the prices low and the service fast.

The phrase evokes comfort food and homestyle dishes, and it is a feeling of nostalgia that many of the main dishes in this chapter bring to mind. Here's a list of some great Blue Plate Special combo platters that you can make using the recipes in this book.

Southern Fried Seitan (page 151); Mashed Potatoes with Homestyle Gravy (page 167); Braised Peas with Radicchio and Shallots (page 175)

Tuna-Free Noodle Casserole (page 133); Bistro Broccolini (page 174); Baked Onion Rings (page 163)

Seitan and Herb Dumplings (page 134); Rosemary Carrots (page 170); Fried Corn Salad (page 91)

Southwestern Wheat-Meat Loaf (page 154); Mashed Potatoes with Jalapeño Gravy (page 167-168); Creamed Corn (page 175)

Salisbury-Style Seitan with Mushrooms (page 132); Double-Stuffed Spuds (page 169); Roasted Brocolli and Bell Peppers (page 173)

Seitan Goulash with Kraut (page 148); Rosemary Carrots (page 170); Parsleyed Noodles (page 156)

All-American Incrediburgers (page 122); Midway French Fries (page 166); Midwest Vinegar Slaw (page 98)

Spaghetti Pie with Arrabbiata Sauce (page 141); Roasted Broccoli and Bell Peppers (page 173)

Sweet Garlicky Ribz (page 150); Cheezy Mac and Greens (page 164); Fried Corn Salad (page 91)

Grilled Seitan with Heirloom Tomatoes (page 144); Double-Stuffed Spuds (page 169); Bistro Broccolini (page 174)

Mexicali Seitan (page 147); Southern-Style Rice and Red Beans (page 172); Farmhouse Tomato Salad (page 91)

Diner Brats (page 119); Baked Beans (page 171); Mustard Mac Slaw (page 99)

Fork-and-Knife Reubens (page 106); Deli Potato Salad (page 96); Quickles (page 170)

Tex-Mex Stackers with Salsa Spread (page 111); Poblano Macaroni Salad (page 90); Fried Avocado Wedges (page 53)

Old-Fashioned Tempeh Burgers (page 123); Midwest Vinegar Slaw (page 98); Portobello Sticks (page 59)

Smokin' BBQ Portabello Sandwiches (page 117); Handcut Potato Chips (page 168); Quickles (page 170)

Chickanini Sandwiches (page 109); Italian Deli Pasta Salad (page 88); Quickles (page 170)

Seitan Po' Boys (page 104); Three-Bean Salad (page 94); Baked Onion Rings (page 163)

Route 66 Seitan Sandwiches (page 114); Beer-Battered Onion Rings (page 162); Sweet-and-Sour Slaw (page 98)

Portobello Popeye Club Sandwiches (page 118); Homestyle Macaroni Salad (page 89); Handcut Potato Chips (page 168)

Black Bean Soup (page 79); Movie Night Potato Skins (page 48); Bistro Chopped Salad (page 87)

Mighty Miso Soup (page 73); Veggie Fried Rice (page 173); Lettuce Wraps (page 55)

Tex-Mex Taco Salad (page 101); Roasted Corn Avocado Salsa (page 50); Baked Poppers with Lime Cream (page 52)

Bistro French Onion Soup (page 72); Not-So-Niçoise Salad (page 93), Cashew Cheeze Stuffed Squash Blossoms (page 62)

Salisbury-Style Seitan with Mushrooms

Serves 4

This is a vegan version of the popular meat-based dish that was standard fare on diner menus and even a popular TV dinner. Serve with a side of mashed potatoes and your favorite vegetable for the ultimate blue plate special.

1/4 teaspoon salt
1/4 teaspoon black pepper
1/4 teaspoon smoked paprika
1/8 teaspoon dried dill weed
1/8 teaspoon ground coriander
1 pound Savory Seitan (page 5) cut into
   1/2-inch thick cutlets
1 tablespoon olive oil
1 tablespoon vegan margarine
2 cups chopped onion
4 cups chopped cremini mushrooms
2 tablespoons dry sherry or vegetable
   broth
3 cloves garlic, minced
2 teaspoons dried thyme
1/4 cup all-purpose flour
2 cups vegetable broth
2 teaspoons vegan Worcestershire sauce

1. In a small bowl, combine the salt, pepper, paprika, dill, and coriander. Rub the spice mixture into both sides of the seitan cutlets.

2. Heat the oil in a large skillet over medium-high heat. Add the seitan and cook until browned, about 5 minutes. Turn the cutlets and brown on the other side, 3 to 5 minutes. Transfer to a plate and set aside.

3. In the same skillet over medium-high heat, add the margarine and onion and cook 3 to 5 minutes, or until the onion begins to soften. Add the mushrooms, sherry, garlic, and thyme and cook 3 minutes, or until the mushrooms are softened. Reduce the heat to medium. Sprinkle the flour into the skillet, stirring for 1 minute. Add the broth and the Worcestershire sauce and cook, stirring until thick, 2 to 3 minutes. Taste and adjust the seasonings.

4. Transfer the reserved cutlets to the skillet and cook until heated through. Serve immediately.

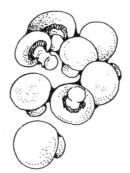

Tuna-Free Noodle Casserole

Serves 4 to 6

Ribbon noodles are combined with a creamy, savory sauce to make this delicious casserole. This casserole can be made ahead and refrigerated until needed. If cooking from the refrigerator, add about 15 minutes to the baking time.

2 tablespoons olive oil
3 tablespoons soy sauce, divided
1 tablespoon rice vinegar
1 teaspoon All-American Spice Blend (page 13) or other spice blend
1 teaspoon smoked paprika
1/2 teaspoon white pepper
1 teaspoon salt, divided
1 1/2 cups cooked or 1 (15-ounce) can chickpeas, drained and rinsed
2 cups vegetable broth
1 cup raw cashews
2 teaspoons Dijon mustard
2 artichoke hearts, packed in water, drained and chopped
8 ounces vegan ribbon-style noodles
2 tablespoons vegan margarine
1/2 cup chopped leek, white part only
1/2 cup diced red bell pepper
5 ounces cremini mushrooms, lightly rinsed, patted dry, and sliced
1/4 cup dry sherry or dry white wine
1 teaspoon dried tarragon
1 teaspoon dried thyme
1 teaspoon dried parsley
1 tablespoon all-purpose flour
1/2 cup cooked peas
Black pepper

CRUMB TOPPING:
1 cup fresh bread crumbs
1/2 teaspoon salt
1/2 teaspoon smoked paprika
1/2 teaspoon dried parsley
1 tablespoon olive oil

1. Preheat the oven to 425°F. Lightly oil a 2 1/2 quart casserole and set aside.

2. In a shallow baking pan, combine the oil, 1 tablespoon of the soy sauce, the vinegar, spice blend, paprika, white pepper, 1/2 teaspoon of the salt, and the chickpeas. Toss to coat, then roast for 30 minutes, stirring occasionally. Remove from the oven and set aside.

3. In a blender, combine the broth and cashews and blend until smooth, at least 3 minutes. Add the mustard and artichoke hearts, and blend until smooth. Set aside.

4. Cook the noodles in a large pot of salted boiling water for 3 to 4 minutes, until al dente. Drain and set aside.

5. Heat the margarine in a large skillet over medium heat. Add the leek, bell pepper, mushrooms, and remaining 1/2 teaspoon salt. Cook for 5 minutes, or until the mushrooms release their liquid. Add the sherry and the remaining 2 tablespoons soy sauce. Cook for 5 minutes, then stir in the tarragon, thyme, and parsley. Sprinkle the flour over the vegetable mixture and stir to coat. Add the reserved cashew mixture, reserved chickpea mixture, peas, and pepper to taste. Stir to mix well and heat through.

6. Preheat the oven to 400°F. In a large bowl, combine the noodles and the reserved chickpea and vegetable mixture. Mix well. Taste and adjust the seasonings and transfer to the prepared casserole dish. Set aside.

7. In a small bowl, combine the topping ingredients and mix well. Spread the crumb mixture over the casserole and cover tightly with foil. Bake 30 minutes, then remove the foil and broil on low until the crumbs are browned and crisp, 3 to 5 minutes. Serve hot.

Seitan and Herb Dumplings

Serves 4

This is my vegan version of a family comfort-food favorite. If you prefer drop dumplings, you can use a teaspoon to drop the dumpling dough into the stew instead of rolling out the dough.

STEW:

1/4 cup olive oil
1/4 cup plus 1 tablespoon all-purpose flour
1 1/2 teaspoons dried thyme
1 teaspoon dried oregano
1/2 teaspoon white pepper
1/8 teaspoon ground cayenne
1/3 cup dry white wine
5 cups vegetable broth
1 teaspoon chicken-flavored vegan bouillon paste, optional
12 ounces Seitan Lite (page 6), cut into 1-inch dice
1 shallot, chopped
1 medium onion, chopped
2 cloves garlic, minced
1 celery rib, chopped
3 carrots, cut into 1/4-inch rounds
2 ounces green beans, cut into 1-inch pieces
1/3 cup peas, fresh or frozen, thawed if frozen
1 tablespoon minced parsley, plus more for optional garnish
1/3 cup soy creamer
Salt and black pepper

DUMPLINGS:

3/4 cup all-purpose flour
1 1/2 teaspoons baking powder
1/2 teaspoon salt
1 tablespoon minced fresh parsley
1 teaspoon minced fresh thyme
3 tablespoons olive oil
1/3 cup soy milk

1. *Stew:* In a large pot, heat the oil over medium heat. Add the flour. Whisking constantly, cook 3 to 5 minutes, or until golden. Add the thyme, oregano, white pepper, and cayenne. Whisk 2 minutes longer then whisk in the wine, broth, and buillion paste, if using. Add the seitan, shallot, onion, garlic, celery, carrots, and green beans. Bring to a boil. Reduce heat to a simmer and cook for 20 minutes. Add the peas, parsley, soy creamer, and salt and pepper to taste. While the stew is simmering, make the dumplings.

2. *Dumplings:* In a small bowl, combine the flour, baking powder, salt, parsley, and thyme. Mix well. Stir in the oil and soy milk and mix well to form a soft but cohesive dough. Add an additional 1 to 2 tablespoons of flour or soy milk, if needed. Transfer the dough to a lightly floured work surface and knead 3 to 4 times. Roll out the dough to about 1/8-inch thickness and cut into 1-inch strips. Cut across the strips to make 1-inch square dumplings.

3. Arrange the dumplings on the stew, cover, and simmer for 15 minutes. Gently turn the dumplings over and simmer 10 minutes longer. Remove one dumpling and cut it open to check for doneness. If it is undercooked, simmer another 5 minutes and test again. Serve immediately, garnished with parsley if desired.

Tempeh Cutlets with Creamy Tomato-Pepper Spaghetti

Serves 4

Spaghetti is a cornerstone of Italian restaurant menus and a life-saver at home for busy nights. This version gets special treatment served with tempeh cutlets and a rich and flavorful sauce. For easy preparation, the sauce may be made ahead of time and the tempeh marinated overnight. For the creamiest sauce, be sure to use soy milk in this dish.

1 pound tempeh

MARINADE:
2 tablespoons olive oil
2/3 cup red wine vinegar
1/4 cup ketchup
1 tablespoon agave nectar
1 tablespoon plus 1 teaspoon onion
   powder
1 tablespoon plus 1 teaspoon dried
   oregano
2 teaspoons red pepper flakes
1 tablespoon vegan Worcestershire sauce
Pinch black pepper

SAUCE:
1 tablespoon olive oil
1 medium onion, chopped
2 cloves garlic, minced
1 red bell pepper, chopped
1 green bell pepper, chopped
1 jalapeño, seeded and minced
2 teaspoon dried basil
1 teaspoon dried oregano
1/2 teaspoon red pepper flakes
1/3 cup chopped sun-dried tomatoes,
   oil-packed or reconstituted
1 tablespoon plus 1 teaspoon all-purpose
   flour
1 1/2 cups soy milk
1 (15-ounce) can tomato sauce
Salt and black pepper
2 tablespoons canola oil
12 ounces spaghetti
Chopped fresh basil, optional garnish

1. Cut the tempeh in half then cut each piece in half horizontally to make 8 cutlets. Steam the tempeh in a saucepan with enough water to cover for 15 minutes. Drain and set aside.

2. *Marinade:* Combine all the marinade ingredients in a 9 x 13-inch pan. Mix well. Add the steamed tempeh to the marinade, cover, and marinate for 1 hour or refrigerate overnight, turning occasionally.

3. *Sauce:* In a large saucepan, heat the olive oil over medium heat. Add the onion and cook 5 minutes. Add the garlic, bell peppers, and jalapeño. Cook 3 minutes. Add the basil, oregano, red pepper flakes, and sun-dried tomatoes. Stir and cook 2 minutes. Add the flour and continue to cook and stir 2 minutes. Add the soy milk. Cook and stir for 2 minutes, or until the sauce thickens. Add the tomato sauce, and salt and pepper to taste. Cook until heated through, about 3 minutes. Keep warm. Preheat the oven to 250°F.

4. Heat the canola oil in a large skillet over medium heat. Remove the tempeh cutlets from the marinade and add to the skillet, in batches, if necessary. Cook for 8 minutes, or until golden brown. Turn and cook the other side for 5 minutes, or until golden brown. Place the cooked cutlets on an oven-proof plate and keep warm in the oven.

5. Cook the spaghetti in a large pot of boiling salted water for 10 minutes, or until al dente. Drain well. Return the drained pasta to the pot. Add the sauce and toss to combine. Transfer the pasta and sauce to four plates, dividing evenly. Top each serving with two tempeh cutlets and garnish with basil, if using. Serve hot.

Tempeh Stroganoff-Stuffed Potatoes

Serves 4

Simple baked potatoes are stuffed to overflowing with tasty tempeh stroganoff for a terrific stick-to-your-ribs dinner. We like them served with sautéed greens on the side.

4 russet potatoes, scrubbed

TEMPEH:

12 ounces tempeh (page 3) steamed, cut into 1/2-inch dice
3/4 cup vegetable broth
3 tablespoons dry red wine or additional broth
1 1/2 tablespoons olive oil
1 1/2 tablespoons soy sauce
1 1/2 tablespoons apple cider vinegar
1/2 tablespoon agave nectar
3/4 teaspoon All-American Spice Blend (page 13) or other spice blend
1/2 teaspoon dried mustard
1/4 teaspoon salt

STUFFING:

2 tablespoons olive oil, divided
3/4 medium onion, chopped
2 teaspoons dried parsley
3/4 teaspoon dried thyme
9 ounces cremini or button mushrooms, lightly rinsed, patted dry, and chopped
2 cloves garlic, minced
1 1/2 tablespoons dry white wine
1 tablespoon vegan margarine
1 1/2 tablespoons Dijon mustard
1 cup vegan sour cream, plus more for optional garnish
Salt and black pepper
2 tablespoons minced fresh parsley
1/4 cup minced scallions

1. Preheat the oven to 350°F. Pierce the potatoes with fork. Place on a baking sheet and bake for 1 hour or until done.

2. *Tempeh:* Combine the tempeh with the roasting broth ingredients in a 9 x 13-inch baking sheet and stir to coat. Bake for 25 to 30 minutes, or until the liquid is absorbed, stirring occasionally.

3. *Stuffing:* Heat 1 tablespoon olive oil in a large skillet over medium heat. Add the onion, parsley, and thyme. Cook 5 minutes, or until the onion begins to turn translucent. Add the mushrooms and garlic, and cook 5 minutes. Add the wine and increase the heat to medium-high for 2 minutes, cooking until the alcohol evaporates. Reduce the heat to low. Add the margarine, mustard, 1/2 cup of the sour cream, and the roasted tempeh cubes. Stir to combine.

4. When the potatoes are cool enough to handle, cut them in half. Using a spoon, gently scoop out the insides, leaving a shell, about 1/4-inch-thick, intact. Place the insides in a large bowl. Add the remaining tablespoon olive oil and the remaining 1/2 cup sour cream. Mash the potatoes.

5. Add the stroganoff mixture to the potato mixture, stirring well to combine. Season with salt and pepper to taste. To serve, mound a portion of the stroganoff mixture in each potato shell, dividing evenly. Place the stuffed potatoes on a baking sheet and bake for 10 minutes. Top with parsley, scallions, and an additional dollop of sour cream, if using.

While the Oven's On

Whenever you've got the oven on, why not roast some green beans, asparagus, or other vegetable for a great side dish? Just toss the amount you want with a little olive oil, sprinkle with salt and pepper, and bake for that last 15 to 20 minutes of baking time, or until tender.

Italian Big Bowl

Serves 4

With vegan sausage, garlic, sun-dried tomatoes, olives and capers, this Italian-style dish is sure to satisfy. If you're not a fan of spicy food, the red pepper flakes may be omitted.

1 pound fettuccine or linguine
2 tablespoons olive oil
6 cloves garlic, sliced
7 ounces Vegan Sausage Links (page 41) or store-bought, cut into 1/4-inch slices
1/2 medium red bell pepper, sliced
2 tablespoons chopped sun-dried tomatoes, oil-packed or reconstituted
1/4 teaspoon fennel seed
1/4 teaspoon red pepper flakes, or more
1/3 cup tomato paste
1/4 cup dry white wine or vegetable broth
1 1/2 tablespoons capers
1/4 cup pitted and quartered kalamata olives
1 to 2 cups cooking water from pasta
1/4 cup chopped fresh basil
Salt and black pepper

1. Cook the fettuccine in a large pot of boiling salted water for 12 minutes or until al dente. Drain the pasta, retaining 2 cups of the cooking water. Return the drained noodles to the pot, toss with a little olive oil, and set aside.

2. Heat the oil in a large skillet over medium heat. Add the garlic. Cook about 3 minutes until it becomes fragrant. Add the sausage and bell pepper and cook until the sausage begins to brown, 5 to 7 minutes.

3. Add the sun-dried tomatoes, fennel, and red pepper flakes. Cook, stirring for 2 minutes, then add the tomato paste, wine, capers, olives, and 1 cup of the pasta cooking water. Reduce heat to low. Add the remaining 1 cup cooking water, if needed, until the sauce is of a consistency that coats the pasta well. Add the basil and season with salt and pepper to taste. Add the sauce to the pot containing the pasta and toss well to combine.

Vegan Parmesan

Here's a recipe for making your own vegan Parmesan.

2 tablespoons almonds
2 tablespoons nutritional yeast
1/4 teaspoon salt
1/2 teaspoon olive oil
Pinch white pepper

Combine all the ingredients in a blender and blend to a powder. Transfer to a small container with a tight-fitting lid and store in the refrigerator.

Italian-Style Seitan with Linguine

Serves 4

Sure, you could hit the Italian joint on your way home from work, but why bother when this delicious homestyle Italian dish can be on the table in minutes.

1 pound linguine or other long pasta
1 tablespoon olive oil
12 ounces Seitan Lite (page 6), cut into
   1-inch strips
Salt and black pepper
1 tablespoon vegan margarine
4 cloves garlic, sliced
1 medium red bell pepper, sliced
2 cups sliced cremini mushrooms
1/2 cup sun-dried tomatoes, oil-packed
   or reconstituted, thinly sliced
1/2 cup sliced pitted kalamata olives
3/4 cup dry white wine or vegetable
   broth
10 ounces fresh baby spinach
Juice of 1/2 lemon
2 teaspoons dried basil
1 teaspoon dried oregano
1/2 teaspoon red pepper flakes

1. Cook the linguine in a large pot of boiling salted water for 10 minutes, or until al dente. Reserve 1 cup of the cooking water, then drain the pasta, toss with a little olive oil, and set aside.

2. While the pasta is cooking, heat the olive oil in a large skillet over medium heat. Season the seitan with salt and pepper, and add to the skillet. Cook for 8 to 10 minutes, turning occasionally, until lightly browned. Remove from the skillet and set aside.

3. Add the margarine to the same skillet over medium heat. Add the garlic, bell pepper, and mushrooms. Cook 3 to 4 minutes, or until the mushrooms soften. Add the sun-dried tomatoes, olives, and wine. Cook, stirring, to deglaze the skillet, until the wine is reduced by half. Add the spinach, reserved seitan, lemon juice, basil, oregano, and red pepper flakes. Season with salt and pepper to taste.

4. When the spinach is nearly wilted, add the cooked, drained pasta to the skillet and heat through, tossing to coat. Add as much of the reserved pasta water as needed to make enough sauce to coat the pasta. Serve hot.

Eggplant Parm with Tomato Basil Sauce

Serves 4

Nothing says comfort food like perfectly seasoned eggplant, combined with a delicious tomato basil sauce, and served over pasta. This sauce can be made ahead and stored in the refrigerator (except for the fresh basil, which is best added at the last minute). Leftover sauce is wonderful on pizza.

SAUCE:
1 tablespoon olive oil
1 large onion, chopped
3 cloves garlic, minced
1 tablespoon plus 1 teaspoon dried basil
2 teaspoons dried parsley
2 tablespoons raisins
2 (28-ounce) cans diced tomatoes,
  undrained
1 teaspoon salt
1/2 teaspoon white pepper
1/2 cup chopped fresh basil

EGGPLANT:
1/4 cup pine nuts
1/2 cup dried bread crumbs
1/4 cup nutritional yeast
1 teaspoon red pepper flakes
1 teaspoon dried parsley
1 clove garlic, minced
1/4 teaspoon salt
1 pound eggplant, cut into 1/4-inch slices
3/4 cup soy milk
3 tablespoons all-purpose flour
Canola oil, for frying
1 pound spaghetti, or other pasta

1. *Sauce:* Heat the oil in a large saucepan over medium heat. Add the onion and cook 5 minutes. Add the garlic, dried basil, and parsley. Cook for 2 minutes then add the raisins, tomatoes, salt, and pepper. Bring to a boil. Reduce to simmer for 30 minutes, stirring occasionally. Add the fresh basil to the sauce a few minutes before serving time. Taste and adjust the seasonings.

2. *Eggplant:* In a blender or food processor, process the pine nuts to a powder. Add the crumbs, yeast, red pepper flakes, parsley, garlic, and salt. Process until combined. Transfer the mixture to a shallow bowl or pie plate. In a second shallow pan, combine the soy milk and flour and mix well.

3. Dip the eggplant in the soy milk mixture, then into the crumb mixture. Pat the crumbs onto the eggplant to coat completely. Place the eggplant slices on a baking sheet. Repeat until all the eggplant slices are coated. If desired, the prepared eggplant can be refrigerated for 30 minutes to help set the crumbs.

4. Preheat the oven to 250°F. Heat a thin layer of oil in a large skillet over medium heat. Working in batches, add the slices and cook 3 to 5 minutes, turning once, until golden brown. Return to the baking sheet as they are cooked, and keep warm in the oven until ready to serve.

5. Cook the spaghetti in a large pot of boiling salted water for 10 minutes, or until al dente. Drain well and return to the pot. To serve, add 2 cups of the sauce to the spaghetti and toss to coat. Arrange a serving of spaghetti on four plates. Top each serving with the eggplant slices, and top with the sauce. Serve hot.

Fettuccine Alfredo

Serves 4

This vegan version of an Italian classic is sure to please. Don't let the unusual ingredients in this recipe fool you. They combine into a creamy and delicious sauce that will leave the whole table guessing what's in it.

3/4 cup raw cashews
1/4 cup plus 2 tablespoons pine nuts
1/2 cup marsala or dry white wine
1 1/2 to 2 cups vegetable broth
3 cloves roasted garlic (page 47)
3 cloves garlic, minced
1 teaspoon salt
3 tablespoons apple cider vinegar
2 tablespoons nutritional yeast
1 1/2 teaspoons prepared yellow
   mustard
1 tablespoon plus 1 teaspoon canned
   mild green chiles
2 tablespoons arrowroot
1/8 teaspoon chili powder
Black pepper
1 pound fettuccine
2 tablespoons chopped fresh parsley

1. Combine the cashews and pine nuts in a blender and grind until powdered. Add the wine, 1 1/2 cups broth, the roasted and raw garlic, salt, vinegar, nutritional yeast, mustard, chiles, arrowroot, chili powder, and black pepper, to taste. Blend until smooth, then transfer to a large saucepan over medium heat. Cook, stirring to heat through, adding more broth to thin, if needed. Taste and adjust the seasonings. Keep warm.

2. Cook the fettuccine in a large pot of boiling salted water for 12 minutes, or until al dente. Drain well then return to the pot. Add the reserved sauce and toss to combine. Serve immediately, sprinkled with the parsley.

● ● ● ● ● ● ● ● ● ●

VARIATION

Broccalfredo. Got extra broccoli? Use it up in this Alfredo variation, using 8 cups broccoli florets and the Fettuccine Alfredo above. When cooking the pasta, add the broccoli to the cooking water for the last 3 minutes of cooking time. Drain the pasta and broccoli then return to the cooking pot. Add the sauce and stir to coat. Garnish with parsley, if desired, and serve.

Spaghetti Pie with Arrabbiata Sauce

Serves 8

Spaghetti pie is a Midwest homestyle favorite that makes great party fare since it can be made ahead of time. My version features a spicy arrabbiata sauce, but for a more traditional flavor, simply omit the red pepper flakes.

1 pound spaghetti
2 tablespoons olive oil, divided
1 1/2 cups hot water
1 1/2 cups texturized vegetable protein granules
1 tablespoon soy sauce
1 large onion, chopped
1 medium red bell pepper, chopped
4 to 6 cloves garlic, minced
1 tablespoon dried parsley
1 tablespoon dried basil
2 teaspoons dried thyme
2 teaspoons dried oregano
1 tablespoon red pepper flakes, or to taste
3/4 cup dry red wine
1 (14.5-ounce) can fire-roasted crushed tomatoes
1 (14.5-ounce) can fire-roasted diced tomatoes, drained
2 (14.5-ounce) cans tomato sauce
Salt and black pepper
1 pound extra-firm tofu, drained
1/4 cup vegan sour cream
1/4 cup vegan cream cheese
1/4 cup fresh lemon juice
1/4 cup nutritional yeast
1 cup soy milk
1 teaspoon garlic powder
1 teaspoon onion powder
1 teaspoon dried parsley
2 teaspoons dried basil
3/4 cup shredded vegan mozzarella cheese, optional

1. Preheat the oven to 350°F. Lightly oil a 9 x 13-inch baking pan or a lasagna pan or spray it with nonstick cooking spray.

2. Cook the spaghetti in a large pot of boiling salted water for 10 minutes, or until al dente. Drain, then toss with 1 tablespoon of the olive oil and transfer to the prepared pan.

3. In a medium bowl, combine the hot water, texturized vegetable protein, and soy sauce. Set aside to rehydrate 10 minutes.

4. Heat the remaining 1 tablespoon olive oil in a large saucepan over medium heat. Add the rehydrated texturized vegetable protein, onion, bell pepper, and garlic. Cook for 10 minutes, or until the vegetables are soft. Add the parsley, basil, thyme, oregano, and red pepper flakes. Cook for 5 minutes, then add the wine, tomatoes, and tomato sauce. Simmer 15 minutes. Season with salt and pepper to taste.

5. In a blender or food processor, combine the tofu, sour cream, cream cheese, lemon juice, yeast, soy milk, garlic powder, onion powder, parsley, basil, and 1/2 teaspoon salt. Blend until smooth. Pour the tofu mixture over the spaghetti, spreading to coat. Spread the tomato sauce mixture over the tofu layer.

6. Cover the pan tightly with foil and bake about 30 minutes, or until the mixture is bubbling. If using cheese, spread on top and broil until melted, for an additional 5 minutes. Serve hot.

Red-Eye Tofu and Vegetable Skewers

Serves 4

Kebobs, skewers, or whatever you like to call them, bistros often feature this fun food on a stick. Here, I'm combining them with a sauce inspired by the red-eye gravy commonly listed on menus in the South.

1 tablespoon olive oil
1/3 cup minced red onion
2 cloves garlic, minced
2/3 cup tomato paste
1/3 cup packed light brown sugar
1/3 cup apple cider vinegar
2 teaspoons liquid smoke
1 teaspoon chili powder
1/2 teaspoon salt
1 tablespoon Dijon mustard
1 tablespoon soy sauce
1 cup brewed coffee
1 tablespoon canola oil
1 pound extra-firm tofu, drained, pressed, and cut into 1-inch dice
1 large red bell pepper, cut into 1-inch dice
1 medium onion, cut into eighths and separated
4 (10-inch) wooden skewers, soaked in water for 1 hour before using

1. Heat the olive oil in a medium saucepan over low heat. Add the onion and garlic. Cook for 5 minutes. Add the tomato paste, brown sugar, vinegar, liquid smoke, chili powder, salt, mustard, soy sauce, and coffee. Bring to a boil. Simmer 15 minutes to allow the flavors to blend and the sauce to thicken.

2. Heat the canola oil in a large skillet over medium heat. Add the tofu and cook until golden brown, 8 to 10 minutes, stirring often so all sides are golden. Transfer to an 8-inch baking dish and pour the sauce over the tofu, tossing to coat. Set aside or refrigerate to marinate for 1 hour or longer.

3. Preheat the grill. Thread the tofu, pepper, and onion alternately onto the skewers.

4. Place the skewers on the grill and cook until slightly charred, 7 to 9 minutes. Turn to grill the other side, 5 to 7 minutes. Baste with the remaining sauce while cooking. Serve immediately.

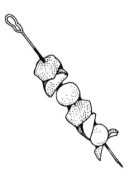

VARIATION

To broil: Preheat the broiler. Place the skewers on a lightly oiled baking sheet. Broil 7 to 9 minutes about 4-inches from the heat source. Baste occasionally. Turn to broil the other side, 6 to 8 minutes, or until slightly charred.

Seitan Katsu with Tonkatsu Sauce

Serves 4

This comfort food from Japan is normally made with meat, but this vegan version is a favorite in my house. It features crispy seitan strips with a deep dark sauce over lightly dressed shredded cabbage, which is the perfect complement. It also makes a fun appetizer, if you serve it family style.

SAUCE:
1 tablespoon olive oil
2 cloves garlic, minced
1 teaspoon minced fresh ginger
3 tablespoons vegan Worcestershire sauce
3 tablespoons agave nectar
3 tablespoons soy sauce
3 tablespoons ketchup
2 teaspoons Dijon mustard
1/4 teaspoon ground allspice
Pinch red pepper flakes, optional

SLAW:
1 small head napa cabbage, shredded, (about 8 cups)
1 1/2 cups shredded red cabbage
2 medium carrots, shredded
Juice of 1 lime
1 tablespoon rice vinegar
1 teaspoon sugar

SEITAN:
16 ounces Seitan Lite (page 6), cut into 1-inch strips
Salt and black pepper
1 cup soy milk
2/3 cup all-purpose flour
1 1/2 cups panko crumbs
Canola oil, for frying

TIP

Double this sauce and enjoy it over any stir-fry, rice, or noodle dish. It stores well in the refrigerator for at least a week.

1. *Sauce:* Heat the oil in a small saucepan over medium heat. Add the garlic and ginger. Cook 2 to 3 minutes, or until fragrant. Reduce the heat to medium and add the remaining sauce ingredients. Stir to combine. Simmer 5 minutes for the flavors to blend and for the sauce to slightly thicken. Remove from the heat and set aside.

2. *Slaw:* Combine all the ingredients in a large bowl. Store in the refrigerator until serving.

3. *Seitan:* Season the seitan strips with salt and pepper and set aside. Place the soy milk in a shallow bowl. Spread the flour on a plate. Place the panko on a separate plate. Line a baking sheet with a brown bag or paper towels for draining.

4. Dip each seitan strip into the soy milk, then dredge it in the flour. Dip the floured strip back into the soy milk, then dredge it in the panko crumbs and arrange on a baking sheet. Repeat until all the seitan is coated.

5. Heat a 1/4-inch layer of oil in a large skillet over medium-high heat until hot. Test the oil by carefully dipping the end of one seitan strip into the oil. It should sizzle. Working in batches, add the seitan to the skillet. Do not overcrowd. Fry the first side until golden brown, about 3 to 5 minutes, then turn and fry the other side until golden, 2 to 4 minutes and arrange on the prepared baking sheet.

6. To serve, divide the slaw evenly on plates. Arrange the strips on top, then drizzle with the sauce. Serve immediately.

Grilled Seitan with Heirloom Tomatoes

Serves 4

Here's another easy dish inspired by the flavors of Little Italy. It's perfect for, lazy, summer entertaining. Heat up the grill and kick back as you enjoy your family, friends, and this amazing dinner. If heirloom tomatoes are unavailable, substitute any variety of fresh ripe tomatoes.

3 tablespoons soy sauce
1/3 cup plus 1 teaspoon balsamic
　　vinegar, divided
1/2 tablespoon olive oil
2 to 3 cloves garlic, minced, divided
1 tablespoon minced fresh rosemary
1 tablespoon fresh thyme
Pinch red pepper flakes
1/8 teaspoon black pepper
4 cutlets Seitan Lite (page 6)
1 pound heirloom tomatoes, seeded,
　　and cut into 1/8-inch dice
2 tablespoons minced fresh basil
1 tablespoon minced fresh parsley
3 tablespoons finely minced onion
1/8 teaspoon salt
1 tablespoon olive oil, for brushing

1. In an 8-inch square pan or other shallow dish, combine the soy sauce, the 1/3 cup vinegar, olive oil, 1 clove garlic, rosemary, thyme, red pepper flakes, and pepper. Stir to combine. Add the seitan cutlets and marinate for 1 hour, or longer.

2. In a medium bowl, combine the tomatoes, basil, parsley, onion, remaining 1 or 2 cloves garlic, the remaining 1 teaspoon vinegar, and salt. Stir to combine. Set aside for 1 hour for the flavors to meld. Do not refrigerate.

3. Preheat the grill. Remove the cutlets from the marinade and brush each side with olive oil. Arrange the cutlets on the grill and cook for 3 to 5 minutes, basting occasionally with the marinade. Turn to cook the other side, 3 to 5 minutes. Serve immediately, topped with the tomatoe mixture.

VARIATION

To cook indoors:

Grill pan: Preheat a grill pan and proceed as above.

Pan fry: Heat a large skillet with just enough oil to cover the bottom over medium heat. Cook the cutlets 4 to 5 minutes, until golden. Turn to cook the second side, 3 to 4 minutes.

21st Century Tacos

If texturized vegetable protein (page 7) is new to you, this flavorful taco recipe is a great way to get acquainted with it. These tacos have been a favorite at our house for more than twenty-five years.

1 1/4 cups hot water
1 1/2 cup texturized vegetable protein granules
1 tablespoon soy sauce
1 teaspoon salt
3 teaspoons ground cumin, divided
1 tablespoon olive oil
1 cup chopped onion
3 cloves garlic, minced
1/2 medium jalapeño or poblano chile, seeded and minced
1 (15-ounce) can tomato sauce
2 teaspoons chili powder
1 teaspoon onion powder
1/2 teaspoon black pepper
1/2 teaspoon dried oregano
1/2 teaspoon liquid smoke
1 teaspoon vegan Worcestershire sauce
1/2 to 1 minced chipotle chile in adobo, or to taste
1/4 to 1/2 cup water
Salt
12 taco shells
Toppings: shredded lettuce, chopped tomatoes, shredded vegan cheese, chopped avocados, chopped pitted olives, salsa, or scallions

1. In a medium bowl, combine the hot water, texturized vegetable protein, soy sauce, salt, and 1 teaspoon of the cumin. Stir to combine, then set aside to rehydrate, about 10 minutes.

2. Heat the oil in a large skillet over medium heat. Add the onion, garlic, and jalapeño. Cook 2 to 3 minutes, or until just fragrant. Add the texturized vegetable protein mixture, tomato sauce, chili powder, onion powder, remaining 2 teaspoons cumin, black pepper, oregano, liquid smoke, and Worcestershire sauce. Stir to combine. Reduce heat to medium-low and add the chipotle and 1/4 cup water. Simmer about 20 minutes for the flavors to combine, stirring occasionally. Add additional 1/4 cup water, if needed. Season with salt to taste.

3. Preheat the oven to 350°F. Place the taco shells on a baking sheet and bake 3 to 4 minutes, or until crisp. To serve, fill the taco shells with the taco filling and add toppings as desired.

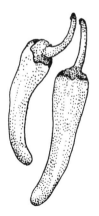

Wet Bean Burritos

Serves 4

Unlike hand-held tacos, these saucy burritos require a knife and fork to enjoy them. This easy recipe can be made ahead. If baking straight from the refrigerator, add 10 to 15 minutes to your baking time. If dried chiles are unavailable, begin with step 2, adding 1 tablespoon chili powder to the onion and garlic. Top with shredded vegan cheese before baking, if desired.

SAUCE:

2 dried guajillo chiles, stemmed and seeded
2 dried pasilla chiles, stemmed and seeded
1 tablespoon olive oil
1/4 cup diced onion
2 cloves garlic, minced
3/4 cup vegetable broth
1 (15-ounce) can tomato sauce
1 tablespoon apple cider vinegar
1/2 teaspoon ground cumin
1/2 teaspoon dried oregano
1/2 teaspoon salt
1/2 teaspoon liquid smoke
1/4 teaspoon ground cayenne

BURRITOS:

1 tablespoon olive oil
1/2 large onion, chopped
1 poblano chile, chopped
8 ounces cremini mushrooms, rinsed, patted dry, and chopped
2 cloves garlic, minced
3 cups cooked or 2 (15-ounce) cans black beans, drained and rinsed
2 teaspoons ground cumin
1 teaspoon chili powder
1 teaspoon dried oregano
1/4 teaspoon red pepper flakes
2 tablespoons tomato paste
Juice of 2 limes
1/4 cup nutritional yeast
12 ounces fresh baby spinach, (about 8 cups packed)
Salt and black pepper
8 (8-inch) flour tortillas
Toppings: shredded lettuce, chopped tomatoes, guacamole, pitted olives, salsa, chopped scallions

1. *Sauce:* Heat a large skillet over medium-high heat. Add the dried chiles and press down on them with a spatula, turning as needed until the color changes slightly, 3 to 5 minutes. Place the chiles in a heatproof bowl with enough boiling water to cover. Set aside for 30 minutes to rehydrate.

2. Heat the oil in a small skillet over medium heat. Add the onion and garlic and cook for 3 minutes, then transfer to a blender or food processor. Drain the chiles and add them to the blender, along with the remaining sauce ingredients. Process until smooth. Taste and adjust the seasonings. Set aside.

3. *Burritos:* Heat the oil in a large skillet over medium heat. Add the onion and cook until it begins to turn translucent, about 5 minutes. Add the poblano and cook 3 minutes. Add the mushrooms and garlic. Cook 3 to 5 minutes, until the mushrooms begin to soften. Add the beans, cumin, chili powder, oregano, red pepper flakes, tomato paste, lime juice, and nutritional yeast. Stir together, then add the spinach. Cook, stirring occasionally, about 5 minutes. Add a splash of broth or water if the mixture is too dry. Season with salt and pepper to taste.

4. Preheat the oven to 400°F. Lightly spray or oil a 9 x 13-inch baking pan. Fill each tortilla with 1/8 of the filling. Roll up and arrange in the baking pan. Repeat until all the burritos are filled. Pour the reserved sauce over the burritos and bake 15 to 20 minutes, until bubbly. Serve hot with toppings as desired.

Mexicali Seitan

Serves 4

This dish is so quick and easy, you'll feel like a short-order cook. It's so versatile, you can serve it over rice, in tortillas, or use in a quick-and-easy taco salad. It can be served with a variety of toppings – avocado puts it over the top. Chipotle chiles in adobo are hot, so use less if you don't like spicy food.

1 tablespoon minced chipotle chile in adobo, or to taste
1 (15-ounce) can crushed tomatoes
1 tablespoon canola oil
16 ounces Savory Seitan (page 5), cut into 1-inch strips
1 medium onion, sliced
1 medium red bell pepper, sliced
1/2 medium green bell pepper, sliced
1 small jalapeño, unseeded and minced
2 cloves garlic, minced
1 teaspoon chipotle chili powder
1/2 teaspoon dried marjoram
1 teaspoon ground cumin
1/2 teaspoon salt
3/4 cup corn kernels, fresh or frozen, thawed
Juice of 1/2 lime
Black pepper
4 (10-inch) flour tortillas or hot cooked rice, for serving
Toppings: chopped avocado, sour cream, chopped tomatoes, pitted sliced black olives, chopped fresh cilantro

1. In a bowl, combine the chipotle with the tomatoes and set aside. Heat the oil in a large skillet over medium heat. Add the seitan, and cook until browned, turning as needed, about 10 minutes. Remove the seitan from the skillet and set aside.

2. In the same skillet over medium heat, add the onion and cook until softened, about 5 minutes. Stir in the bell peppers, jalapeño, and garlic. Cook for 3 minutes. Add the chili powder, marjoram, cumin, and salt. Cook for 1 minute then add the tomato mixture, corn, lime juice, and black pepper to taste. Return the seitan to the skillet and heat until hot. Taste and adjust the seasonings. Serve immediately spooned into tortillas or over rice, with as many of the toppings as desired.

Seitan Goulash with Kraut

Serves 4

There's something about pairing beer with sauerkraut that works well, probably because both are fermented. If desired, 1 1/4 cups texturized vegetable protein chunks may be substituted for the seitan. If using, add them with the beer and broth, along with an extra 1/2 cup of broth.

1 tablespoon olive oil
1 medium onion, chopped
1 stalk celery, chopped
1 medium green bell pepper, chopped
12 ounces Savory Seitan (page 5), cut into 1-inch chunks
2 cups quartered baby Portobello mushrooms
3 cloves garlic, minced
2 medium carrots, cut into 1/4-inch slices
Salt
2 tablespoons Hungarian paprika
1/2 teaspoon ground cayenne
1 teaspoon caraway seeds
1/4 teaspoon dried dill weed
1 cup vegan beer, such as Magic Hat #9
1 cup vegetable broth
1 (15-ounce) can diced tomatoes, with juice
2 cups sauerkraut, rinsed and drained
2 tablespoons tomato paste
1 tablespoon chopped fresh parsley
1/4 cup vegan sour cream, plus more for serving
Black pepper
Parsleyed Noodles (page 156)
1 tablespoon chopped fresh parsley or dill, optional garnish

1. Heat the oil in a large saucepan over medium heat. Add the onion, celery, bell pepper, seitan, mushrooms, garlic, carrots, and a pinch of salt. Cook 5 minutes, or until the onion begins to turn translucent. Add paprika, cayenne, caraway, and dill. Cook, stirring for 2 minutes. Add the beer, broth, diced tomatoes (with juice), sauerkraut, and tomato paste. Stir to combine and bring to a boil. Reduce the heat to a simmer and partially cover. Cook 30 minutes, adding additional broth if the mixture is dry. Stir in the parsley, sour cream, and salt and pepper to taste.

2. To serve, spoon the noodles onto plates and top with the goulash. Top with a dollop of sour cream and fresh herbs, if using.

Vegan Beer and Wine

It's true that many beers and wines aren't vegan, but new ones are becoming available all the time. Find out what's vegan at these online resources. They are frequently updated and have large databases. You can also ask the sales clerk at your local liquor store, as doing so will show an increasing demand for vegan beer and wine. Along the same lines, a quick e-mail to the brewery or winery should give you sound information and also indicate interest.

For wine:

http://vegans.frommars.org/wine/
http://www.barnivore.com/wine

For beer:

http://www.barnivore.com/beer
http://www.veganvanguard.com/vegism/beer.html

Cajun Pot Pie

Serves 4

Vegan sausage, vegetables, and beans combine for a savory filling, topped with a black pepper crust. This isn't the pot pie you grew up on. Inspired by the large Cajun population in Louisiana, this regional version is rustic, hearty, and spicy. For a more traditional variation, see below.

CRUST:

1 cup all-purpose flour
1 tablespoon sugar
1 tablespoon nutritional yeast
1/4 teaspoon salt
1/4 teaspoon cracked black pepper
1/4 cup chilled vegan margarine
1/4 cup chilled vegan shortening
1 tablespoon white vinegar
2 tablespoons chilled water

FILLING:

2 tablespoons olive oil
8 ounces red potatoes, cut into 1/2-inch dice
1 leek, chopped, white part only
1/2 celery rib, chopped
1 small carrot, chopped
1/2 cup green beans, trimmed, and cut into 1-inch pieces
1/2 cup peas, fresh or frozen, thawed
2 cups packed chopped Swiss chard
1 1/2 cups cooked or 1 (15-ounce) can black eyed peas, drained and rinsed
12 ounces Vegan Sausage Links (page 41), cut into 1/2-inch dice
1 teaspoon smoked paprika
1 teaspoon chili powder

SAUCE:

3 tablespoons olive oil
3 tablespoons all-purpose flour
1 teaspoon dried basil
1/2 teaspoon ground cayenne
1/2 teaspoon dried oregano
1/2 teaspoon dried thyme
1/2 teaspoon salt
1 cup vegetable broth
1/2 tablespoon apple cider vinegar

1. *Crust:* In a food processor, combine the flour, sugar, nutritional yeast, salt, and pepper. Mix to combine. Add the margarine and shortening. Pulse until the mixture resembles small peas. Drizzle in the vinegar and water. Mix until the dough forms a ball. Flatten into a disk and wrap in plastic wrap. Refrigerate one hour.

2. *Filling:* Heat the oil in a large skillet over medium heat. Add the potatoes, leek, celery, and carrot. Cook 5 minutes. Add the remaining ingredients, stirring to combine. Cook 5 minutes, stirring occasionally. If the mixture sticks to the skillet, add a splash of water.

3. *Sauce:* Heat the oil in a small saucepan over medium heat. Add the flour and whisk together. Cook, stirring, for 5 minutes. Add the remaining ingredients. Whisk together and cook until thick, about 5 minutes. Add the sauce to the skillet with the filling and stir to combine. Taste and adjust the seasonings. Preheat the oven to 375°F.

4. *To assemble:* Roll out the crust to a 14-inch round, about 1/4-inch thick. Transfer the filling to a 10-inch pie plate. Place the crust on top of the filling. Crimp the edge. Cut 2 to 3 slits in the top to let steam escape. Place on a baking sheet to catch the drips. Bake 35 minutes, or until golden and bubbly. Let cool 5 minutes before serving.

● ● ● ● ● ● ● ● ● ●

VARIATION

For a more traditional pot pie, omit the black pepper from the crust and omit the cayenne from the sauce. In the filling, omit the chili powder, substitute white beans for the black eyed peas and 12 ounces diced Savory Seitan (page 5) for the Vegan Sausage Links.

Sweet Garlicky Ribz

Serves 4

A soul food favorite, serve these tasty ribz with corn on the cob and Taters and Strings (page 165) or your favorite sides. If smoked salt is unavailable, substitute 1 teaspoon salt and 1 teaspoon liquid smoke.

SAUCE:
1/3 cup olive oil
3/4 cup minced onion
6 to 8 cloves garlic, minced
1 tablespoon smoked paprika
1 1/2 teaspoons chili powder
1 teaspoon salt
Pinch black pepper
1/3 cup dark brown sugar
1/3 cup apple cider vinegar
1 tablespoon vegan Worcestershire sauce
2 teaspoons liquid smoke
2 (15-ounce) cans tomato sauce

RIBZ:
3/4 cups vegetable broth plus 2
  tablespoons, divided
1/4 cup texturized vegetable protein
  granules
2 cups vital wheat gluten
1 tablespoon instant tapioca
1 tablespoon plus 1 teaspoon smoked
  paprika
1 teaspoon chili powder
2 teaspoons garlic powder
1 teaspoon onion powder
1 teaspoon smoked salt
1/2 teaspoon ground black pepper
1/4 cup ketchup
1/4 cup dry red wine
2 tablespoons toasted sesame oil
2 teaspoons vegan Worcestershire sauce

1. *Sauce:* Heat the oil in a large saucepan over medium heat. Add the onion and garlic and cook 3 to 5 minutes, until the onion is translucent. Add the remaining ingredients. Simmer 30 minutes. Taste and adjust the seasonings. Set aside until needed.

2. *Ribz:* Heat 1/4 cup plus 2 tablespoons broth in a small saucepan until hot. Add the texturized vegetable protein and set aside for 10 minutes to rehydrate. In a medium bowl, combine the vital wheat gluten, tapioca, spices, salt, and pepper and mix well. Set aside.

3. In a small bowl, combine the remaining 1/2 cup broth with the ketchup, wine, sesame oil, and Worcestershire sauce and stir to combine. Add the texturized vegetable protein and the wet ingredients to the dry ingredients. Stir together, then mix well, kneading with your hands for 3 to 4 minutes. Let sit 10 minutes, then transfer to a work surface. Prepare a steamer.

4. Divide the mixture into 2 pieces. Pat each piece flat, rolling and shaping into 4 x 8-inch rectangles, just under 1-inch thick. Set aside for 2 minutes.

5. Using a sharp knife, cut each piece of gluten almost through to the bottom at 1-inch intervals to create 8 "ribz." Be sure to leave the ribz attached at the bottom. Transfer the ribz to the center of a 16-inch long piece of foil. Fold the opposite sides of the foil over the ribz. Fold the ends over. Gently pat the foil closed, making 2 packets. They do not need to be sealed tightly. Transfer to the steamer. Steam 45 minutes, then set aside to cool. Refrigerate until ready to grill.

6. Preheat a grill. Brush both sides of the ribz with the sauce, using about 1/3 of the sauce on each piece. Transfer to the grill and cook about 5 to 7 minutes, or until brown and marked. Baste occasionally. Turn over to cook the second side, about 5 minutes, until brown. Baste occasionally. To serve, pull apart and serve with the remaining sauce.

VARIATION

These ribz are best cooked on an outdoor grill but may also be cooked indoors on a grill pan or baked in the oven.

TO COOK ON A GRILL PAN: Cook the ribz 5 to 7 minutes, basting with the sauce. Turn to cook the other side, basting occasionally, about 5 minutes, or until brown and marked.

TO BAKE IN THE OVEN: preheat the oven to 375°F. Lightly oil a baking sheet. Brush ribz with about 1/3 of the sauce. Cover tightly with foil. Bake 15 minutes. Uncover, baste the ribz and turn over. Bake 10 more minutes.

Southern Fried Seitan

Serves 4

Although associated with the South, the non-vegan counterpart to this dish, fried chicken, is hugely popular in fast food restaurants, diners, and even upscale restaurants offering versions of comfort food. The crispy herb coating is the perfect complement for the cutlets. Tip: See Dredging Done Right (page 50).

1 teaspoon salt
1 teaspoon sweet paprika
1/2 teaspoon dried thyme
1/2 teaspoon onion powder
1/2 teaspoon garlic powder
1/2 teaspoon dried oregano
1/4 teaspoon black pepper
1/4 teaspoon ground cayenne
1 cup all-purpose flour
1/2 cup soy milk
2 tablespoons cornstarch
4 cutlets Seitan Lite (page 6)
Canola oil, for cooking

1. In a shallow bowl or pan, combine the salt, paprika, thyme, onion power, garlic powder, oregano, pepper, cayenne, and flour. Mix well to combine. In another shallow bowl, combine the soy milk and cornstarch. Mix with a fork until blended.

2. Dredge each cutlet in the soy milk mixture, then in the flour mixture. Dip each cutlet in the soy milk mixture again, then again in the flour mixture, and transfer to a baking sheet.

3. Heat 1/4-inch of oil in a large skillet over medium heat. Add the cutlets and cook 2 to 4 minutes, until golden. Turn to cook the other side, 2 to 3 minutes. Drain on paper towels. Serve hot.

Brewpub Tater-Tot Pie

Serves 4

This new twist on the old-fashioned Shepherd's Pie is sure to be greeted by smiles around the table at your house. Tater Tots, once a popular dish in school lunches and TV dinners, are made from shredded potatoes which are then compressed and made into nuggets. When baked, the outside crisps. For a more traditional version, substitute mashed potatoes for the topping.

2 cups texturized vegetable protein granules
2 cups hot water
2 tablespoons soy sauce
1 tablespoon olive oil
1 tablespoon vegan margarine
1 large onion, chopped
2 large carrots, chopped
1/2 cup chopped celery
2 large Portobello mushroom caps, lightly rinsed, patted dry, degilled and chopped
2 teaspoons All-American Spice Blend (page 13) or other spice blend
2 teaspoons dried thyme
1 teaspoon dried oregano
1/2 cup vegan beer, such as Sam Smith's Lager
1/2 cup vegetable broth
1/4 cup plus 2 tablespoons tomato paste
Salt and black pepper
1 pound frozen Tater Tots, partially thawed
Smoked paprika, for dusting

1. Lightly oil a 3-quart casserole. Preheat the oven to 400°F. In a medium bowl, combine the texturized vegetable protein, water, and soy sauce and set aside for 10 minutes to rehydrate.

2. In a large skillet, heat the olive oil and margarine over medium heat. Add the onion, carrots, and celery. Cook 3 minutes. Add the mushrooms, texturized vegetable protein, spice blend, thyme, and oregano. Cook and stir about 5 minutes, or until the texturized vegetable protein is browned and the mushrooms are soft. Add the beer, broth, and tomato paste. Season with salt and pepper to taste. Stir to combine and cook for 5 minutes to allow the flavors to blend. Transfer to the prepared casserole dish and set aside.

3. Cut the Tater Tots roughly in half and spread them evenly on top of the casserole. Sprinkle with smoked paprika. Bake for 40 minutes or until golden brown on top. Let stand 5 minutes before serving.

Blue Plate Special Wheat-Meat Loaf

Serves 4

Seitan is also known as "wheat-meat," and it is especially good in this savory loaf. Serve with cooked greens and the Mashed Potatoes with Homestyle Gravy (page 167) for a nostalgic Blue Plate Special. Leftovers make great sandwiches, too.

3/4 cup texturized vegetable protein
    granules
3/4 cup hot water
3/4 cup fresh bread crumbs
1/4 cup soy milk
8 ounces Savory Seitan (page 5), cut into
    large chunks
1 tablespoon olive oil
1 cup minced onion
2 cloves garlic, minced
3/4 cup minced green or red bell pepper
2 teaspoons onion powder
1 teaspoon garlic powder
1 teaspoon smoked paprika
1/2 teaspoon dried mustard
1/2 teaspoon dried sage
1/2 teaspoon dried thyme
 2 teaspoons soy sauce
1 teaspoon vegan Worcestershire sauce
3/4 cup vital wheat gluten
1/3 cup ketchup
2 tablespoons minced parsley
1/4 teaspoon salt
1/4 teaspoon black pepper

1. Preheat the oven to 350°F. Lightly oil a baking sheet. Combine the hot water with the texturized vegetable protein. Set aside for 10 minutes to rehydrate. In a large bowl, combine the bread crumbs and soy milk.

2. Finely mince the seitan in a food processor, then transfer to the bowl containing the bread crumb mixture.

3. Heat the oil in a large skillet over medium heat. Add the onion, garlic, and bell pepper. Cook 3 to 4 minutes, or until the vegetables are soft. Transfer to the bowl containing the seitan. Add the remaining ingredients, and the reserved rehydrated texturized vegetable protein. Knead the ingredients together well, squeezing and kneading, for about 5 minutes. Taste and adjust the seasonings.

4. Transfer to the prepared baking sheet and shape into a 4 x 8-inch oval loaf. Bake for 45 minutes. After 30 minutes, check to see if it is browning too much. If so, cover with foil for the remaining time. Let stand 5 minutes before serving.

Southwestern Wheat-Meat Loaf

For something different, try this zesty Southwestern spin. It's especially good topped with the Jalapeño Gravy (page 168) and served with mashed potatoes and cooked greens.

1/2 cup texturized vegetable protein granules
1/2 cup hot water
8 ounces Savory Seitan (page 5), cut into large chunks
1 chipotle chile in adobo
1 tablespoon olive oil
3/4 cup minced onion
1/2 cup minced green bell pepper
1 tablespoon minced jalapeño
2 cloves garlic, minced
2 teaspoons dried oregano
2 teaspoons ground cumin
1 teaspoon chili powder
1 teaspoon ground coriander
1 teaspoon smoked paprika
1 teaspoon browning sauce, optional
2 teaspoons soy sauce
1/2 cup corn kernels, fresh or frozen, thawed if frozen
1/2 cup vital wheat gluten
1/3 cup ketchup

1. Preheat the oven to 350°F. Lightly oil a baking sheet. Combine the hot water with the texturized vegetable protein to rehydrate. Set aside for 10 minutes.

2. Combine the seitan and chipotle in a food processor. Process until ground. Transfer to a large mixing bowl.

3. Heat the oil in a large skillet over medium heat. Add the onion. Cook 3 to 4 minutes. Add the bell pepper, jalapeño, garlic, oregano, cumin, chili powder, coriander, and smoked paprika.

4. Cook about 5 minutes, or until the vegetables are soft. Transfer to the seitan bowl. Add the remaining ingredients, and the reserved rehydrated texturized vegetable protein. Knead the ingredients together well, squeezing and kneading, for about 5 minutes.

5. Transfer to a baking sheet and shape into a 4 x 8-inch oval loaf. Bake for 1 hour. After 30 minutes, check to see if it is browning too much. If so, cover with foil for the remaining baking time. Let sit 5 minutes before serving.

Pesto Lasagna with Slow-Roasted Tomatoes and Mushrooms

Serves 4 to 6

Slow-roasting the tomatoes turns them into intense little flavor bombs. They're also delicious as a bruschetta topping or in salads. Both the tomatoes and sauce can be made ahead of time, for easy assembly. If baking the lasagna from the refrigerator, add an extra 10 minutes to the baking time.

SLOW-ROASTED TOMATOES:
1 quart ripe cherry tomatoes, halved
2 tablespoons olive oil
1/2 teaspoon dried basil
1/4 teaspoon dried thyme
1/2 teaspoon salt
Pinch black pepper

TOMATO SAUCE:
1 tablespoon olive oil
1 cup chopped onion
2 cloves garlic, minced
1/4 cup chopped sun-dried tomatoes, oil-packed or reconstituted
1 teaspoon red pepper flakes
1 tablespoon dried basil
1 teaspoon dried thyme
1 teaspoon dried oregano
2 (15-ounce) cans tomato sauce
Salt and black pepper
Pinch sugar
1/4 cup chopped fresh basil

LASAGNA:
1 tablespoon olive oil
1/4 cup chopped onion
12 ounces cremini mushrooms, rinsed, patted dry, cut into 1/4-inch slices
1 teaspoon dried thyme
1 tablespoon fresh lemon juice
3/4 cup Besto Pesto (page 68), or store-bought
8 ounces extra-firm tofu, drained, pressed, and crumbled
12 ounces lasagna noodles
Vegan Parmesan (page 137) or store-bought, optional

1. *Slow-Roasted Tomatoes:* Preheat the oven to 200°F. Line a 9 x 13-inch baking sheet with parchment paper. Place all the ingredients on the baking sheet. Stir to coat. Bake for 4 to 5 hours, checking and stirring every hour. Tomatoes should be shriveled and collapsing, but still retain moisture.

2. *Sauce:* Heat the oil in a large saucepan over medium heat. Add the onion and cook until softened, 5 minutes. Add the garlic, sun-dried tomatoes, and dried herbs. Cook 2 to 3 minutes. Add the sauce, salt, pepper, and sugar and bring to a boil. Reduce heat to low and simmer for 15 minutes. Add the fresh basil, then taste and adjust the seasonings.

3. *Lasagna:* Heat the oil in a medium skillet over medium heat. Add the onion and cook until softened, 5 minutes. Add the mushrooms and thyme and cook 5 to 8 minutes, until the mushrooms are softened and their juices begin to evaporate. Add the lemon juice and cook 2 minutes. Taste and adjust the seasonings.

4. In a large pot over high heat, cook the lasagna in boiling salted water for 9 minutes, or until al dente. Drain and rinse under cold water. Set aside. Combine the crumbled tofu and pesto in a medium bowl. Mix well and set aside.

5. *To assemble:* Preheat the oven to 375°F. Lightly oil a 9 x 13-inch pan. Ladle 1/2 cup of the tomato sauce into the pan. Arrange a layer of noodles on top. Spread the tofu mixture evenly over the noodles and top with another layer of noodles. Spread the roasted tomatoes on top, followed by a layer of noodles, a layer of mushrooms, and the remaining noodles. Pour the remaining tomato sauce on top and sprinkle with Parmesan, if using. Cover tightly with foil and bake 40 minutes. Remove foil and bake 5 minutes longer. Let stand 5 minutes before cutting.

Beer-Simmered Seitan Stroganoff with Cracked Pepper

Serves 4

Seitan, onions, bell peppers, and mushrooms combine to create a satisfying comfort food dish that is a cross between seitan au poivre and seitan stroganoff and is especially good served over Parsleyed Noodles (below). If you don't have tamarind paste, substitute 1 teaspoon vegan Worcestershire sauce.

1 pound Savory Seitan (page 5), cut into 1-inch dice
1 1/2 teaspoons smoked paprika, divided
1 1/2 teaspoons cracked black pepper
1 tablespoon olive oil
1 large onion, chopped
1 cup chopped green bell pepper
1 cup chopped orange or yellow bell pepper
3 cups sliced cremini mushrooms
1 clove garlic, minced
2 1/2 cups vegan beer, such as Sam Smith's Lager
1 1/2 teaspoons dried parsley
1/4 cup tomato paste
1 tablespoon tamarind paste (see headnote)
Salt
Parsleyed Noodles (recipe follows)

1. In a shallow bowl, combine the seitan with 1 teaspoon of the smoked paprika and cracked pepper. Toss to coat and set aside.

2. Heat the olive oil in a large skillet over medium high heat. Add the onion and the remaining 1/2 teaspoon smoked paprika. Cook 3 to 5 minutes until soft. Add the reserved seitan. Cook another 3 minutes, until the seitan is just starting to brown. Add the bell peppers. Cook another 3 minutes. Reduce the heat to medium and cook for 2 minutes. Add the mushrooms and garlic. Cook 3 minutes, or until the mushrooms begin to soften.

3. Add the beer to deglaze the pan, then stir in the parsley, tomato paste, tamarind paste, and salt to taste. Reduce to simmer for 10 to 15 minutes, until the mixture is saucy and well combined. Serve hot over the noodles.

Parsleyed Noodles

Serves 4

These noodles make a quick and flavorful sidedish for any seitan dish. Keep a close eye on the noodles, as it is easy to overcook them.

1 pound vegan ribbon-style noodles
2 tablespoons vegan margarine, cut into small pieces
1/2 cup chopped fresh parsley

Cook the noodles in a large pot of salted boiling water for 4 minutes, or until tender. Drain well. To the same pot, add the margarine, then return the noodles to the pot and add the parsley. Stir well and serve immediately.

Margherita Pizza with Roasted Red Pepper Sauce

Makes 2 pizzas

One of America's favorite comfort foods is made here with a roasted red pepper sauce. For a more traditional sauce, use Easy Marinara Sauce (page 54) or Tomato Basil Sauce (page 139).

DOUGH:

3/4 to 1 cup warm water
1 teaspoon agave nectar
2 1/4 teaspoons active baking yeast
2 cups all-purpose flour
1/2 cup whole wheat pastry flour
1 tablespoon nutritional yeast
2 teaspoons salt
1 teaspoon dried Italian herbs, optional
2 tablespoons plus 1 teaspoon olive oil, divided

SAUCE:

1 tablespoon olive oil
1/2 cup minced onion
3 cloves garlic, minced
1/2 teaspoon dried thyme
1/2 teaspoon dried basil
1/4 teaspoon ground fennel
1/4 teaspoon red pepper flakes
Salt and black pepper
1/4 cup dry red wine, optional
1 cup chopped roasted red bell peppers (page 28) or store-bought
1 (15-ounce) can diced tomatoes, undrained
1 tablespoon capers
1 tablespoon agave nectar

TOPPINGS:

6 to 8 ripe Roma or plum tomatoes, cut into 1/4-inch slices
2 to 2 1/2 cups shredded vegan mozzarella cheese
1 cup finely chopped basil

1. *Dough:* In a small bowl, combine 3/4 cup warm water, agave nectar, and yeast. Set aside for 5 minutes or until bubbly. In a large bowl, combine the flours, nutritional yeast, salt, and herbs, if using. Add the yeast mixture and the 2 tablespoons olive oil. Stir to combine. Add the remaining 1/4 cup water, as needed, to make a cohesive dough and transfer to a floured work surface. Knead about 10 minutes, or until the dough is smooth and shiny. Shape into a ball.

2. Lightly oil a large bowl with the remaining 1 teaspoon olive oil. Transfer the dough to the bowl and turn the dough to coat it with oil. Cover the bowl with a clean towel and set aside in a warm place to rise for an hour.

3. *Sauce:* Heat the oil in a medium saucepan over medium heat. Add the onion, garlic, herbs, and red pepper flakes. Season with salt and pepper to taste. Cook 5 minutes, stirring until fragrant. Add the wine, if using, and cook 5 minutes. Add the remaining ingredients. Bring to a boil, then reduce heat to medium and simmer 15 to 20 minutes to thicken. For a smoother sauce, use an immersion blender or transfer to a blender and blend until smooth. Cool completely before using.

4. Preheat the oven to 500°F. If using a pizza stone, place it in the oven. If using baking sheets or pizza pans, lightly oil them. Lightly flour a work surface. Divide the dough into 2 pieces. Place one piece of dough on the work surface and pat into a disk. Turn it over and lightly flour. Roll out the dough into a 12-inch round. Transfer to the baking sheet or stone. Repeat with the remaining dough.

5. *Toppings:* Top each pizza with a thin layer of the sauce, then a layer of tomato slices, followed by the cheese, spreading evenly. Place the pizzas in the oven and immediately reduce the temperature to 475°F. Bake 10 to 14 minutes, or until the cheese is melted and the crust is lightly browned. Top with chopped basil and cut into wedges.

Chicago-Style Deep-Dish Pizza

Makes 1 pizza

The story goes that deep-dish pizza was invented in the early 1940s at Pizzeria Uno in Chicago. It caught on quickly and is still offered in pizza shops today. For Chicago pizza, the cheese is placed directly on the crust, with the sauce and toppings on top of the cheese. This works well with vegan cheeses that can sometimes be slow to melt.

DOUGH:
3/4 cup warm water
1 teaspoon agave nectar
2 1/4 teaspoons active baking yeast
1 cup all-purpose flour
1 cup white wheat flour
3/4 teaspoon salt
3 tablespoons olive oil
Cornmeal, for dusting

SAUCE:
1 (28-ounce) can whole plum tomatoes, undrained
1 teaspoon dried basil
1/2 teaspoon dried parsley
1/2 teaspoon dried oregano
Pinch fennel seeds
2 to 4 cloves garlic, minced
1/4 teaspoon salt
Pinch black pepper

TOPPINGS:
1 tablespoon olive oil, plus more for drizzling
3 1/2 ounces spicy Vegan Sausage Links (page 41) or store-bought, finely minced
1/2 teaspoon red pepper flakes
1 cup sliced cremini mushrooms
1 cup shredded vegan mozzarella cheese
1/2 teaspoon dried oregano
2 tablespoons Vegan Parmesan (page 137) or store-bought
1 cup tightly packed chopped fresh baby spinach

1. *Dough:* In a small bowl, combine the warm water, agave nectar, and baking yeast. Set aside for 5 minutes or until the yeast bubbles. In a large bowl, combine the flours and salt. Stir together. Add the yeast mixture and the olive oil. Mix well to form a cohesive dough. Transfer to a lightly floured work surface and knead about 5 minutes, adding flour as needed. Dough will remain tacky, but shouldn't be sticky. Shape into a ball. Lightly oil a large bowl and transfer the dough to the bowl, turning so that the top is coated with oil. Cover with a clean towel. Let rise in a warm place until doubled, about 1 1/2 hours.

2. *Sauce:* Drain the tomatoes in a colander for 10 minutes, gently squeezing them to break them up. Transfer to a medium bowl, add the remaining sauce ingredients, and set aside.

3. *Toppings:* Heat the olive oil in a small skillet over medium heat. Add the sausage and the red pepper flakes. Cook 2 to 3 minutes until fragrant and the sausage has lightly browned. Transfer to a plate and set aside. Add the mushrooms to the same skillet, and cook over medium heat, stirring, until they release their juice, about 4 minutes. Cook until the liquid evaporates and the mushrooms are nearly dry. Set aside.

4. *Assembly:* Preheat the oven to 500°F. Generously oil the bottom and sides of a 10-inch cast iron skillet with olive oil. Sprinkle with cornmeal. Place the rack at the lowest level in the oven. On a lightly floured work surface, roll out the dough into a 14-inch circle. Gently transfer the dough to the skillet, pressing it up the sides. Let the dough rest 15 minutes.

5. Spread the mozzarella evenly on the crust, then top with the reserved sausage and mushrooms, and other toppings, if using. Spread the tomato sauce on top, then sprinkle with oregano and Parmesan.

6. Bake for 20 minutes. Remove from the oven. Spread the spinach evenly on top of the pizza and lightly drizzle with olive oil. Return the pizza to the oven and reduce the temperature to 400°F. Bake 5 to 10 minutes, or until the crust is golden brown. Let the pizza stand 10 minutes before cutting.

● ● ● ● ● ● ● ● ● ● ●

VARIATIONS

Add any or all of these additional toppings to your pizza:

- 1/2 small onion, sliced into thin rings and separated
- 1/2 green bell pepper, cut into thin strips
- 3 tablespoons chopped pitted black olives

CHOICE OF SIDES

Turn your favorite main dish into a "Blue Plate Special" by teaming it with these tempting sides. We've all been there: a restaurant menu full of choices, but not many of them vegan. When that happens, I usually order several sides, and before the meal is over, my dinner companions are wishing I had ordered for them. Choose from crispy Beer-Battered Onion Rings, Mac and Cheeze, or maybe Midway French Fries, reminiscent of the fresh-cut fries you get at a county fair. Baked Beans, popular in New England back in colonial times, are dressed up in this modern take, and they go especially well with All-American Incrediburgers.

Beer-Battered Onion Rings

Serves 4

Onion rings are a classic American side that are always a favorite, whether served at your favorite diner or pub. Now you can enjoy them at home – they're especially good served alongside the All-American Incrediburgers (page 122).

1 cup soy milk
1 tablespoon apple cider vinegar
1 large Vidalia or other sweet onion (1 pound), cut into 1/2-inch rings
2 cups all-purpose flour, divided
1 teaspoon salt
3/4 teaspoon garlic powder
1/2 teaspoon onion powder
Few grinds black pepper
1 to 1 1/4 cups vegan beer, such as Killian's Irish Red
Canola oil, for frying (see page 67)

1. In a shallow bowl, combine the soy milk and vinegar and mix well, then set aside for a few minutes to curdle.

2. Separate the onion slices into rings and transfer them to the soy milk mixture. Let sit 1 hour or longer, stirring occasionally so that the onion rings are soaked.

3. Line a baking sheet with a brown bag or paper towels for draining. In a deep fryer, heat the oil to 375°F or heat 1-inch of oil in a large skillet over medium heat.

4. In a shallow bowl, combine 1 cup of the flour, salt, garlic powder, onion powder, and pepper.

5. In a second shallow bowl, combine 1 cup beer with the remaining 1 cup flour. If the mixture is too thick, add a little more beer. The batter should coat the onion rings well, but drip off.

6. Remove the rings one at a time from the milk mixture and dredge them in the dry flour mixture, then in the beer mixture. Carefully place the battered onion ring into the oil and fry until golden, 3 to 5 minutes, working in batches so the oil doesn't get too crowded. Remove the cooked onions from the oil and drain on the baking sheet. Serve hot.

Baked Onion Rings

Serves 4

These onion rings may not have the deep-fried decadence of the Beer-Battered Onion Rings, but they're lower in calories and have a crispy outer coating and fantastic flavor.

2 cups soy milk
2 tablespoons apple cider vinegar
1 large Vidalia or other sweet onion (1 pound), cut into 1/2-inch-thick slices
1 cup all-purpose flour
1 cup dried bread crumbs
1 cup panko crumbs
1/2 teaspoon dried parsley
1/4 teaspoon garlic powder
1/4 teaspoon salt
Pinch black pepper
Olive oil or nonstick cooking spray

1. Lightly oil 2 large baking sheets. Preheat the oven to 350°F. In a shallow bowl, combine the soy milk and vinegar and set aside for a few minutes to curdle. Separate the onion slices into rings and add them to the soy milk mixture, stirring to coat.

2. Place the flour in a shallow bowl or pie plate. In a second shallow bowl, combine the bread crumbs, panko, parsley, garlic powder, salt, and pepper.

3. Remove the onion rings from the milk mixture and dip them in the flour mixture. Dip them into the milk mixture again, then into the crumb mixture. Place the coated onion rings on the prepared baking sheet. Continue until all the onion rings are dipped, working in batches.

4. Spray the onion rings with oil or nonstick cooking spray. Bake 20 minutes, then turn and spray them again with oil. Bake 15 to 20 minutes longer, or until golden brown. Serve hot.

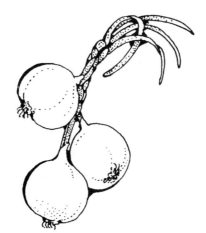

Cheezy Mac and Greens

Serves 4

Nearly every restaurant offers a mac and cheese, even if it's only on the kid's menu. This updated version can be enjoyed by both children and adults, and it's a great way to get kids to eat their spinach.

8 ounces elbow macaroni
4 cups tightly packed fresh baby spinach, cut in a fine chiffonade
2 tablespoons vegan margarine
1 tablespoon minced onion
2 cloves garlic, minced
2 tablespoons all-purpose flour
2 1/2 cups soy milk
1/4 cup nutritional yeast
1 teaspoon prepared yellow mustard
1/2 teaspoon dried mustard
1/2 teaspoon white pepper
4 ounces extra-firm tofu, drained, pressed, and crumbled
2 tablespoons vegan sour cream
Pinch grated nutmeg
2 teaspoons white miso paste
Salt and black pepper

1. Cook the macaroni in a large pot of boiling salted water for 8 to 10 minutes, or until al dente. Drain well and return the macaroni to the same pot off the heat. Stir the spinach into the macaroni. Set aside.

2. In a medium saucepan, melt the margarine over medium heat. Add the onion and garlic and cook 5 minutes, until soft. Stir in the flour. Cook about 2 minutes to remove the raw flour taste. The mixture will be clumpy and pasty.

3. Add the soy milk, yeast, prepared mustard, dried mustard, white pepper, tofu, sour cream, and nutmeg. Whisk together to blend then cook, stirring, over low heat. Add a little more soy milk if the mixture seems too thick. Remove from heat. Mix in the miso paste.

4. Pour the sauce over the macaroni and spinach and stir to combine. Season with salt and pepper, then taste and adjust the seasonings. Serve hot.

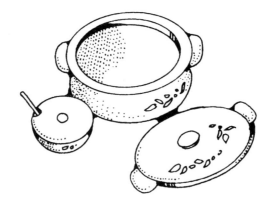

Stovetop Mac and Cheeze

Serves 6 to 8

Macaroni and cheese is one of America's ultimate comfort foods. Here's an easy and tasty vegan version that I hope you'll enjoy as much as we do.

1 pound elbow macaroni or other small
   pasta shape
1/4 cup olive oil
1/2 cup minced onion
2 cloves garlic, minced
2 1/2 cups soy milk, divided
1 cup nutritional yeast
2 1/2 teaspoons dried mustard
2 1/2 teaspoons garlic powder
1 1/4 teaspoons onion powder
1 1/4 teaspoons dried basil
1 1/4 teaspoons dried thyme
1 teaspoon salt
3 tablespoons cornstarch
Salt and black pepper

1. Cook the macaroni in a large saucepan of boiling salted water for 8 to 10 minutes, or until al dente. Drain well and return to the saucepan. Set aside.

2. Heat the oil in a medium saucepan over medium heat. Add the onion and garlic and cook 3 minutes, or until softened. Whisk in 2 cups of the soy milk, the yeast, mustard, garlic powder, onion powder, basil, thyme, and salt.

3. Combine the cornstarch with the remaining 1/2 cup soy milk, mixing until smooth. Add to the saucepan, whisking to combine. Bring to a boil, then reduce heat. Simmer gently to thicken, stirring. Adjust the seasonings. Pour the sauce over macaroni and stir to coat. Serve immediately.

Taters and Strings

Serves 4

This "vegetable of the day" is a two-in-one side dish that's quick, easy, and especially good served with the Salisbury-Style Seitan with Mushrooms (page 132) for the ultimate Blue Plate Special.

1 1/2 pounds small red potatoes,
   scrubbed, and cut into 1/2-inch pieces
2 to 3 tablespoons olive oil
Salt and black pepper
12 ounces fresh green beans, trimmed
2 tablespoons fresh lemon juice
2 tablespoons fresh minced parsley
2 teaspoons fresh minced rosemary

1. Preheat the oven to 400°F. Arrange the potatoes in a 9 x 13-inch baking pan. Add 2 tablespoons olive oil and season with salt and pepper, to taste. Bake 25 minutes, stirring once, about halfway through.

2. Add the green beans and lemon juice, stirring to coat with the oil. Add the remaining 1 tablespoon oil, if needed. Bake an additional 15 minutes, or until the beans are tender. Remove from the oven and stir in the parsley and rosemary. Serve hot.

Midway French Fries

Serves 4 to 6

We like these with the skins still on for extra crunch, but you can peel the potatoes, if you prefer. Serve them with vinegar for an old-fashioned county fair experience. If you don't have a deep fryer, these may also be cooked in a large, heavy bottomed pot in 2 inches of oil over medium heat. For more information, see Before You Deep Fry (page 67). Double frying French fries gives them a crispy outside, but keeps the inside texture soft.

4 russet potatoes (2 pounds), scrubbed
Canola oil, for cooking
Salt and black pepper

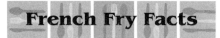

French Fry Facts

Properly cooked French fries really don't absorb that much oil. Food scientists have done tests checking the volume of oil before and after frying. Using the correct oil temperature reduces absorption and produces better tasting food.

French fries boomed in the United States when soldiers returned home from fighting in Belgium and France after World War I.

Older potatoes tend to make the best fries because their sugars more easily convert to starches, helping the fries brown better.

More than one-fourth of all potatoes sold in the United States are in the form of fries. The average American eats thirty pounds of French fries a year.

1. Cut the potatoes into 1/4-inch strips and place them in a large bowl with enough cold water to cover. Place the bowl in the refrigerator or add a few ice cubes to the water to keep the water cold. Keep chilled for at least 1 hour, or as long as overnight, if refrigerated.

2. Heat the oil in a deep fryer to 325°F. Cover a baking sheet with a brown bag or paper towels for draining.

3. Working in batches, blot a handful of the cold fries until very dry. Gently place the fries in the fryer and cook for 7 to 8 minutes. The potatoes should just start to turn translucent. Remove the potatoes from the fryer and drain on the prepared baking sheet. Repeat until all the potatoes are fried. Let the fries cool completely to room temperature, at least 15 minutes.

4. Turn the heat on the fryer to 375°F. Working in batches, refry the fries for 3 to 5 minutes, or until they reach the desired crispness. Remove and drain on the baking sheet. Season with salt and pepper while still hot. Serve hot.

Mashed Potatoes with Homestyle Gravy

Serves 4 to 6

Enjoy this comfort food favorite topped with a creamy gravy and served with Salisbury-Style Seitan with Mushrooms (page 132) or Southern Fried Seitan (page 151). For a spicy gravy, try the Jalapeño Gravy on the following page. Add another side dish, and make yourself a Blue Plate Special (see pages 130-131).

3 pounds Yukon Gold potatoes, cut into
　1-inch dice
1 teaspoon salt
3 tablespoons vegan margarine, diced
1/4 cup soy milk
Salt and black pepper
Homestyle Gravy (recipe follows)

1. Combine the potatoes in a large saucepan with enough water to cover and 1 teaspoon salt. Bring to a boil over high heat, then reduce to a simmer. Cook for 20 minutes, or until the potatoes are fork tender. Drain well.

2. Transfer the potatoes back into the saucepan, off the heat. Add the margarine and mash with a potato masher. Add the soy milk and stir with a fork. Season with salt and pepper, to taste. Serve hot topped with the gravy.

Homestyle Gravy

Makes 2 cups

For holiday meals, or anytime, this deeply flavored rich-tasting gravy will remind you of Mom's.

1/3 cup olive oil
1/2 cup minced onion
2 cloves garlic, minced
1/2 teaspoon dried sage
1/2 teaspoon dried thyme
2 tablespoons dry red wine, optional
1/3 cup all-purpose flour
2 cups vegetable broth
1 teaspoon soy sauce
1 teaspoon vegan Worcestershire sauce
1 tablespoon nutritional yeast
1 teaspoon minced fresh parsley
1/8 teaspoon salt
Pinch black pepper

1. In a medium saucepan, heat the oil over medium heat. Add the onion and garlic and cook 3 to 4 minutes, or until the onion is tender. Add the dried herbs and wine, if using. Cook 2 to 3 minutes.

2. Whisk in the flour, cook 3 minutes to remove the flour taste, continuing to whisk. The mixture will be clumpy and pasty.

3. Drizzle in the broth, continuing to whisk. Add the remaining ingredients and whisk until thickened, about 3 minutes. Taste and adjust the seasonings. Serve hot.

Jalapeño Gravy

Makes 2 1/2 cups

For a zesty change of pace, try this spicy but flavorful gravy on the mashed potatoes. It also makes a great sauce for sautéed seitan or tempeh or the Southwestern Wheat-Meat Loaf (page 154).

1/3 cup olive oil
1/3 cup minced jalapeño, seeded
1/3 cup all-purpose flour
2 3/4 to 3 cups vegetable broth
1/3 cup nutritional yeast
1 1/2 teaspoons garlic powder
3/4 teaspoons onion powder
1 1/2 teaspoons adobo sauce
Salt and black pepper

Heat the olive oil in a small saucepan over medium heat. Add the jalapeño and cook 3 to 5 minutes. Stir in the flour and cook 2 to 3 minutes to reduce the flour taste, stirring continuously. Whisk in the broth, yeast, garlic powder, onion powder, and adobo sauce. Season with salt and pepper to taste. Cook, stirring, until thickened. Taste and adjust the seasonings and serve hot.

Handcut Potato Chips

Serves 4

Ordinary potato chips can become a divine taste experience when you make them yourself. They are an extra-special treat when eaten still warm from the fryer. After draining on paper towels, try dusting these chips with different seasonings, such as chili powder or garlic salt. For vinegar chips, add 2 tablespoons apple cider vinegar to the soaking water.

2 russet potatoes, about 8 ounces, scrubbed
2 teaspoons salt
Canola oil, for frying

1. Cut the potatoes into paper thin slices and transfer them to a medium bowl with enough cold water to cover. Add the salt and refrigerate for at least 1 hour. Line a baking sheet with a brown bag or paper towels for draining.

2. Heat the oil in a skillet or deep fryer to 370°F. Working in batches, blot the potato chips dry, then gently transfer them to the skillet and fry until golden, 3 to 5 minutes. Drain on the prepared baking sheet, sprinkling on additional salt, if needed.

Double-Stuffed Spuds

Serves 4

The twice-baked potato of steakhouse fame gets a new look (and taste) with these double-stuffed spuds. The Coconut 'Bacon' Bits (below) used in these potatoes are also delicious on salads, potato skins, or sprinkled on burgers and other sandwiches.

4 russet potatoes, scrubbed
1/3 cup soy milk
2 tablespoons vegan margarine
3 tablespoons vegan sour cream
1 tablespoon nutritional yeast
2 teaspoons white miso paste
1 teaspoon prepared yellow mustard
1/2 teaspoon salt
Pinch black pepper
1 tablespoon fresh chopped chives
2 tablespoons Coconut 'Bacon' Bits
   (recipe follows), optional
1/8 teaspoon smoked paprika

1. Preheat the oven to 400°F. Pierce the potatoes with a fork 3 to 4 times and arrange them on a baking sheet. Bake for 1 hour, then set aside until cool enough to handle. Slice 1/2-inch off the top of the potatoes, and set the tops aside. Use a spoon to scoop out the insides of the potatoes, leaving about 1/4-inch of the outer potato intact.

2. Place the insides of the potatoes in a medium bowl. Add the soy milk, margarine, sour cream, nutritional yeast, miso, mustard, salt, and pepper. Mash well. Stir in the chives and the Coconut "Bacon" Bits, if using. Taste and adjust the seasoning.

3. Divide the stuffing mixture evenly among the potato skins. Dust with paprika. If desired, place the reserved tops back on the potatoes. Transfer the potatoes to the baking sheet and bake for 20 minutes. Serve hot.

Coconut 'Bacon' Bits

Makes 1/2 cup

This recipe is an unusual and surprising way to capture the smoky flavor of bacon. With just the right crunch, it's far more flavorful than store-bought vegan bacon bits. In addition, it's easy to make and stores well.

1 tablespoon soy sauce
1 teaspoon maple syrup
1/4 teaspoon prepared yellow mustard
1/4 teaspoon cracked black pepper
1/4 teaspoon toasted sesame oil
1 teaspoon liquid smoke
1/8 teaspoon smoked paprika
1/2 cup unsweetened flaked coconut
   (not shredded)

1. Preheat the oven to 300°F. Line a 9 x 13-inch baking sheet with parchment paper. Combine all the ingredients on the baking sheet. Stir to coat. Spread the mixture evenly on the sheet.

2. Bake about 20 to 30 minutes, checking frequently until dry and nicely browned but not burnt. It will crisp as it cools. When completely cool, transfer to a container with a tight-fitting lid. It can be stored at room temperature for up to 2 weeks. To recrisp, bake at 300°F. for 3 minutes.

Rosemary Carrots

If you enjoyed finding raw carrot sticks in your lunchbox as a kid, try this grown-up side-dish that combines this colorful vegetable with fragrant rosemary and a splash of lemon juice. It takes very little effort and adds color to the plate. Instead of rosemary, you can substitute fresh dill, also a wonderful accent for carrots.

5 large carrots, cut into 1/4-inch slices
1/2 teaspoon minced fresh rosemary or
   1/8 teaspoon dried
1/2 teaspoon olive oil
2 teaspoons fresh lemon juice
Salt and black pepper

Place the carrots in a steamer basket over a large pot of boiling water. Steam for 5 to 7 minutes, or until tender, then transfer to a serving bowl. Add the rosemary, olive oil, lemon juice, and salt and pepper to taste. Stir to combine. Serve hot.

Quickles

Makes about 2 cups

In American diners and delis, pickles are a familiar addition to a sandwich platter. Some people like to place pickle slices inside the sandwich, while others prefer to eat them separately. Easy to make, these great tasting pickles are ready in no time and will keep for up to a month in the refrigerator. For less heat, omit the jalapeño.

3 to 4 Kirby or other pickling cucumbers,
   cut into 1/8-inch rounds (about 2
   cups)
1/2 small onion, cut into 1/8-inch slices
1/2 small green bell pepper, cut into 1/8-
   inch slices
1/2 medium jalapeño, quartered
   lengthwise, optional
6 sprigs fresh dill
1 cup apple cider vinegar
1/2 cup sugar
2 cloves garlic, peeled and smashed
1 tablespoon pickling spices
1 tablespoon salt

1. In a medium heatproof bowl, combine the cucumbers, onion, bell pepper, jalapeño, if using, and dill. Set aside.

2. In a medium saucepan, combine the vinegar, sugar, garlic, pickling spices, and salt. Bring to a boil, then reduce the heat to a simmer and cook, stirring, until the sugar is dissolved, about 5 minutes.

3. Pour the vinegar mixture over the vegetable mixture and transfer to an airtight container. The pickles will settle and become immersed in the pickling liquid. Refrigerate for at least 2 hours before serving so the flavors will meld.

Baked Beans

Serves 6 to 8

In diner speak, baked beans are sometimes called "million on a platter." They're great served at a cookout with the Diner Brats (page 119). Instead of beer, 1/4 cup brewed coffee combined with 1/4 cup vegetable broth may be substituted.

1 tablespoon olive oil
4 ounces Seitan Breakfast Strips (page 42) or store-bought vegan bacon, diced
1 medium onion, chopped
1 1/2 cups cooked or 1 (15-ounce) can black beans, drained and rinsed
1 1/2 cups cooked or 1 (15-ounce) can kidney beans, drained and rinsed
1 1/2 cups cooked or 1 (15-ounce) can navy beans, drained and rinsed
3/4 cup Smokin' Chipotle BBQ Sauce (page 117) or store-bought
1/2 cup vegan beer, such as Beck's Dark Lager
1 tablespoon Dijon mustard
1 tablespoon vegan Worcestershire sauce
1 tablespoon soy sauce
1 to 2 tablespoons minced chipotles in adobo
1/8 teaspoon black pepper

1. Preheat the oven to 400°F. Lightly oil a 2 1/2 quart casserole and set aside. Heat the oil in a large skillet over medium high heat. Add the seitan and cook for 5 minutes, stirring occasionally, until browned.

2. Reduce the heat to medium. Add the onion and cook 5 minutes, or until translucent. Remove from the heat and stir in the remaining ingredients.

3. Transfer the mixture to the prepared casserole dish and bake, stirring occasionally, for 45 minutes, or until bubbly and hot. Let sit 10 minutes before serving.

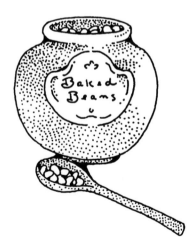

Southern-Style Rice and Red Beans

Serves 4

A favorite green of Southern cooking gets a special quick-cooking treatment, giving them a fresher taste, in this updated version of a traditional southern dish. Liquid smoke adds a smoky flavor that complements the collards. Serve with hot sauce on the side.

2 tablespoons olive oil
8 ounces collard greens, washed, ribs removed and cut in a fine chiffonade
1 cup chopped onion
1/2 cup chopped red or green bell pepper
1/3 cup minced celery
3 cloves garlic, minced
6 ounces Vegan Sausage Links (page 41) or store-bought, minced
1 1/2 cups cooked or 1 (15-ounce) can red beans, drained and rinsed
1 teaspoon liquid smoke
1 teaspoon All-American Spice Blend (page 13) or other spice blend
1 tablespoon minced parsley
2 cups cold cooked long-grain white or brown rice
Salt and black pepper
Hot sauce, for serving

1. Heat the oil in a large cast iron or nonstick skillet over medium heat. Add the collards and cook 10 minutes, or until tender, stirring occasionally.

2. Add the onion, bell pepper, celery, garlic, and sausage. Cook until the vegetables are softened, 5 to 7 minutes.

3. Add the beans, liquid smoke, spice blend, parsley, rice, and salt and pepper to taste. Cook and stir 5 minutes to heat throughout. Taste and adjust the seasonings. Serve hot.

Veggie Fried Rice

Serves 4

This delicious fried rice is packed full of fresh vegetables, giving it more flavor than the usual rice you get in Chinese take-out. For a spicier version, substitute 1 teaspoon chili oil for the toasted sesame oil.

1 teaspoon toasted sesame oil
1 teaspoon peanut oil
1 cup minced onion
1 teaspoon minced fresh ginger
2 cloves garlic, minced
1/2 cup minced red bell pepper
Salt and black pepper
1 cup chopped napa cabbage
1 cup chopped cremini mushrooms
1 cup snow peas, cut into 1/2-inch pieces
1/3 cup chopped scallions
1/2 chopped bean sprouts
1/4 teaspoon five-spice powder
3 cups cold cooked long-grain white or
   brown rice
2 tablespoons soy sauce
1 tablespoon rice vinegar

1. In a large nonstick skillet or wok, heat both oils over medium heat. Add the onion, ginger, garlic, bell pepper, and salt and pepper to taste. Cook, stirring, for 1 to 2 minutes, or until fragrant. Add the cabbage and mushrooms, and cook 1 to 2 minutes to soften.

2. Stir in the snow peas, scallions, bean sprouts and five-spice powder, and cook 1 to 2 minutes longer. Add the rice, soy sauce, and rice vinegar. Cook, stirring, for 5 minutes or until the mixture is well combined and the rice is fried. Taste and adjust the seasonings. Serve hot.

Roasted Broccoli and Bell Peppers

Serves 4

This colorful dish is a flavorful side and a delicious way to enjoy nutrient-rich broccoli.

1 medium head broccoli, trimmed and
   cut into florets
1 medium red bell pepper, cut into 1/4-
   inch slices
2 tablespoons olive oil
Salt and black pepper

Preheat the oven to 400°F. In a 9 x 13-inch pan, combine the broccoli, bell pepper, and oil, stirring to coat. Season with salt and pepper to taste. Roast 20 to 25 minutes, or until the broccoli is tender. Serve hot or at room temperature.

Bistro Broccolini

Broccolini is often a served on the side in upscale bistros. Recreate it yourself with this recipe. For a more homestyle version, substitute broccoli in the variation below. Either way, it's a fast and flavorful addition to any meal. It is especially good served with Grilled Seitan with Heirloom Tomatoes (page 144).

2 tablespoons pine nuts
2 tablespoons olive oil
2 bunches broccolini, ends trimmed
2 cloves garlic, minced
1/2 cup vegetable broth
Juice of 1/2 lemon
1/2 teaspoon balsamic vinegar, optional

1. Heat a large skillet over medium heat. Add the pine nuts and toast until golden, about 5 minutes. Remove and set aside. Reduce heat to medium.

2. To the same skillet, add the olive oil and broccolini. Cook, stirring occasionally, for 4 to 5 minutes, or until the broccolini is bright green. Add the garlic and cook 1 minute longer. Add the broth and cover the skillet to steam the broccolini until tender, 5 to 6 minutes. Remove the lid to allow the broth to evaporate. Add the reserved pine nuts, lemon juice, and vinegar, if using. Stir to combine. Serve hot.

VARIATION

Instead of broccolini, substitute 1 medium head of regular broccoli. To prepare it, cut off the florets and slice the stalks into 1/4-inch-thick slices, so they will cook evenly with the florets.

Braised Peas with Radicchio and Shallots

Serves 4

Green peas are ubiquitous in American cooking. The quick-cooking method used here preserves the fresh taste of the peas. Shallots and radicchio add a sophisticated nuance.

2 teaspoons olive oil
2 tablespoons minced shallot
Salt
3 cups fresh or frozen peas, thawed if frozen
1/4 cup chopped radicchio
2 tablespoons vegetable broth, divided
2 teaspoons minced fresh parsley
Black pepper

1. Heat the oil in a large skillet over medium heat. Add the shallot and a pinch of salt. Cook 3 to 4 minutes, until softened. Add the peas, radicchio, and 1 tablespoon of the broth. Cover and cook 2 minutes.

2. Remove the lid and add the remaining 1 tablespoon of broth to deglaze the pan. Add the parsley and season with salt and pepper to taste. Cook until the broth is evaporated. Serve hot.

Creamed Corn

Serves 4

TV dinners, a 1950s favorite modeled after the Blue Plate Specials, often included a corn side dish. With a Midwestern homestyle remake, this version is best made with fresh corn cut from the cobs, but frozen corn can be substituted.

1/2 tablespoon olive oil
1/2 cup minced onion
1 clove garlic, minced
1/3 cup minced green bell pepper, optional
1/2 teaspoon dried basil or 2 teaspoons minced fresh basil, optional
Salt
4 cups corn kernels (about 5 to 6 ears)
1 cup soy creamer
1 tablespoon agave nectar
Black pepper

1. In a medium saucepan over medium heat, combine the oil, onion, garlic, bell pepper, if using, basil, if using, and a pinch of salt. Cook about 2 minutes, until fragrant.

2. Add the corn, creamer, and agave nectar. Bring to a simmer. Cover and cook 10 minutes, until the corn is tender, stirring occasionally.

3. Using an immersion blender, cream as much of the corn as desired, leaving some kernels whole. If using a blender, blend 1/2 of the corn mixture until smooth, then return to the saucepan. Season with salt and pepper to taste. Serve hot.

menu

THE DESSERT CASE

As kids, we enjoyed sweet treats like cookies, cakes, and pies, without a care in the world. However, as adults, we tend not indulge so often. When we do, we really want our desserts to taste great and these vegan desserts fill the bill. For a taste of true Americana, try Mom's Apple Pie or, for a modern twist on the classic, dig into my Apple Butterscotch Pie. You'll also find luscious cakes, a tasty cheezecake, cookies, crisps, cobblers, and puddings, so I hope you always save room for dessert.

Mom's Apple Pie

Serves 6 to 8

Piled high with cinnamon-spiced apples, this is the quintessential American dessert. Serve this pie with a scoop of vegan ice cream on the side, if desired.

8 or 9 McIntosh, or other red baking
   apple, peeled and cut into 1/4-inch
   slices (about 8 cups)
1/2 cup sugar
1/3 cup light brown sugar
1/4 cup all-purpose flour
1 1/4 tablespoons ground cinnamon
1/2 teaspoon ground ginger
Juice of 1/2 lemon
Pinch salt
Fast-and-Easy Pie Crust (recipe follows)
   or 2 store-bought crusts

1. Preheat the oven to 425°F. Place an oven rack on the lowest level in the oven.

2. In a large bowl, combine the apples, sugar, brown sugar, flour, cinnamon, ginger, lemon juice, and salt. Stir to coat the apples, then set aside.

3. On a lightly floured surface, roll out half of the pie dough to a 13 to 14-inch round, less than 1/4-inch thick. Add flour to the work surface and dough as needed. Gently transfer to a 9-inch pie plate, pressing it to fill the pan, allowing the excess to hang over the sides. Transfer the apple mixture to the pie plate.

4. Roll out the remaining pie dough and gently arrange it over the apples. Cut any overhanging dough that exceeds 1-inch. Use your fingers to seal the dough, rolling the dough from the bottom crust up and onto the top crust to form a rim around the pie. Crimp the edge with your fingers. Cut 4 or 5 slits in the top crust to allow steam to escape.

5. Place the pie on a pie ring or baking sheet to catch the drips. Bake 20 minutes, or until golden brown. Remove from the oven and cover loosely with foil. Bake 30 minutes longer, or until the filling bubbles. Cool slightly before cutting.

Fast-and-Easy Pie Crust

Makes 2 crusts

Even if you just need enough dough for a single crust pie or 1 batch of turnovers (page 178), make the full recipe and freeze the remainder, wrapped airtight. When you're ready to bake with it, thaw overnight in the refrigerator.

2 cups all-purpose flour
1/4 cup sugar
1/2 teaspoon salt
1/2 cup cold vegan margarine, diced
1/2 cup cold vegan shortening, diced
1 tablespoon apple cider vinegar
5 tablespoons cold water

1. In a food processor, combine the flour, sugar, and salt. Pulse to mix. Add the diced margarine and shortening. Pulse to mix until the mixture resembles small peas. Add the vinegar and water through the feeder tube and pulse until the mixture is combined and forms a ball. Divide in half and pat each half into a flat disk. Wrap the disks in parchment paper or plastic wrap. Refrigerate for 1 hour before using.

To blind-bake a crust: Some single-crust pies require that the crust be baked prior to filling. To do this, prick the bottom and sides of the crust with a fork. Line with a piece of foil or parchment paper and some loose dried beans. Bake in a 425°F oven until golden, 12 to 15 minutes. Remove from the oven. Remove the foil and beans. Let the crust cool on a rack then fill as desired.

2. To bake a pie, remove the dough from the refrigerator and transfer to a lightly floured work surface. Using a lightly floured rolling pin, roll from the center outward until you have an even flat round about 14-inches across and about 1/8 to 1/4-inch thick. Add flour to the work surface as needed. Transfer to a 9 or 10-inch pie plate and gently press so that the crust fits the pan. Repair any tears with wet fingers, if needed.

3. If using for a double crust pie, fill according to the recipe. Roll out the second crust and transfer to top of pie. Crimp and bake as directed in recipe. If using for a single crust pie, crimp the edge, if desired.

The American Love Affair with Dessert

Most popular American desserts have their roots in other countries. For example, apple pie, the classic American dessert, was made in Europe in the 1300s, while the cheesecake, a deli favorite, is believed to have been served in ancient Greece at the first Olympic games in 776 B.C.

Colonial Americans had a clear preference for fruit-based dishes, thanks to the abundance of fruits in their new country. Adapting the recipes they brought with them, they often served fruit dishes for a main dish or first course. To this day, many New Englanders still eat pie for breakfast. In the late 1800s, fruit shifted into a dessert role. Those early fruit desserts went by many names:

- **Crisp** – a baked layer of fruit with a crumb topping.
- **Crumble** and **Buckle** – usually a single layer cake made with blueberries and a streusel topping.
- **Cobbler** – deep dish fruit dessert with a biscuit crust.
- **Grunt** (Massachusetts), **Slump** (the rest of New England) – a cobbler dessert cooked on top of the stove.

Apple Butterscotch Pie

Serves 6 to 8

This delicious pie combines the best features of an apple pie and an apple crisp. Some store brands of butterscotch chips are not vegan, so be sure to read the labels to be certain.

1 Fast-and-Easy Pie Crust (page 178) or store-bought
1/2 cup sugar
1/4 cup all-purpose flour
1 1/2 teaspoons ground cinnamon
1/8 teaspoon ground nutmeg
1/8 teaspoon salt
6 to 7 Granny Smith or other crisp apples, peeled, cored, and cut into 1/8-inch slices (about 7 cups)
1 tablespoon fresh lemon juice

CRUMB TOPPING:
1/2 cup all-purpose flour
1/4 teaspoon ground cinnamon
2 tablespoons sugar
Pinch salt
3 tablespoons canola oil
1/2 cup butterscotch chips (see headnote)

1. On a lightly floured work surface, gently roll the dough out to a 14-inch round, less than 1/4-inch thick. Carefully arrange the dough in a 9-inch pie pan, pressing the dough into the pan with your fingers and repairing any tears with wet fingers. Press the dough up the sides of the pan and cut off any that hangs over the outside of the pan by more than 1-inch. Roll the end of the dough up to create an edge on the crust and crimp with your fingers or a fork. Refrigerate until needed.

2. In a large bowl, combine the sugar, flour, cinnamon, nutmeg, and salt, and mix well. Add the apple slices and lemon juice and toss to coat completely. Transfer the apple mixture to the prepared crust.

3. Preheat the oven to 400°F. Place a rack in the lowest level of the oven. Bake the pie for 15 minutes. While it is baking, prepare the crumb topping. In a small bowl, combine the flour, cinnamon, sugar, and salt. Drizzle in the oil. Mix together with a fork or your fingers until the mixture clumps together. Stir in the butterscotch chips and set aside.

4. Remove the pie from the oven and sprinkle the crumb topping evenly over the pie. Reduce the temperature to 375°F. Bake an additional 30 minutes, or until top is golden and filling is bubbly. Transfer the pie to a rack to cool for 30 minutes before serving.

VARIATION

If butterscotch chips are unavailable, substitute 2 tablespoons light brown sugar, and you'll still have an apple pie that may just rival Mom's.

Crispy Bottom Peanut Butter 👍 ☺
Pie with Chocolate Fudge Sauce

Serves 8

Peanut butter and chocolate are a perfect dessert combo. This make-ahead pie will wow your guests (even unexpected drop-ins) with a decadent treat.

3 tablespoons vegan margarine
3/4 cup vegan chocolate chips
2 cups vegan puffed rice cereal
8 ounces vegan cream cheese, room temperature
1 cup smooth peanut butter
1/4 cup agave nectar
1/4 cup sugar
2 tablespoons fresh lemon juice
1/4 cup soy creamer or soy milk
1 teaspoon pure vanilla extract
Chocolate Fudge Sauce (recipe follows)

1. Lightly oil a 9-inch pie plate. Melt the margarine and chocolate chips in the microwave or over a double boiler. When melted and smooth, add the cereal, stirring to coat. Transfer the mixture to the pie plate and press into the bottom and sides to form a crust. Freeze for 30 minutes or longer.

2. Using a mixer, combine the cream cheese, peanut butter, agave nectar, sugar, lemon juice, soy creamer, and vanilla until smooth. Pour into the prepared crust and place in the freezer for another 30 minutes. After the pie is frozen, cover tightly with plastic wrap and foil.

3. Remove the pie from the freezer about 10 minutes before serving for easier cutting. Top with chocolate fudge sauce.

Chocolate Fudge Sauce 🕐 ☺

Makes about 1/2 cup

Flexible and delicious, you can make this sauce as thin or thick as you like. It's handy for that sudden urge for a milkshake or to drizzle over various desserts, such as the Banana Split Cake (page 190). If you're feeling adventurous, add 1/2 teaspoon of an extract such as mint, orange, or raspberry.

1/2 cup soy milk
1 tablespoon brewed coffee
2 tablespoons maple syrup
2 tablespoons unsweetened cocoa powder
3 tablespoons vegan semisweet chocolate chips
Pinch salt
1/2 teaspoon pure vanilla extract
1/2 tablespoon vegan margarine

1. In a small saucepan over medium heat, combine the soy milk, coffee, maple syrup, cocoa, chocolate chips, and salt. Whisk together and bring to a low boil. Whisking constantly, simmer for 8 to 10 minutes, or until it reaches the desired consistency. Remove from the heat.

2. Whisk in the vanilla and margarine. For a thinner sauce, add a little more soy milk. Serve warm or at room temperature. To store, transfer it to a bowl, cover, and refrigerate. Properly stored, it will it keep for up to 1 week.

Double-Dark Mississippi Mud Pie

Serves 8 to 10

If you don't have an ice cream maker, you can make this pie as a mousse-style pie by simply omitting the ice cream maker instructions and pouring the filling directly into the crust. The rest of the recipe remains the same. Or substitute 1 quart of store-bought vegan ice cream, such as Temptation's Coffee Ice Cream, and soften it before spreading in the crust.

2 3/4 cup vegan chocolate cookies
2 tablespoons sugar
1 tablespoon instant espresso coffee
  crystals or 2 tablespoons instant
  coffee granules
1/4 cup vegan margarine, melted
Mocha Vegan Ice Cream (page 183)
1/2 cup Soyatoo! Soy Whip (see below)

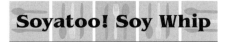

Soyatoo! Soy Whip

Soyatoo! Soy Whip whipped topping whips into a smooth whipped cream-like topping. It is available in natural food stores or online (see Resources, page 199). If unavailable, Soyatoo canned topping may be used to spread on top of the pie.

1. Preheat the oven to 400°F. Lightly oil a 9-inch pie plate. Process the cookies in a food processor or blender until they are crumbs. Add the sugar and instant espresso, and process to blend. Drizzle in the margarine, processing to combine. Transfer the crumb mixture to the pie plate and press into the bottom and sides of the pan. There will be an extra 1/2 to 3/4 cup of crumbs. Set them aside. Bake the crust for 5 to 6 minutes. Set aside to cool completely before filling.

2. Spread the ice cream evenly into the crust and smooth the top. Spread the remaining cookie crumbs evenly over the ice cream, gently pressing them into the ice cream. Cover tightly with plastic wrap and freeze until solid, about 2 hours.

3. Pour the Soyatoo into a medium bowl and use an electric mixer to whip it on high for 3 to 5 minutes, or until peaks form. Spread the whipped Soyatoo evenly over the frozen pie in a decorative way. Return the pie to the freezer, uncovered, for 20 minutes, then remove from the freezer and cover tightly with plastic wrap and foil. Return to the freezer until read to serve.

4. To serve, remove the pie from the freezer and set aside for 5 to 10 minutes, or until soft enough to cut.

Mocha Vegan Ice Cream

Makes 1 quart

An important component of the "mud pie" on the previous page, this delicious ice cream can also be enjoyed on its own with a garnish of fresh berries, if desired. If instant espresso coffee is unavailable, substitute 1/2 cup instant coffee granules.

1 (12-ounce) package extra-firm silken tofu
3/4 cup sugar
1/4 cup unsweetened cocoa
1 tablespoon arrowroot
1/4 cup instant espresso coffee crystals
1/4 teaspoon salt
1 cup soy creamer
1 cup unsweetened coconut milk
1/4 cup vegan semisweet chocolate chips
3 tablespoons Kahlua liqueur
1 teaspoon pure vanilla extract

1. Process the tofu in a blender or food processor until smooth and creamy. Set aside.

2. In a medium saucepan, combine the sugar, cocoa, arrowroot, instant espresso, and salt, and whisk until well mixed. Place the saucepan over medium heat and whisk in the soy creamer and coconut milk. Bring just to a boil, then remove from heat and add the chocolate, Kahlua, and vanilla, whisking until the chocolate melts.

3. Add the mixture to the tofu in the blender or food processor. Process until the mixture is completely smooth. Transfer to a bowl and refrigerate at least 4 hours or overnight.

4. Freeze the reserved mixture in an ice cream maker about 25 minutes, or according to the manufacturer's directions.

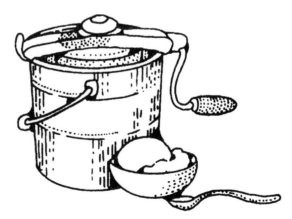

Peachy Keen Cobbler

Serves 4

This luscious cobbler is a rite of summer when peaches are at their peak, but since peach season is short, plan ahead by freezing cobbler filling for fall or winter (see sidebar below).

FILLING:

6 to 8 peaches, peeled, pitted, and sliced
   (6 cups)
1/3 cup all-purpose flour
1/3 cup sugar
Juice of 1/2 lemon
1 teaspoon pure vanilla extract
3/4 teaspoon ground cinnamon
Pinch ground nutmeg

TOPPING:

1 cup all-purpose flour
2 teaspoons baking powder
1/4 teaspoon salt
2 tablespoons sugar
Zest of 1/2 lemon
2 tablespoons canola oil
1/4 cup plus 3 tablespoons soy milk

1. *Filling:* Preheat the oven to 375°F. In a medium bowl, combine the peaches with the flour, sugar, lemon juice, vanilla, cinnamon, and nutmeg. Mix well, then transfer to a 1 1/2-quart casserole dish.

2. *Topping:* In a small bowl, combine the flour, baking powder, salt, sugar, and lemon zest. Mix well. Add the oil and soy milk, stirring to combine. Drop the dough mixture by heaping spoonfuls (about 1/4 cup) onto the top of the fruit filling. Bake 40 to 45 minutes, or until the top is golden brown and the topping is baked throughout.

Freeze Your Filling

Place a plastic freezer bag in a 1 1/2-quart casserole dish. Prepare the fruit according to the recipe, then transfer it to the plastic bag. Freeze, remove from the dish, and keep the bag of filling in the freezer. When ready to use, remove frozen filling from the bag, return to casserole dish, and thaw. Then add topping and bake as directed.

Apple Crisp

Serves 4

This crisp is just like my mom makes. You can vary the texture and flavor of the crisp by trying different kinds of apples or by cutting them into different size slices. Leave the peel on one of the apples if you prefer a rustic look.

7 to 8 McIntosh or other cooking apples, peeled, cored, and thinly sliced
Juice of 1/2 lemon
3/4 cup all-purpose flour
3/4 cup light brown sugar
Pinch salt
1 teaspoon ground cinnamon
1/3 cup vegan margarine

1. Preheat the oven to 375°F. Place the apples in an 8-inch square baking pan. Add the lemon juice and toss to coat. Set aside.

2. In a medium bowl, combine the flour, brown sugar, salt, and cinnamon. Stir together. Add the margarine and use your fingers to crumble the mixture until it resembles small peas.

3. Spread the topping evenly over the apples. Bake 30 to 40 minutes, or until the top is golden brown and the apples are cooked to the desired doneness. Serve warm or at room temperature.

Cherry Turnovers

Makes 5 to 6

A cousin to the classic fruit pie, these little "hand pies" can be enjoyed on the go. They pack well for lunches and picnics, too.

1 1/2 cups fresh or 1 (15-ounce) can pitted tart red cherries, drained
2 tablespoons sugar
2 tablespoons agave nectar
Zest of 1/2 lemon
Pinch salt
2 tablespoons cornstarch
1/2 teaspoon pure vanilla extract
1/4 teaspoon almond extract
1/2 recipe Fast-and-Easy Pie Crust (page 178)
1 to 2 tablespoons soy milk

1. In a small saucepan, combine the cherries, sugar, agave nectar, zest, and salt. Stir gently to not break up the cherries. Bring to a boil and add the cornstarch. Boil about 1 minute or until thickened. Remove from the heat and stir in the vanilla and almond extracts. Set aside to cool.

2. Preheat the oven to 375°F. Line a baking sheet with parchment paper. On a lightly floured surface, roll out the pie crust to less than 1/4-inch thickness. Cut into 4-inch squares.

3. Spoon about 2 tablespoons filling in the center of each turnover. Fold two opposite corners together and press to seal along the edges. Arrange the turnovers on the baking sheet. Crimp the edges with a fork and pierce the top once with a fork. Continue, rolling the dough as needed, until it is all used.

4. Lightly brush the tops of the turnovers with soy milk. Bake 14 to 18 minutes, or until golden. Cool on a baking rack for at least 10 minutes before serving.

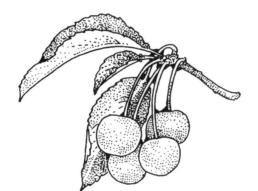

Chocolate Chip Quick Cake 🕐 ☺

Serves 4 to 6

This delicious cake is part shortcake, part quick bread, and all old-fashioned. Best of all, it's wonderfully easy to make.

1/2 cup soy milk
1 and 1/2 teaspoons apple cider vinegar
1 teaspoon pure vanilla extract
1 3/4 cups all-purpose flour
2 1/2 tablespoons sugar
1 1/2 teaspoons baking powder
1/2 teaspoon salt
1/3 cup diced vegan margarine
1/4 cup vegan semisweet chocolate chips
Sliced strawberries, for serving

1. Preheat the oven to 450°F. Lightly oil a baking sheet and set it aside. In a small bowl, combine the soy milk and vinegar and set aside to curdle for 2 minutes. Add the vanilla.

2. In a medium bowl, combine the flour, sugar, baking powder, and salt, and whisk to blend. Crumble the margarine into the flour mixture, working it in with your fingers to the size of small peas.

3. Make a well in the center of the flour mixture, then add the reserved liquid ingredients. Using a fork, stir the dough until just mixed. Add another tablespoon of either flour or soy milk to get a rough but manageable dough. Fold in the chocolate chips.

4. Transfer the dough to a lightly floured work surface and knead a few times with floured hands. Pat the dough into a 1-inch thick round and place on the baking sheet.

5. Bake 16 to 18 minutes, or until golden. Cool on a rack. When ready to serve, cut like a pie and top with strawberries.

Spiced Chocolate Pudding Cake

Serves 6 to 8

This moist and flavorful all-in-one cake makes its own sauce while it bakes. It's quick to make and disappears just as fast.

1 cup all-purpose flour
1/2 cup plus 3 tablespoons unsweetened
  cocoa powder, divided
2 teaspoons baking powder
1/2 cup sugar
1/2 teaspoon salt
3/4 teaspoon ground cinnamon, divided
1/8 teaspoon ground cayenne
1/2 cup soy milk
1/4 cup maple syrup
2 tablespoons canola oil
1 teaspoon pure vanilla extract
3/4 cup packed dark brown sugar
1 cup brewed hot coffee
3/4 cup hot water
Vegan ice cream, optional

1. Preheat the oven to 350°F. In a medium bowl, combine the flour, 1/2 cup cocoa, baking powder, sugar, salt, 1/2 teaspoon cinnamon, and cayenne.

2. In a small bowl, combine the soy milk, maple syrup, oil, and vanilla and add to the dry ingredients. Mix well, then spread into an 8-inch square baking pan.

3. In a small bowl, combine the brown sugar, remaining 3 table-spoons cocoa, and remaining 1/4 teaspoon cinnamon. Sprinkle over the top of the cake. Immediately pour the hot coffee and hot water over the top of the cake.

4. Bake 40 minutes or until the cake begins to pull away from the sides of the pan. Serve warm with ice cream, if using.

Pineapple Upside-Down Cake

Serves 4 to 6

The idea of an upside-down cake has been around since the Middle Ages, but the American version boomed in popularity when canned pineapple became widely available in the early 1900s.

TOPPING:
3 tablespoons vegan margarine
1/2 cup packed light brown sugar
1/4 teaspoon ground ginger
1/8 teaspoon ground allspice

CAKE:
4 (1/4-inch) slices fresh or canned
  pineapple
1 tablespoon dried unsweetened
  cherries
1 tablespoon ground flaxseed
3 tablespoons hot water
3 tablespoons vegan margarine
3/4 cup soy milk
1/2 teaspoon pure vanilla extract
1 1/2 cups all-purpose flour
1 cup sugar
1/4 teaspoon salt
1/4 teaspoon ground cinnamon
2 1/4 teaspoons baking powder

1. *Topping:* Melt the margarine in a small saucepan over medium heat. Stir in the brown sugar, ginger, and allspice. Set aside.

2. *Cake:* Preheat the oven to 375°F. Lightly spray an 8-inch square baking pan with nonstick cooking spray. Spread the reserved topping evenly in the baking pan. Arrange the pineapple slices in the pan, filling the cored holes of the pineapple with dried cherries. Set aside.

3. In a small bowl, combine the flaxseed and water. Mix vigorously with a fork. Place the margarine in a medium bowl and stir until smooth and creamy. Stir in the soy milk, reserved flax mixture, and vanilla and mix until smooth. Add the flour, sugar, salt, cinnamon, and baking powder and mix well. The batter will be thick. Spread the batter evenly in the baking pan.

4. Bake 30 to 35 minutes, or until golden and the sides of the cake begin to pull away from the baking pan. Let cool in the pan 20 minutes, then invert onto a serving platter.

Banana Split Cake

Serves 8 to 10

As vegans, we don't need to miss out on this old-fashioned ice cream parlor favorite. This easy dessert will have your guests asking for seconds – and the recipe.

1 tablespoon ground flaxseed
3 tablespoons hot water
1 cup all-purpose flour
2 tablespoons unsweetened cocoa
1/2 cup light brown sugar
2 teaspoons baking powder
1/2 teaspoon baking soda
1/4 teaspoon salt
2 tablespoons canola oil
1 teaspoon pure vanilla extract
1/2 cup water
1 pint vegan vanilla ice cream
1 large ripe banana, peeled, and cut into
   1/2-inch slices
1 cup halved strawberries
1/4 cup chopped fresh pineapple
Chocolate Fudge Sauce (page 181)

1. Preheat the oven to 375°F. Lightly oil a 9-inch springform pan. In a small bowl, combine the flax seeds and hot water. Stir vigorously with a fork to combine. Set aside.

2. In a medium bowl, combine the flour, cocoa, brown sugar, baking powder, baking soda, and salt. Use an electric mixer to combine. To the dry ingredients, add the flax mixture, oil, vanilla, and water and blend well with an electric mixer. Scrape the batter into the prepared pan. Bake for 12 to 15 minutes, or until a toothpick inserted in the center of the cake comes out clean. Remove from the oven and let cool completely.

3. Let the ice cream soften until it is a spreadable consistency, then spread it evenly on top of the cake. Cover with plastic wrap against the surface of the ice cream and freeze for at least 1 hour.

4. To serve, arrange a row of banana slices around the perimeter of the top of the cake. Arrange two rows of strawberry halves inside the row of banana slices. Spoon the pineapple into the center of the cake. Cut the cake into wedges, then remove the outer ring from the pan. Arrange the cake slices on dessert plates and drizzle with chocolate fudge sauce.

Maple Cupcakes with Cinnamon Cream Cheese Frosting

👍 ☺

Makes 1 dozen

These cupcakes are similar to the ones made by moms during the Depression. At that time, eggs and butter were rationed, so bakers were encouraged to use inexpensive substitutes, such as mayonnaise, which gave baked goods a unique texture and a mildly tangy undercurrent. Of course, I take this a step further and use vegan mayo.

CUPCAKES:
1/4 cup plus 2 tablespoons vegan margarine, room temperature
1/4 cup vegan mayonnaise
3/4 cup plus 1 tablespoon soy milk
1/2 cup maple syrup
1 teaspoon maple extract
1 teaspoon pure vanilla extract
2 tablespoons light brown sugar
2 cups all-purpose flour
1 teaspoon baking powder
1/2 teaspoon baking soda
1/2 teaspoon salt
1/2 teaspoon ground cinnamon

FROSTING:
1/3 cup vegan cream cheese, room temperature
1/3 cup vegan margarine, room temperature
1 teaspoon pure vanilla extract
1/2 teaspoon ground cinnamon
Pinch salt
1 1/2 cups confectioners' sugar

1. *Cupcakes:* Preheat the oven to 350°F. Line a cupcake pan with cupcake papers. In a medium bowl, combine the margarine, mayonnaise, soy milk, maple syrup, and the extracts. Mix with an electric mixer until creamy. Add the brown sugar and mix until smooth.

2. Add the remaining dry ingredients and mix well. Spoon the batter into the cupcake pan, filling the cups about three-quarters full. Bake 20 to 22 minutes or until a toothpick inserted in the center of a cupcake comes out clean. Cool completely on a baking rack before frosting.

3. *Frosting:* Combine all the frosting ingredients in a medium bowl and use an electric mixer to cream until smooth. If the mixture is too thick, add 1 tablespoon soy milk. If it's too thin, add a little more confectioners' sugar. Spread the frosting on the cooled cupcakes.

New York-Style Cheesecake

Serves 8 to 10

Traditionally, a New York-style cheesecake is made with heavy cream. No dairy here, but this vegan version has the same rich flavor and creamy texture that you might remember from the deli. Because it is made the day before serving, it is very convenient for holidays or get-togethers.

CRUST:

1 1/2 cups vegan graham cracker crumbs
   (9 crackers)
1 1/2 tablespoons sugar
4 1/2 tablespoons canola oil

FILLING:

4 (8-ounce) packages vegan cream
   cheese, room temperature
1 1/3 cups sugar
2 teaspoons pure vanilla extract
1/4 cup all-purpose flour
1/2 cup soy milk
1 tablespoon fresh lemon juice

TOPPING:

1/2 cup vegan sour cream
2 tablespoons sugar
1 teaspoon pure vanilla extract
Canned cherry or blueberry pie filling,
   or fresh fruit, optional

1. *Crust:* Preheat the oven to 350°F. Spray a 9 or 10-inch spring-form pan with nonstick cooking spray. In a small bowl, combine the crumbs, sugar, and canola oil. Mix well. Press the crumb mixture evenly into the bottom of the prepared pan. Bake for 8 minutes, or until golden. Remove and let cool completely.

2. *Filling:* Preheat the oven to 350°F. Combine all the ingredients in a large bowl and use an electric mixer to mix until smooth. Pour the filling into the cooled crust. Bake 40 to 45 minutes, or until the center of the cheesecake is set. The cheesecake may appear jiggly, but if your oven temperature is accurate, trust the time.

3. *Topping:* In a small bowl, whisk the sour cream, sugar, and vanilla until smooth. Pour the topping over the hot cheesecake when it is finished baking. Place the cheesecake back into the oven and immediately turn the heat off. Leave the cheesecake in the oven for 1 hour.

4. Remove from the oven and cool on a baking rack. When completely cool, refrigerate overnight. Serve topped with pie filling or fruit, if using.

● ● ● ● ● ● ● ● ● ● ●

VARIATION

Mini Cheesecakes: You can use the above recipe to make mini cheesecakes in four (4-inch) springform pans. Decrease the baking time to 30 to 35 minutes.

Oatmeal Raisin Cookies

Makes 3 dozen

Similar to the oatmeal cookies found in big name coffee shops, these are well-worth making at home. To reduce the cookies' tendency to spread, bake just 6 to 8 cookies on a parchment-covered baking sheet. For best results, be sure that your dough is chilled and the oven is up to temperature.

2 cups old-fashioned oats
1 cup all-purpose flour
1 cup sugar
1/2 cup dark brown sugar
1 teaspoon baking powder
1 teaspoon baking soda
1 teaspoon ground cinnamon
1/2 teaspoon salt
1/2 cup vegan margarine
1/2 cup canola oil
1 teaspoon pure vanilla extract
1 tablespoon maple syrup
1 cup raisins

1. In a medium bowl, whisk together the oats, flour, sugars, baking powder, baking soda, cinnamon, and salt.

2. In a large bowl, cream together the margarine, oil, vanilla, and maple syrup. Slowly, mix the dry ingredients into the wet ingredients until well mixed. Stir in the raisins. Refrigerate the dough for 1 hour or longer.

3. Preheat the oven to 350°F. Line two baking sheets with parchment paper. Drop the cookies onto the prepared baking sheets, using about 2 tablespoons of dough for each cookie and placing them at least three inches apart. Bake 12 to 14 minutes, or until golden brown. Let the cookies cool on the sheet for 5 minutes, then transfer to a cooling rack. If moved too soon, the cookies will crumble.

Apricot Cream Cheese Cookies ☺

About 3 dozen

A fluted pastry wheel cutter gives these bakery-style cookies pretty crimped edges, but a pizza cutter works well, too. For the filling, you'll get the best results by using the bright orange apricots that have been dried with sulphur dioxide rather than the brownish ones.

4 ounces vegan cream cheese, room
  temperature
4 ounces vegan margarine, room
  temperature
1 teaspoon pure vanilla extract
1 cup all-purpose flour
1 cup plus 2 tablespoons dried apricots
1/2 cup water
3 tablespoons agave nectar
1 1/2 tablespoons fresh lemon juice
1/8 teaspoon ground cinnamon
Confectioners' sugar, for dusting
  (optional)

1. In a medium bowl, combine the cream cheese, margarine and vanilla. Use an electric mixer to cream until smooth. Add the flour and mix well. The mixture will be sticky, but will form a soft dough. Divide the dough in half and shape into two disks. Wrap each disk separately in plastic wrap. Refrigerate overnight.

2. In a small saucepan, combine the apricots, water, agave nectar, lemon juice, and cinnamon and bring to a boil. Reduce the heat to medium and simmer 10 minutes, then transfer to a blender and blend until smooth. Set aside to cool before using. The consistency should be thick enough to hold its shape when dropped from a spoon.

3. Line 2 baking sheets with parchment paper. Preheat the oven to 375°F. On a lightly floured work surface, roll out one of the chilled dough pieces until it is about 1/8-inch thick. Cut into 2 1/2-inch squares, and spoon 1 teaspoon of filling in the center of each square. Do not overfill. Dampen two opposite corners with wet fingers and pinch together. Seal them well. Arrange the cookies on the baking sheet about 2-inches apart. Gently tuck the end under each cookie to prevent it from popping open.

4. Bake for 10 to 12 minutes, or until lightly browned. Transfer to cooling racks. If desired, the cookies may be dusted with confectioners' sugar before serving.

Lime-Avocado Cream in Puff Pastry

Serves 8

This easy and colorful dessert will surprise your family and friends with its secret ingredient: avocado. If raspberries are unavailable, another type of berry, such as strawberries or blueberries, may be substituted.

1 sheet frozen vegan puff pastry, thawed
1 ripe Hass avocado, pitted, peeled, and
  cut in chunks
1/4 cup agave nectar
1/4 cup fresh lime juice
1/4 cup soy creamer
1 teaspoon pure vanilla extract
1/2 cup confectioners' sugar
Zest of 1 lime
2 cups fresh berries of choice

1. Preheat the oven to 400°F. Lightly spray a baking sheet with nonstick cooking spray. On a lightly floured surface, roll out the puff pastry to a 9 x 12-inch rectangle. Cut the rectangle into quarters, then cut each of the quarters in half to create 8 rectangles. Transfer to the baking sheet. Bake 10 to 12 minutes or until golden brown. Transfer to a cooling rack.

2. In a food processor or blender, combine the avocado, agave nectar, lime juice, soy creamer, vanilla, sugar, and zest. Process until smooth. Use immediately or refrigerate until needed.

3. To serve, cut each pastry rectangle in half horizontally. Place each pastry bottom on a plate and top with 2 to 3 tablespoons of the avocado cream. Place the top of each pastry rectangle on top of the avocado cream. Top each pastry with another dollop of avocado cream and 1/4 cup of berries. Serve immediately.

Mom's Tapioca Pudding

Serves 4

With a couple of minor substitutions, this pudding is just like my Mom used to make. Be sure to use soy milk in this recipe as other nondairy milks don't give the best results.

2 tablespoons instant tapioca
1/4 cup sugar
2 cups soy milk
1/8 teaspoon salt
2 tablespoons cornstarch
1 teaspoon pure vanilla extract

1. Combine all ingredients except the vanilla in a medium saucepan. Whisk together and let sit 5 minutes to soften the tapioca. Place over medium heat and bring to a rolling boil. Continue to whisk and cook until thickened, about 3 minutes.

2. Remove from heat and whisk in the vanilla. Pour into dessert cups. Serve warm, or refrigerate for 1 hour to serve chilled.

Cherry Chocolate Bread Pudding with Vanilla Sauce

Serves 6

Originally an innovative way to use stale bread, today's decadent bread pudding variations bear little resemblance to this dish's humble roots. The comfort factor, however, remains the same.

BREAD PUDDING:
1/2 cup dried unsweetened cherries
2 tablespoons brandy, whiskey, or apple juice
1 cup soy creamer
2 tablespoons vegan margarine
3 tablespoons agave nectar
3 tablespoons light brown sugar
1/4 teaspoon ground cinnamon
Pinch salt
3/4 cup soy milk
2 tablespoons tapioca flour
1/2 teaspoon pure vanilla extract
1 loaf day-old French bread, cut or torn into 1-inch pieces, about 8 cups
1/4 cup vegan semisweet chocolate chips
1/2 teaspoon unsweetened cocoa

1. *Bread Pudding:* Lightly oil a 9-inch baking dish and set aside. Place the cherries and brandy in a large bowl and set aside to soak.

2. In a medium saucepan, combine the soy creamer, margarine, agave nectar, brown sugar, cinnamon, and salt. Whisk frequently over medium heat for 2 minutes, or until well blended and hot.

3. In a small bowl, whisk together the soy milk and tapioca flour until smooth, then add to the mixture in the saucepan. Continue to cook, whisking until thick, 2 to 3 minutes. Remove from heat. Whisk in the vanilla and let cool slightly. Preheat the oven to 375°F.

4. Add the bread to the bowl with the cherries. Pour the liquid mixture over the bread and stir to coat. Set aside for 5 minutes to soak, stirring occasionally. Add the chocolate chips and transfer to the baking dish. Dust the top with cocoa. Bake 25 minutes, or until lightly browned. If a crisper top is desired, broil 3 to 5 minutes under the broiler.

VANILLA SAUCE:

1/2 cup soy creamer
1/4 cup vegan margarine
1/4 cup agave nectar
1/4 cup soy milk
2 tablespoons Bird's Custard Powder (see Tip)
1 teaspoon pure vanilla extract

TIP

Bird's Custard Powder is a cornflour based product invented by Alfred Bird in the early 1800s. Alfred's wife couldn't eat traditional British custard because she was allergic to eggs. Look for it in the international section of your supermarket. If Bird's Custard Powder isn't available, make the Vanilla Drizzle variation instead of the Vanilla Sauce for the bread pudding.

5. *Sauce:* Heat the soy creamer, margarine, and agave nectar in a small saucepan over medium heat, stirring frequently with a whisk.

6. Pour the soy milk into a small bowl and whisk in the custard powder until smooth, then add it to the mixture in the saucepan and bring to a full boil, whisking constantly until the mixture thickens, about 3 minutes. Remove from the heat and stir in the vanilla. If the mixture is too thick, add a little more soy milk.

7. To serve, spoon the warm bread pudding into bowls and drizzle with the sauce.

● ● ● ● ● ● ● ● ● ● ●

VARIATION

Vanilla Drizzle. Make this easy drizzle as an alternative to the Vanilla Sauce to serve over the bread pudding.

   1/4 cup canola oil
   1/2 cup soy creamer
   1 teaspoon pure vanilla extract
   1 cup confectioners' sugar

In a medium bowl, whisk together the oil, soy creamer, vanilla, and confectioners' sugar until smooth. Drizzle over the warm bread pudding.

Vanilla Espresso Shake

Serves 2

Whenever we travel to Vermont, we always stop at the wonderful Strong Hearts Cafe in Syracuse, New York. It's the halfway point on our trip and serves amazing vegan food. They make many flavors of milkshake there, and they inspired this one. You might wonder why you need a recipe for a shake, but I'm betting you'll be glad you have this one.

1 1/2 cups vegan vanilla ice cream
1/4 cup soy creamer
1 teaspoon pure vanilla extract
3/4 teaspoon instant espresso crystals or
   1 1/2 teaspoons instant coffee crystals

Combine all the ingredients in a blender. Blend until thick and creamy. Pour into glasses and serve immediately.

Resources

While it's convenient to shop locally, it's nice to know where you can find vegan items on the Internet. Whether you're looking for basic ingredients or specialty items, you can find most anything you need from these online retailers:

Bob's Red Mill Whole Grain Store
www.bobsredmill.com
Phone: 800-349-2173

In addition to texturized vegetable protein, Bob's also carries a long list of grains, mixes, and other baking supplies.

Cosmo's Vegan Shoppe
www.cosmosveganshoppe.com
Phone: 800-260-9968

Another super-store, you can get everything you need for personal use, home, and the vegan kitchen.

Ethical Planet
www.ethicalplanet.com
Phone: 224-636-7150

An all-vegan store that's earth friendly, cruelty free, and organic. They also carry clothes, household goods, supplements, and more.

Food Fight Grocery
www.foodfightgrocery.com
Phone: 503-233-3910

Smaller and more eclectic than some of the other stores, Food Fight offers specialty foods along with vegan lifestyle goods.

Herbivore Clothing
www.herbivoreclothing.com
Phone: 503-281-TOFU

Although they don't carry food items, Herbivore is a great source for clothing, books, and accessories.

King Arthur Flour
www.kingarthurflour.com
Phone: 800-827-6836

An employee-owned company, King Arthur carries a huge line of flours and other baking goods.

Mail Order Catalog for Healthy Eating
www.healthy-eating.com
Phone: 800-695-2241

One of the first businesses to make natural foods accessible via mail-order, this is a terrific source for texturized vegetable protein and many other items.

Pangea
www.veganstore.com
Phone: 800-340-1200

Pangea carries a wide variety of vegan goods as well as ingredients, such as white chocolate chips.

Penzey's Spices
www.penzeys.com
Phone: 800-741-7787

Various locations across the country, this store is like a candy shop for cooks with wonderful scents everywhere you turn. The choices are many and the herbs and spices are always high quality.

Vegan Essentials
www.veganessentials.com
Phone: 866-88-VEGAN

Vegan Essentials carries a wide range of items for a vegan lifestyle, including vegan cheeses.

Index

About the Author

For Ohio native and author, Tamasin Noyes, developing recipes for *American Vegan Kitchen* came naturally. She has worked as a committed cookbook tester for many well-known vegan cookbook authors and has cooked in several restaurants. She grew up helping her mom in the kitchen and has loved comfort food since she was a kid. Tami also enjoys discovering vegan food options when traveling whether it's in a small town cafe, a local diner, or a metropolitan bistro.

"I love cooking because of the creativity in taking basic vegan ingredients and transforming them into delicious new dishes," she says. "Improvising and creating recipes in the kitchen is a way to put yourself out there and discover common ground with others. I especially like the practicality of cooking (we all have to eat), as well as the art of it. To me, vegan cooking is the most nurturing thing we can do for our planet and those we love, and I've dreamed of creating comfort food for vegans for a long time."

In addition to developing recipes, Tami enjoys food photography and took all the photographs for the *American Vegan Kitchen* photo insert. For more of Tami's great recipes and food photos, visit her blog at www.veganappetite.com.

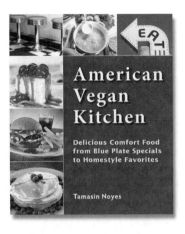

Need more copies of *American Vegan Kitchen?*

Discounts are available to bookstores, distributors, and other resellers. For discount information contact the publisher@veganheritagepress.com. For announcements of upcoming titles, go to www.veganheritagepress.com, or write to Vegan Heritage Press, P.O. Box 628, Woodstock, VA 22664-0628.

Keep up with author Tami Noyes and her recipes by subscribing to her blog: www.veganappetite.com.

VEGAN HERITAGE PRESS
Paperback, 268 pages, 7½ x 9
ISBN 13: 978-0-9800131-0-8
ISBN 10: 0-9800131-0-0

Vegan Fire & Spice
200 Sultry and Savory Global Recipes

by Robin Robertson

Take a trip around the world with delicious, mouth-watering vegan recipes ranging from mildly spiced to nearly incendiary. Explore the spicy cuisines of the U.S., South America, Mexico, the Caribbean, Europe, Africa, the Middle East, India, and Asia with *Red-Hot White Bean Chili, Jambalaya, Szechuan Noodle Salad, Vindaloo Vegetables,* and more.

Organized by global region, this book gives you 200 inventive and delicious, 100% vegan recipes for easy-to-make international dishes, using readily available ingredients. Best of all, you can adjust the heat yourself and enjoy these recipes hot – or not.

For more about Robin Robertson's cookbooks, visit her website www.globalvegankitchen.com. or blog at http://veganplanet.blogspot.com.

Coming Soon!
The Official Revised Edition of **Apocalypse Chow**, now with 80 great recipes!

VEGAN HERITAGE PRESS
Paperback, 245 pages, 7 x 7
ISBN 13: 978-0-9800131-2-2
ISBN 10: 0-9800131-2-7

Vegan Unplugged
How to Eat Well When the Power Goes Out

by Jon Robertson with recipes by Robin Robertson

No fridge? No stove? No microwave? No problem. *Vegan Unplugged* is your go-to source for gourmet pantry cooking in a variety of worst-case scenarios. Make tasty meals whenever the power goes out from storms, hurricanes, and blackouts. Cook your way through quarantines, home renovations, visits with the in-laws, and other disasters.

Just because your kitchen is powerless doesn't mean you have to be. *Vegan Unplugged* provides easy, practical tips on how to shop for, store, and quickly prepare nonperishable pantry foods. Make great dishes such as Almost-Instant Black Bean Chili, Pantry Pasta Salad, Fire-Roasted Blueberry Cobbler, and more. This book is a "must have" for anyone who wants to be ready for anything with great-tasting, nutritious pantry cuisine.